Entrepreneurship in the Globalized World

ENTREPRENEURSHIP in the Globalized World

Edited by

M. Sarngadharan

Director,
SNES Institute of Management Studies and Research, Kozhikode

and

Sona Padman

Assistant Professor,
SNES Institute of Management Studies and Research, Kozhikode

New Century Publications
New Delhi, India

NEW CENTURY PUBLICATIONS
4800/24, Bharat Ram Road,
Ansari Road, Daryaganj,
New Delhi - 110 002 (India)

Tel.: 011-2324 7798, 4358 7398, 6539 6605
Fax: 011-4101 7798
E-mail: indiatax@vsnl.com • info@newcenturypublications.com
www.newcenturypublications.com

Editorial office:
LG–7, Aakarshan Bhawan,
4754-57/23, Ansari Road, Daryaganj,
New Delhi – 110 002

Tel.: 011-4356 0919

First Published: **2014**

ISBN: **978-81-7708-379-8**

Published by New Century Publications and printed at Salasar Imaging Systems, New Delhi.

Designs: Patch Creative Unit, New Delhi.

PRINTED IN INDIA

About the Book

Entrepreneurship is the quality of being an entrepreneur, i.e. one who *undertakes an enterprise*. The term puts emphasis on the risk and effort taken by individuals who both own and manage a business.

Globalisation implies widening and deepening integration with the *globe*, i.e. with people and processes abroad. The trend towards the evolution of a global society is generally thought of in economic terms and the context of consequences of the revolution in communication technologies. There is undoubtedly much greater economic integration among the nations of the world today. Globalisation has also resulted in the creation of a new business framework. More changes can be expected in the business scenario, specifically in terms of openness, adaptiveness and responsiveness.

The world has been changing at a fast pace. An increasing need is being felt for a paradigm shift in the relationship between industry and academicians. Improvement in the competence of workforce assumes special significance in Indian context where low productivity is a problem of greater dimension than unemployment. The competence and dedication of workforce depends largely on the improvement in the basic determinants of quality education. This necessitates knowledge, either imported or home spun, through research.

The present volume contains 14 research papers—authored by experts on managerial practices—on the changing business management practices in India in various areas.

About the Editors

Dr. M. Sarngadharan is presently Director, SNES Institute of Management Studies and Research, Kozhikode (affiliated to the University of Calicut). He secured his M.Com. degree from the University of Kerala (1975) and Ph.D. in Commerce from the University of Calicut (1986). He has authored 14 books and 469 articles. He has also served as Dean, Faculty of Commerce, University of Kerala and Member Senate, Cochin University of Science and Technology. He has participated in several international conferences and visited Spain, UK, Singapore, Malaysia and Nepal. He is the chief editor of *Journal of Business Studies* published from Trivandrum.

Ms. Sona Padman is currently Assistant Professor at SNES Institute of Management Studies and Research, Kozhikode (affiliated to the University of Calicut). She secured her MBA degree from Birla Institute of Technology and Science (BITS), Pilani in Rajasthan. She is the associate editor of JMAR, a half-yearly research journal published from Kozhikode. She has contributed a number of research articles in reputed journals and edited volumes.

Contents

Contributors

Sarat Sarngadharan	Project Management Professional and Software Engineer, Central European University Business School, Budapest, Hungary.
Sona Padman	Assistant Professor, SNES Institute of Management Studies and Research, Kozhikode.
Rajagopalan P.	Professor, SNES Institute of Management Studies and Research, Kozhikode.
M. Sarngadharan	Director, SNES Institute of Management Studies and Research, Kozhikode.
Usha P.M.	Associate Professor, SNES Institute of Management Studies and Research, Kozhikode.
Leena George	Assistant Professor, Department of Commerce, Kristu Jayanti College, Bengaluru.
Suresh Chandra Bihari	Professor, Banking and Finance, IBS, Hyderabad.
Pankaj M. Madhani	Associate Professor, ICFAI Business School (IBS), Ahmedabad.
Ambilikumar V.	Associate Professor, Kerala University of Fisheries and Ocean Studies, Kochi.
Shamla N.K.	Associate Professor, SNES Institute of Management Studies and Research, Kozhikode.
Anil Kumar K.	Associate Professor, Department of Commerce, Government Arts College, Thiruvananthapuram.
Ajesh S.R.	Assistant Professor, Department of Commerce, Devaswom Board College, Kollam.

Preface

An entrepreneur is an individual who organizes and operates a business or businesses, taking on financial risk to do so. The entrepreneur is commonly seen as an innovator of new ideas, and business processes. Management skill and strong team building abilities are often perceived as essential leadership attributes for successful entrepreneurs. A growing body of work shows that entrepreneurial behaviour is dependent on social and economic factors. Some of the most significant influences on an individual's decision to become an entrepreneur are workplace peers and the social composition of the workplace. The ability of entrepreneurs to innovate is thought to relate to innate traits such as extroversion and a proclivity for risk-taking.

In political economics, entrepreneurship is the quality of being an entrepreneur, i.e. one who *undertakes an enterprise*. The term puts emphasis on the risk and effort taken by individuals who both own and manage a business, and on the innovations resulting from their pursuit of economic success.

Entrepreneurship in this sense may result in new organizations or may be part of revitalizing mature organizations in response to a perceived opportunity. The most obvious form of entrepreneurship is that of starting new businesses. In recent years, the term has been extended to include social and political forms of entrepreneurial activity.

Entrepreneurial activities are substantially different depending on the type of organization and creativity involved. Entrepreneurship ranges in scale from solo projects to major undertakings creating many job opportunities.

The acts of entrepreneurship are often associated with true uncertainty, particularly when it involves bringing something really novel to the world, whose market never exists. However, even if a market already exists, there is no guarantee that a market exists for a particular new player in the cola category.

Globalisation implies widening and deepening integration

with the *globe*, i.e. with people and processes abroad. The trend towards the evolution of a global society is generally thought of in economic terms and in terms of the consequences of the revolution in communication technologies. There is undoubtedly much greater economic integration among the nations of the world today. Globalisation is widely seen as the most important factor that could influence economies of nations the world over in the new millennium. The rapid advancement in information technology and communications has made it not just possible but absolutely essential for economies of the world to adapt or fall by the wayside.

Globalisation has also resulted in the creation of a new business framework. More changes can be expected in the business scenario specifically in terms of openness, adaptiveness and responsiveness. The most important dimensions of economic globalisation are: (a) breaking down of national barriers; (b) international spread of trade, financial and production activities, and (c) growing power of transnational corporations and international financial institutions in these processes. While economic globalisation is a very uneven process, with increased trade and investment being focused in a few countries, almost all countries are greatly affected by this process.

A major feature of globalisation is the growing concentration and monopolisation of economic resources and power by transnational corporations and by global financial firms and funds. This process has been termed transnationalisation, in which fewer and fewer transnational corporations are gaining a large and rapidly increasing proportion of world economic resources, production and market shares. Where a multinational company used to dominate the market of a single product, a big transnational company (TNC) now typically produces or trades in an increasing multitude of products, services and sectors. Through mergers and acquisitions, fewer and fewer of these TNCs now control a larger and larger share of the global market, whether in commodities, manufactures or services.

The world has been changing at a fast pace. An increasing need is being felt for a paradigm shift in the relationship between industry and academicians. Improvement in the competence of work force assumes special significance in Indian context where low productivity is a problem of greater dimension than unemployment. Both scarcity and surpluses are observed to co-exist in the employment market due to mismatch between skills and requirements of emerging employment opportunities. This mismatch is likely to become more acute in the process of rapid structural changes and modernization of the Indian economy under globalization. The competence and dedication of work force depends largely on the improvement in the basic determinants of quality education. This necessitates knowledge, either imported or home spun, through research.

It is in this backdrop that an attempt has been made in this edited volume to collect and compile select papers on the changing business management practices in India in various areas with a view to provide knowledge to the trainers, trainees, teachers, taught, researchers and practitioners.

This volume would not have been possible without the strong support provided by the contributors of the papers. We place on record our deep appreciation and gratitude to all the scholars for their co-operation and contributions.

Finally, we express our sincere thanks to New Century Publications, New Delhi for providing technical and editorial support to make this venture a success.

Kozhikode

M. Sarngadharan
Sona Padman

1

Change Management Strategies for Enhanced Working Results

Sarat Sarngadharan

The term *change management* is quite common in the management literature. Furthermore, managerial interest in the topic has been stimulated by the comments of Peter Drucker as to whether one can manage change at all or merely lead or facilitate its occurrence within an organization. Change management is the process by which an organization gets to its future state—its vision. While traditional planning processes delineate the steps on the journey, change management attempts to facilitate that journey. Therefore, creating change starts with creating a vision for change and then empowering individuals to act as change agents to attain that vision. The empowered change management agents need plans that provide a total systems approach, wherein everything is realistic and future-oriented. Change management depicts the effective mechanism of strategies and programmes that enable the change agents to achieve the proposed vision.

Change management is an approach to shifting individuals, teams, and organizations from a current state to a desired future state. It is an organizational process aimed at helping change stakeholders to accept and embrace changes in their business environment or individuals in their personal lives. In some project management contexts, change management refers to a project management process wherein changes to a project are formally introduced and approved. Change management uses basic structures and tools to control any organizational change. The goal is to maximize benefits and minimize the change impacts on workers and avoid distractions.

Organizational change is a structured approach in an organization for ensuring that changes are smoothly and successfully implemented, and that the lasting benefits of change are achieved. In the modern business environment, organizations face rapid change like never before. Globalization and the constant innovation of technology results in a constantly evolving business environment. Recent phenomenon like social media and mobile adaptability have revolutionized business and the effect of this is an ever increasing need for change, and therefore change management.

The growth in technology also has a secondary effect of increasing the availability and, therefore, accountability from knowledge. Easily accessible information has resulted in unprecedented scrutiny from the stakeholders and media. Prying eyes and listening ears raise the stakes for failed business endeavours and increase the pressure on struggling executives. With the business environment experiencing so much change, organizations must then learn to become comfortable with change as well. Therefore, the ability to manage and adapt to organizational change is an essential ability required in the workplace today.

Types of Change

Changes in an organization can often be identified as one of the four types—operational, strategic, cultural and political—with the definite possibility of overlap among them. Operational changes affect the way the ongoing operations of the business are conducted, such as the automation of a particular area. Strategic changes occur in the strategic business direction, e.g. moving from an inpatient to an outpatient focus. Cultural changes affect the basic organizational philosophies by which the business is conducted, e.g. implementing a continuous quality improvement (CQI) system. Political changes in staffing occur primarily for political reasons of various types, such as those that occur at top patronage job levels in government agencies.

These four different types of change typically have their

greatest impacts at different levels of the organization. For example, operational changes tend to have their greatest impacts at the lower levels of the organization, right on the firing line. People working at the upper levels may never notice changes that cause significant stress and turmoil to those attempting to implement the changes. On the other hand, the impact of political changes is typically felt most at the higher organizational levels. As the name implies, these changes are typically made not for results-oriented reasons but for reasons such as partisan politics or internal power struggles. When these changes occur in a relatively bureaucratic organization, as they often do, those working at the bottom often hardly notice the changes at the top.

Micro and Mega Changes

A more practical model divides changes into micro changes and mega changes. It is basically possible to differentiate between the two: micro changes—differences in degree; and mega changes—differences in kind. Using an information system as an example, modifications, enhancements, improvements, and upgrades would typically be micro changes, while a new system or a very major revision of an existing one would be a mega change. This scheme works surprisingly well for communication within organizations as long as it is to be remembered that one person's micro change is often another person's mega change. So while the system designers think they are making a minor change to enhance the total system, an individual end user may see the change as a mega change and resist it vehemently. When designing the *total people strategy* for any system, it is important to involve a variety of people from the very beginning, to clearly understand how groups function in the organization and how the work is really is carried out.

In order to implement change, the following steps are crucial:

- Identifying what roles they themselves are occupying in the process.

- Identifying what roles the others involved in the process are playing, being careful to recognize multiple roles.
- Identifying carefully which role is speaking when one is communicating with those playing multiple roles.
- Monitoring throughout the process whether any role is changing.

Change Management Theories

Theories about how organizations change draw on many disciplines, from psychology and behavioural science to engineering and systems thinking. The underlying principle is that change does not happen in isolation—it influences the whole organization (system) around it, and all the people touched by it. In order to manage change successfully, it is, therefore, essential to attend to the wider impacts of the changes. While considering the tangible impacts of change, it is important to consider the personal impact on those affected, and their journey towards working and behaving in new ways to support the change. The change curve is a useful model that describes the personal and organizational process of change in more detail.

In 1974, Watzlawick, Weakland, and Fisch concluded in their research on change management that the earlier theories explained first-order and second-order changes: First-order change is a variation in the way the processes and procedures have been carried out in a given system, leaving the system itself relatively unchanged. Some examples are, creating new reports, creating new ways to collect the same data, and refining existing processes and procedures.

Second-order change occurs when the system itself is changed. This type of change usually occurs as the result of a strategic change or a major crisis such as a threat against system survival. Second-order change involves a redefinition or rethinking of the business of the organization and the way it is to be conducted. For instance, in the banking business automated teller machines redefined the way that many banking functions are conducted worldwide. These two orders of change represent extremes. First-order change involves doing better what the organization already does, while second-order change alters the core ways the organization conducts business or even the basic business itself.

Golembiewski, Billingsley, and Yeager subsequently added another level of change, defining middle-order change as lying somewhere between the extremes of first- and second-order change. Middle-order change represents a compromise; the magnitude of change is greater than first-order change, yet it neither affects the critical success factors nor is strategic in nature. Kurt Lewin is credited with combining theories from psychology and sociology into the field theory in social psychology. Lewin focused on motivation and the motivational concepts that underlie an individual's behaviour. Lewin believed that there is tension in a person whenever a psychological need or an intention exists, and the tension is released only when the need or intention is fulfilled. The tension may be positive or negative. These positive and negative tension concepts were translated into a more refined understanding of conflict situations and, in turn, what Lewin called force fields.

Change management is, therefore, a very broad field, and change management approaches vary widely, from organization to organization and from project to project. Many organizations and consultants subscribe to formal change management methodologies. Change management focuses on people, and is about ensuring change—is thoroughly, smoothly and lastingly implemented.

Due to the growth of technology, modern organizational change is largely motivated by exterior innovations rather than internal moves. And when these developments occur, the organizations that adapt the quickest create for themselves a competitive advantage. Meanwhile, the companies that refuse to change get left behind and this can result in drastic profit and/or market share loss. Organizational change directly affects all departments from the entry level employee to the upper management. With the recent developments like social media marketing and smart phone applications, the entire company must learn how to handle these new changes to the organization. Whether it is the CMD determining how to incorporate social media, or the secretary representing themselves and their company responsibly online, change occurs rapidly in today's ever developing world. When determining which latest techniques or innovations to adopt, there are four major components viz, Levels, goals and strategies; Measurement system; Sequence of steps; and Implementation and organizational change.

Kotter's Model of Change Management

The Kotter's eight step organizational change management model is being practiced in business enterprises globally. The essence underlying in the model can be summarized as shown below:

- Increase urgency—inspire people to move, make objectives real and relevant.
- Build the guiding team—get the right people in place with the right emotional commitment, and the right mix of skills and levels.
- Get the vision right—get the team to establish a simple vision and strategy and focus on emotional and creative aspects necessary to drive service and efficiency.
- Involve as many people as possible, communicate the essentials, simply, and to appeal and respond to people's needs.
- Remove obstacles, enable constructive feedback and lots of support from leaders.
- Reward and recognize progress and achievements.
- Create short-term wins and set aims that are easy to achieve with manageable numbers of initiatives.
- Finish current stages before starting new ones.

Resistance to Change

Resistance to change is an ongoing problem. At both the individual and the organizational levels, resistance to change impairs concerted efforts to improve performance. Many corporate change efforts have been initiated at tremendous cost only to be halted by resistance among the organization's employees. Organizations as a whole also manifest behaviour similar to that of individuals when faced with the need to change. The relationship between individual and organizational resistance to change is important. An organization is a complex system of relationships between people, leaders, technologies, and work processes. From these interactions, emerge organizational behaviour, culture, and performance.

These emergent properties and behaviours are tightly linked in two directions to the lower-level interactions. Organizational resistance to change is an emergent property, and individual resistance to change can give rise to organizational resistance. A self-reinforcing loop of increasing resistance can develop as individuals create an environment in which resistance to change is the norm. That environment, in turn, encourages increased resistance to change among individual employees. The self-reinforcing nature of this loop can be tremendously powerful, defeating repeated attempts to break out of it.

Studies of system dynamics frequently reveal that major problems that everyone considers external are actually the unintended consequences of internal policies. The basic dynamic behind this phenomenon is that the organization is made up of a network of circular causal processes: A influences B, which then influences C, which in turn influences A, i.e. the snake bites its own tail. Understanding these internal organizational dynamics is a prerequisite for leading effective change processes.

All change involves loss. In many a cases, change requires at the minimum that individuals give up familiar routines. In some cases, the loss is substantial, affecting position, power, networks of friends and colleagues, and so on. In all these situations, rituals of transition can be crucial in assisting people to grieve and let go off the old and move on to the new. The strategies for overcoming the barriers to change are quite diverse and touch on every aspect of the organization. No organization can begin using all the strategies at the same time or even in a short period of time.

A better approach is to focus on one or two until they become part of the normal way of operating, i.e., until they become engrained in people's habits. Only then, is it time to introduce another strategy. In this way, over time, the organization gradually improves its abilities to learn rapidly, to adapt to new conditions, and to embrace change.

Rules of Management of Change

Managing organizational change will be more successful if the well set principles are applied appropriately. Achieving personal changes more successful too if the same approach is used wherever found relevant. Change management entails thoughtful planning and sensitive implementation, and above all, consultation with, and involvement of, the people affected by the changes. If change is forced on people, normally problems arise. Change must be realistic, achievable and measurable. These aspects are especially relevant to managing personal change. Before starting organizational change, ask and find out solutions to the following queries:

- What does the organization want to achieve with this change, why, and how will it know that the change has been achieved?
- Who is affected by this change, and how will they react to it?
- How much of this change can the organization achieve on its own?
- What parts of the change do the organization's principles need help with?

These aspects also relate strongly to the management of

human resources. Aesop's Fables section has other short and beautifully simple analogies useful for illustrating aspects of causing or dealing with change, for example:

- The Crow and the Pitcher (change being provoked by pressure or necessity).
- The North Wind and the Sun (gentle persuasion rather than force).
- The Lion and The Ass (enforced change—might is right).
- The Crab and his Mother (lead by example and evidence—or you'll not change people).
- The Miller, his Son and the Ass (no single change is likely to please everyone—everyone wants something different).
- The Oak and the Reeds (the need for tolerance—changer or 'changes').
- The Rich Man and the Tanner, (time softens change—given time people get used to things).
- The Ass and the Mule (agree to reasonable change now or you can risk far worse enforced change in the future).

Components of Change Management

The components of change management, in general, include the following:

- Change management process.
- Readiness assessments.
- Communication and communication planning.
- Training managers for change management.
- Employees training and development.
- Sponsored activities and sponsored roadmaps.
- Resistance management.
- Data collection.
- Feedback analysis and corrective action.
- Recognizing success.

Change Management Process: The change management process is the sequence of steps or activities that a change management team or project leader would follow to a project or change. Based on Prosci's research, most change management processes contain three phases—preparing for change (preparation, assessment and strategy development); managing change (detailed planning and change management implementation); and reinforcing change (data gathering, corrective action and recognition. Change process management is a necessary component for any organizational performance improvement process to succeed, including programs like: six sigma, business process reengineering, total quality management, organizational development, restructuring and continuous process improvement (CPI).

Readiness Assessment: Assessments are tools used by a change management team or project leader to assess the organization's readiness to change. Readiness assessments can include organizational assessments, culture and history assessments, employee assessments, sponsor assessments and change assessments. Each tool provides the project team with an insight into the challenges and opportunities they may face during the change process. Assessing the scope of the change provides answers to the following queries:

- How big is this change?
- How many people are affected?
- Is it a gradual or radical change?

In the same manner, assessing the readiness of the organization impacted by the change, reveals:

- What is the value-system and background of the impacted groups?
- How much change is already going on?
- What type of resistance can be expected?

Such being the case, it is advisable to assess the strengths of the change management team and then assess the change sponsors and take the initial steps to enable them to effectively lead the change process.

Communication and Communication Planning: Many managers take it granted that if they communicate clearly with their employees, their job successfully is done. However, there are many reasons why employees may not hear or understand what their managers are narrating the first time around. In fact, the messages need to be repeated 6 to 7 times before they are cemented into the minds of employees. That is because each employee's readiness to hear depends on many factors.

Effective communicators carefully consider three components: the audience, what is said and when it is said. For example, the first step in managing change is building awareness around the need for change and creating a desire among employees. Therefore, initial communications are typically designed to create awareness around the business reasons for change and the risk of not changing. Likewise, at each step in the process, communications should be designed to share the right messages at the right time, from the right source, in the right manner to the right person. Communication planning, therefore, begins with a careful analysis of the audiences, key messages and the timing for those messages. The change management team or project leaders must design a communication plan that addresses the needs of front-line employees, supervisors and executives. Each audience has particular needs for information based on their role in the implementation of the change.

Training Managers for Change Management: Supervisors have to play a key role in managing change. Ultimately, the direct supervisor has more influence over an employee's motivation to change than any other person at work. However, in many a cases, supervisors as a group can be the most difficult to convince of the need for change and can be a source of resistance. It is vital for the change management team and executive sponsors to gain the support of supervisors and to build change leadership. Individual change management activities should be used to help these supervisors through the change process.

Once managers and supervisors are on board, the change management team must prepare a coaching strategy. They need to provide training for supervisors including how to use individual change management tools with their employees.

Employees Training and Development: Training is the cornerstone for building knowledge about the change and the required skills. Project team members have to develop training requirements based on the skills, knowledge and behaviours necessary to implement the change. The training requirements serve as the starting point for the training group or the project team to develop training programs.

Sponsored Activities and Sponsored Roadmap: Business leaders and executives play a vital sponsor role in change management. The change management team must develop a plan for sponsor activities and help key business leaders for executing the plans. Sponsorship should be viewed as the most important success factor. It is imperative to avoid the chances of confusing the notion of sponsorship with support. The CEO of the company may support the project, but that is not the same as sponsoring initiative. Sponsorship involves active and visible participation by the senior business leaders throughout the process. Unfortunately many executives do not know what this sponsorship looks like. A change agent's or project leader's role includes helping senior executives to implement the right things to sponsor the project.

Resistance Management: Resistance from employees and managers is normal. Persistent resistance, however, can weaken a project. The change management team needs to identify, understand and manage resistance throughout the organization. Resistance management is the processes and tools used by managers and executives with the support of the project team to manage employee resistance.

Data Collection, Feedback Analysis and Corrective Action: Employee involvement is a necessary and integral part of managing change. Managing change is not a one way street. Feedback from employees is a key element of the change management process. Analysis and corrective action based on this feedback provides a robust cycle for implementing change.

Recognizing Success: Early successes and long-term wins must be recognized and celebrated. Individual and group recognition is also a necessary component of change management in order to cement and reinforce the change in the organization. The final step in the change management process is the after-action review. It is at this point that one can stand back from the entire program, evaluate successes and failures, and identify process changes for the next project. This is part of the ongoing, continuous improvement of change management for the organization and it ultimately leads to change competency.

Guiding Principles for Change Management

Successful change management is more likely to occur if the following are included for a systematic and comprehensive framework of change management. It may help the executives to understand what to expect, how to manage their own personal change, and how to engage the entire organization in the process.

Address the Human Side Systematically: Any significant transformation creates *people issues*. New leaders are asked to step up, jobs changed, new skills and capabilities developed. In the process there is every possibility that the employees would be uncertain and resistant. Dealing with these issues on a reactive, case-by-case basis puts speed, morale, and results at risk. A formal approach for managing change—beginning with the leadership team and then engaging key stakeholders and leaders—should be developed early, and adapted often as change moves through the organization.

This demands as much data collection and analysis, planning, and implementation discipline by way of redesigning the strategy, systems, or processes. The change management approach should be fully integrated into program design and decision-making, both informing and enabling the strategic direction. It should be based on a realistic assessment of the organization's history, readiness, and capacity to change.

Start at the Top: Because change is inherently unsettling for people at all levels of an organization, when it is on the horizon, all eyes may turn to the CEO and the leadership team for strength, support, and direction. The leaders themselves must embrace the new approaches first, both to challenge and to motivate the rest of the institution. They must speak with one voice and model the desired behaviours. The executive team also needs to understand that, although its public face may be one of unity, it, too, is composed of individuals who are going through stressful times and need to be supported. Executive teams that work well together are best positioned for success. They are aligned and committed to the direction of change, understanding the culture and behaviours the changes intend to introduce, and can model those changes themselves.

Involve Every Layer: As transformation programmes progress from defining strategy and setting targets to design and implementation, they affect different levels of the organization. Change efforts must include plans for identifying leaders throughout the company and pushing responsibility for design and implementation. This would bring about cascading effect throughout the organization which means a chemical or physiological process that occurs in successive stages, each of which is dependent on the preceding one, and often producing a cumulative effect. At each layer of the organization, the leaders who are identified and trained must be aligned to the company's vision, equipped to execute their specific mission, and motivated to make the change a reality.

A major multi-line insurer with consistently flat earnings decided to change performance and behaviour in preparation for going public. The company followed this *cascading leadership* methodology, training and supporting teams at each stage. First, 10 officers set the strategy, vision, and targets. Next, more than 60 senior executives and managers designed the core of the change initiative. Then 500 leaders from the field drove implementation. The structure remained in place throughout the change program, which doubled the company's earnings far ahead of schedule. This approach is simultaneously helpful to the organization in identifying its next generation of leadership.

Make the Formal Case: Individuals are inherently rational and will question to what extent change is needed, whether the company is headed in the right direction, and whether they want to commit personally to making change happen. They will look to the leadership for answers. The articulation of a formal case for change and the creation of a written vision statement are invaluable opportunities to create or compel leadership-team alignment. Three steps should be followed in developing the case: First, confront reality and articulate a convincing need for change. Second, demonstrate faith that the organisation has a viable future and the leadership to get there. Finally, provide a road map to guide behaviour and decision-making. Leaders must then customize this message for various internal audiences, describing the pending change in terms that matter to the individuals.

Create Ownership: Leaders of large change programs must over perform during the transformation and be the zealots who create a critical mass among the work force in favour of change. This requires more than mere buy-in or passive agreement that the direction of change is acceptable. It demands ownership by leaders willing to accept responsibility for making change happen in all of the areas they influence or control. Ownership is often best created by involving people in identifying problems and crafting solutions. It is reinforced by incentives and rewards. These can be tangible (for example, financial compensation) or psychological (for example, camaraderie and a sense of shared destiny).

Communicate the Message: Too often, change leaders make the mistake of believing that others understand the issues, feel the need to change, and see the new direction as clearly as they do. The best change programs reinforce core messages through regular, timely advice that is both inspirational and practicable. Communications flow in from the bottom and out from the top, and are targeted to provide employees the right information at the right time and to solicit their input and feedback. Often, this demands over communication through multiple, redundant channels.

Assess the Cultural Landscape: Successful change programs pick up speed and intensity as they cascade down, making it critically important that leaders understand and account for culture and behaviours at each level of the organization. Companies often make the mistake of assessing culture either too late or not at all. Thorough cultural diagnostics can assess organizational readiness to change, bring major problems to the surface, identify conflicts, and define factors that can recognize and influence sources of leadership and resistance. These diagnostics identify the core values, beliefs, behaviours, and perceptions that must be taken into account for successful change to occur. They serve as the common baseline for designing essential change elements, such as the new corporate vision, and building the infrastructure and programs needed to drive change.

Address Culture Explicitly: Once the culture is understood, it should be addressed as thoroughly as any other area in a change program. Leaders should be explicit about the culture and underlying behaviours that will best support the new way of doing business, and find opportunities to model and reward those behaviours. This requires developing a baseline, defining an explicit end-state or desired culture, and devising detailed plans to make the transition. Organizational culture is an amalgam of shared history, explicit values and beliefs, and common attitudes and behaviours. Change programs can involve creating a culture (in new organisations or those built through multiple acquisitions), combining cultures (in mergers or acquisitions of large companies), or reinforcing cultures (in, say, long-established consumer goods or manufacturing companies). Understanding that all companies have a cultural centre—the locus of thought, activity, influence, or personal identification—is often an effective way to jump-start culture change.

Prepare for the Unexpected: No change program goes completely in accordance with a plan. People react in unexpected ways; areas of anticipated resistance fall away; and the external environment shifts. Effectively managing change requires continual reassessment of its impact and the organization's willingness and ability to adopt the next wave of transformation. Fed by real data from the field and supported by information and solid decision-making processes, change leaders can then make the adjustments necessary to maintain momentum and drive results.

Speak to the Individual: Change is both an institutional journey and a very personal one. People spend many hours each week at work; many think of their colleagues as a second family. Individuals (or teams of individuals) need to know how their work changes, what is expected of them during and after the change program, how they are measured, and what success or failure means for them and those around them. Team leaders should be as honest and explicit as possible. People will react to what they see and hear around them, and need to be involved in the change process. Highly visible rewards, such as promotion, recognition, and bonuses, should be provided as dramatic reinforcement for embracing change. Sanction or removal of people standing in the way of change would reinforce the institution's commitment.

Key Elements for Success

In recent years, many change management gurus have focused on soft issues, such as culture, leadership, and motivation. Such elements are important for success, but managing these aspects alone is not sufficient to implement transformation projects. Soft factors do not directly influence the outcomes of many change programs. For instance, visionary leadership is often vital for transformation projects, but not always. The same can be said about communication with employees. Moreover, it is not easy to change attitudes or relationships; they are deeply ingrained in organizations and people. And although changes in, say, culture or motivation levels can be indirectly gauged through surveys and interviews, it is tough to get reliable data on soft factors.

The key elements for success of change management can be on the following lines:

- Plan long-term broadly—a sound strategic vision, not a specific detailed plan (the latter is impossible to predict reliably). Detailed five years plans are out of date two weeks after they are written. Focus on detail for establishing and measuring delivery of immediate actions, not medium-to-long-term plans.
- Establish forums and communicating methods to enable immediate review and decision-making. Participation of interested people is essential. This enables their input to be gained, their approval and commitment to be secured, and automatically takes care of communicating the actions and expectations.
- Empower people to make decisions at a local operating level—delegate responsibility and power as much as possible (or at least encourage people to make recommendations which can be quickly approved).
- Remove (as far as is possible) from strategic change and approval processes and teams (or circumvent) any ultra-cautious, ultra-autocratic or compulsively-interfering executives. Autocracy and interference are the biggest obstacles to establishing a successful and sustainable dynamic culture and capability.
- Encourage, enable and develop capable people to be active in other areas of the organization via 'virtual teams' and 'matrix management'.
- Scrutinise and optimise ICT (information and communications technology) systems to enable effective information management and key activity team-working.
- Use workshops as a vehicle to review priorities, agree

broad medium-to-long-term vision and aims, and to agree short term action plans and implementation method and accountabilities.

- Adjust recruitment, training and development to accelerate the development of people who contribute positively to a culture of empowered dynamism.

It may be concluded that the change management processes may include creative marketing to enable communication between change audiences, as well as deep social understanding about leadership's styles and group dynamics. As a visible track on transformation projects, organizational change management aligns groups' expectations, communicates, integrates teams and manages people training.

It makes use of performance metrics, such as financial results, operational efficiency, leadership commitment, communication effectiveness, and the perceived need for change to design appropriate strategies, in order to avoid change failures or resolve troubled change projects. Just as the state of *unconscious incompetence,* needs to be developed into *conscious competence* to provide a basis for training, so that a person's subjective emotion needs to be developed into objectivity before beginning to help them handle change.

Nobody is immune from subjectivity, ignorance or denial. The lessons and reminders found in stories and analogies can help to show a new clear perspective. It is not always easy or perhaps even possible to consider matters at such depth, but try to persuade others above in their ivory towers to think about the fundamental integrity of the situation, instead of short-term profit.

References

Davies, P. (1999), What is Evidence-based Education?, *British Journal of Educational Studies*, 47, 108-121.

Kohn, A. (2006), Abusing Research: the Study of Homework and other Examples, Phi Delta Kappan, September, 9-21.

Kotter, J. (1990), A Force for Change, New York: The Free Press.

Kotter, J. (2011), Change Management vs. Change Leadership: What's the Difference?, Forbes online.

Phillips, J.R. (1983), Enhancing the Effectiveness of Organizational Change Management, *Human Resource Management*, 22(1/2), 183-199.

2

Entrepreneurial Competency for Successful Business

Sona Padman

The term entrepreneurship is often used synonymously with the term entrepreneur. Though, they are two sides of the same coin, conceptually they are different. Entrepreneurship is the indivisible process which flourishes when the interlinked dimensions of individual psychological entrepreneurship, entrepreneur traits, social encouragement, business opportunities, government policies, availability of plenty of resources and opportunities contribute towards the common good and development of the society and economy. Entrepreneurship is the process of identifying opportunities in the market place, arranging the resources required to pursue these opportunities and investing the resources to exploit the opportunities for long-term gains. It involves creating wealth by bringing together resources in new ways to start and operate an enterprise. Cole opined that entrepreneurship is the purposeful activity of an individual or a group of associated individuals undertaken to initiate, maintain and aggrandize profit by production or distribution of economic goods and services.

Entrepreneurship is a creative process of organizing, managing an enterprise and assuming the risk involved in the enterprise. It is a process of creating something new and assuming the risks and rewards as detailed below:

- It creates something new of value to the entrepreneur and customers.
- It requires the duration of the necessary time and effort.
- It involves risk taking—financial, psychological and social.

- It needs reward in the form of profit, personal satisfaction and independence.

Entrepreneurship is therefore about learning the skills needed to assume the risk of establishing a business, developing the winning strategies and executing them with all the vigour, persistence and passion needed to win any game. It serves as a linchpin between invention, innovation, and introduction of new products and services in the marketplace and also enables the entrepreneurs to act as engines of growth in the economy. Entrepreneurship is linked to entrepreneurial opportunities, the compelling forces enabling entrepreneurs to introduce or develop new products or services.

It is simply concerned with what an entrepreneur actually does—the utilization of resources in managing an enterprise and assuming the risks and maximizing profit from the business venture. It is a very dynamic process of creating incremented wealth for the well being of both the entrepreneur and individuals in society. Successful entrepreneurship requires the entrepreneur to posses certain managerial skills. These skills are the ability to conceptualize and plan effectively; ability to manage other individuals, ability to manage time effectively and to learn new techniques in handling business operations; and ability to adopt to change and to handle changes in the environment.

Sustainable Economic Growth and Entrepreneurship

Economic development is the process of structural transformation of an economy towards a modern, technologically advanced economy based on services and manufacturing. This process involves not only qualitative changes to the nature of an economy, but also application of quantitative changes in terms of the productivity and output per person. If these qualitative and quantitative changes result in unambiguous improvements in human welfare, it is generally seen as *economic development*. The entrepreneurship, in the context of global financial and economic crisis, more and more convincingly, is accepted as instrument that guarantees sustainable future growth.

Governments face plenty of transformative challenges in their attempts to safeguard the economic recovery, such as increasing scarcity of natural resources, significant demographic shifts, and the environmental and social implications of climate change, which increasingly force them to rely on corporate sector support. For these reasons, nowadays entrepreneurs are recognized as general drivers of economic and social progress, and rapidly growing entrepreneurial initiatives are considered as important source of innovation, employment and productivity growth.

On that background, entrepreneurship is considered as the fourth production factor. In general, entrepreneurship is depicted as a very important factor for economic development; to create jobs, ease fiscal burden, and to provide competition. The entrepreneurs with their ability to scan, analyze and identify opportunities in the environment transform them into business proposition through creation of economic entities. Through efficient and effective utilization of national resources, they act as catalysts for economic development and agents of social transformation and change.

The diversity of activities that characterizes rich countries can be attributed to the supply of entrepreneurs. They play a vital role for the economic development of a country.

Common Characteristics Associated with Entrepreneurs

A review of literature related to entrepreneurial characteristics reveals the existence of a large number of factors that can be consolidated into a much smaller set of profile dimensions such as the following:

- Total commitment, determination and perseverance.
- Drive to achieve and grow.
- Opportunity utilisation and goal orientation.
- Taking initiative and personal responsibility.
- Persistent problem solving.
- Realism and a sense of humour.
- Seeking and using feedback.

- Internal locus of control.
- Calculated risk taking and risk seeking.
- Need for status and power.
- Integrity and reliability.

In a broader perspective, entrepreneurship can also be characterized as the interaction of the following characteristics:

- Entrepreneurial ability.
- Entrepreneurial skills.
- Entrepreneurial personality.
- Entrepreneurial motivation.
- Entrepreneurial cognition.
- Entrepreneurial self-efficacy.

Entrepreneurial Ability: It is the possession of abilities necessary for starting and nurturing a new enterprise, especially in a competitive environment. That is, the ability to start, nurture and grow businesses to both profitability and survival. It comprises of the talent or skills required, first of all to perceive business opportunities and thereafter to exploit them. The Lucas Model (1978) emphasized that those who were endowed with superior ability would become entrepreneurs, whilst those possessed inferior ability would become employees.

Entrepreneurial Skills: Entrepreneurial skills are simply business skills, which an individual acquires to enable him function effectively in the turbulent business environment. Agbonifoh (1999) defined entrepreneurial skills as skills relating to identifying business opportunities and receiving a sustainable income from these opportunities. The acquisition of entrepreneurial skills means combining personal characteristics, financial resources within one's environment and taking advantage of them for rewarding outcome.

Brouwer (2002) opined that entrepreneurial skills means possessing the ability to find and evaluate business opportunities, gather the necessary resources, initiate appropriate action to ensure success; and implement actions to take advantage of the opportunities for rewarding outcome. There is a pattern to entrepreneurial skills that can be explained by reference to the following three dimensions:

- **Technical Skills:** Ability to perform the key operations of the business. Some technical skills are: specific operation technology; communication; interpersonal relations; organizational ability; coordinating team members; and environmental observation.
- **Management Skills:** Ability to organize and efficiently manage the operations. The basic management skills required are: planning; formulating goals; decision-making; motivating; marketing; accounting; and negotiation.
- **Entrepreneurial Skills:** Ability to identify market opportunities and create strategies to capture those opportunities like: inner discipline; risk-seeking; innovation; change-orientation; persistence; and vision.

Entrepreneurial Personality: The entrepreneurial personality combines the psychological and sociological characteristics of an entrepreneur. A few of them are listed below.

Psychological Characteristics inclusive of being highly confident; risk taker; motivated reasoning; thirsting for the right answer; thinking logically and being practical.

Sociological Characteristics consisting of inconsistency in planning; blend with the environment; cognitive dissonance; ability to comprehend chaos; and lateral thinking—thinking may not be supported rationally.

Entrepreneurial Motivation: In common perception, entrepreneurs are after money and they engage in profit making. True, profit—as understood in terms of the residual income of the owner after meeting all the expenses incurred on the engagement and utilisation of other factors of production—is the reward of entrepreneurship just as salary is to men and women in employment and professional fee is to those in profession. So everybody works for money. But people certainly don't work for money alone. After all, money is required not for its own sake, but for the sake of the needs of the person that it can fulfil.

Money, thus, is not the need as such. It is teleological (to put it more simply, distantly) related to the internally felt needs (such as need for food) and socially acquired needs (such as status symbols). This leads us to the needs framework of studying entrepreneurial motivation. This framework serves the important purpose of enabling us to understand what motivates an entrepreneur.

McClelland identified three types of manifest needs, namely, Need for Achievement (N-ach.), Need for Power (N-pow.) and Need for Affiliation (N-aff.). If a man speculates about who is boss, he has a concern for power, notes McClelland. If a man readily thinks about interpersonal relationships, then he has a concern for affiliation. But entrepreneurial behaviour is so much singularly attributed to the need for achievement. N-ach concerns issues of excellence, competition, challenging goals and overcoming difficulties that will make an entrepreneur feel self-worthy and self-reliant.

Entrepreneurial Cognition: Entrepreneurial cognitions are the knowledge structures that people use to make assessments, judgments or decisions involving opportunity evaluation, venture creation and growth. Hindle (2004) opined that entrepreneurial cognition is all about *understanding how entrepreneurs use simplifying mental models to put back together previously unconnected information that helps them to identify and invent new products or services and to assemble the necessary resources to start and grow the business.* Bloom (Richey 2000) classifies cognitive learning objectives and consequently cognitive competences hierarchically as: (i) *knowing* of concepts, rules, procedures and theories, (ii) *understanding the knowledge* with capabilities of self-change, foresight, integration and forecasting, (iii) *using the knowledge* in terms of operation, problem solving, and knowledge transfer, (iv) *analysis* with capabilities of information interpretation, (v) *synthesis* with capability of new conceptual links creation and experimentation, and (vi) *evaluation* with the capabilities of value judgments about the use of different methods, technical solutions and products (Dermol 2010). In consensus to this, Pagon, Banutai and Bizjak (2008) define the following types of cognitive competences: divergent thinking, critical thinking, problem solving, strategic thinking, analytical skills, and numerical abilities.

Entrepreneurial Self-efficacy: Self-efficacy can be defined as a person's belief about his or her ability and capacity to accomplish a task or to deal with the challenges of life (Bandura 1993; 1997). It seems that self-efficacy affects the individuals' beliefs about possibilities to realise the objectives, as well as their personal choices, desires, efforts and perseverance—even in case of setbacks or obstacles (Boyd and Vozikis 1994). On the other hand, if individuals perceive that a given behaviour exceeds their capacity, they do not react–even in cases when society encourages such behaviour. Empirical studies show that self-efficacy has a reciprocal effect on entrepreneurial competences. Absorption of competences and past performance enhances self-efficacy and helps to strengthen the desire and improve future performance. This applies vice versa as well—self-efficacy affects the acquisition of competences and individual performance. Boyd and Vozikis (1994) note that self-efficacy is obtained through life stages, it is developed in line with experience since it enables the development of complex cognitive, social, linguistic and/or motor skills.

Entrepreneurial Competency

A pertinent starting point in conceptualizing entrepreneurial competencies is to first define competence. Competence can be defined as the ability of implementation, especially of something physical, mental or financial, or as a legal power to achieve something. It is either a natural skill or an acquired skill or talent. As identified by Lans et al. (2008) competences are a mix of knowledge, skills and attitudes.

They can also be defined as broader personal characteristics necessary for superior behaviour, but also as an outcome of a proper application of knowledge (Brown 1993). Competency was first popularized by Boyatzis (1982).

He opined that *competency is a capacity that exists in a person that leads to behaviour that meets the job demands within the parameters of organizational environment, and that, in turn brings about desired results*. Le-Brasseur, Blanco and Dodge (2002) note that when considering competences the emphasis is on *behaviour* and *performance*. They understand competency as 'an effective performance of a task or activity in a job setting, due to the underlying characteristics of the individual: motives, traits, skills, self-image, social role, or knowledge and experience.' Gibb (1990, 21), defines competence as an ability to perform certain tasks for which knowledge, skills, attitudes and motivations are necessary.

Entrepreneurial competencies include those clusters of related knowledge, attitudes, and skills which an entrepreneur must acquire through managerial training and development to enable him produce outstanding performance, and maximize profit, while managing a business venture or an enterprise. Quite often, less attention is paid to these critical success variables; rather attention is focused mainly on financial resources.

Business or entrepreneurial failures are readily attributed to inadequacy of financial resources. This calls for a shift in paradigm, in rethinking about entrepreneurial failures, by focusing on entrepreneurial competencies as the missing links to successful entrepreneurship. The small-scale business enterprises can achieve high level of productivity through the application of what he calls the people-based approaches or techniques, such as employee motivation, organizational communication, employee training and development, participation in decision making, among others. Emphasis must be re-focused in developing entrepreneurial competencies in the entrepreneurs to enable them contribute maximally to the economic development of the society.

Entrepreneurial Competencies and Entrepreneurship

Entrepreneurial competencies have to play a crucial in entrepreneurship. On a critical analysis of the present day situation in India, it can be seen that the following factors contribute favourably as links to successful entrepreneurship.

Time Management: Time is a scare resource, it is irreplaceable and irreversible. It means a business man must choose the best and wisest way to spend it. In fact, time has been now recognized as one of the factors of production in the world of managerial excellence. In order to achieve more in the day to day business, the entrepreneur must be thoroughly equipped with the skills for managing his/her time effectively. The entrepreneur needs to learn how to manage his time effectively by carrying out activities such as: quick decision-making habits, keeping diaries, delegating duties, avoiding unnecessary interruptions, properly conducted meetings, avoiding queues, selecting and following priorities. A successful entrepreneur is an effective time manager.

Communication: Communication is the exchange of ideas from the sender to the receiver. The specific goals of communication in an organization are to influence, inform and/or to express feelings. The entrepreneur, therefore, requires effective communication skills for several reasons: Communication process helps the entrepreneur effect the managerial functions of planning, organizing, staffing, influencing, interacting, controlling, and coordinating. It facilitates distribution of work to various categories of staff. It is an effective tool for staff participation in decision-making and entrepreneurial effectiveness.

It enhances the development of actual understanding among all organizational members and helps to create good public relations or image for an organization. Communication is an instrument for maintaining staff discipline and in asserting authority over subordinates and it serves a means of transmitting information, work instructions and feedback at the workplace. It is obvious therefore, that communication is the most important tool the entrepreneur uses in getting things done and the basis for understanding, for coordinating and for action. In carrying out this vital managerial responsibility, the entrepreneur must learn to communicate in correct, clear, short and courteous manner in order to accomplish the desired goals.

Human Resources Management: The human resources of most companies are the most difficult to obtain, the most expensive to maintain and the hardest to retain. Capital and materials are of equal importance to the organization but, inanimate and unemotional; they demand no understanding of human needs and motivations for their effective utilization. All the activities of any enterprise are initiated and determined by the persons who make up the institution. Plans, offices, computer automated equipment and all else that a modern firm uses, are unproductive except for human effort and direction. The human resources as the most dynamic of all the organization's resources that need considerable attention from the organization's management if they are to realize their full potential in their work The entrepreneur needs to put in place both human resources and capital resources (money, machinery, materials and methods) in order to achieve the overall organizational goals and objectives.

Without acquisition of human resource management skills, the capital resources earlier mentioned cannot be effectively used. The effective management of the human resources of an organization determines the success or failure of the organization because all other resources (inanimate) depend on the human element. The obvious justification for small-scale business organization to pay serious attention to human resources management function since this contributes significantly to entrepreneurial success. The entrepreneur must follow important procedures for interviewing, hiring, evaluating and preparing job description for new employees. Instituting an effective organizational culture can also be useful in human resources management.

Marketing Management: Marketing skills in the growth stage of a new venture are also critical to a venture's continued success. As the company grows, it will need to develop new products and services to maintain its distinctiveness in a competitive market. This should be an ongoing process based on information regarding changing. Marketing is crucial to the survival and growth of any organization. It is only marketing that brings revenue into the organization which is used to settle bills, acquire assets, carry out expansion, pay dividends and taxies and embark on community projects as part of its social responsibility.

In essence, all the funds generated by an entrepreneur are dependent on marketing. The marketing function interrelates with almost all other functional areas of business such as accounting, finance, production, engineering and human resources. The marketing function is central and strategic to a firm's success. The importance of marketing management skill of an entrepreneur cannot be overemphasized. It is a matter how lofty the entrepreneur's ideas, techniques and products are—effective marketing must be applied in order to reap the dividends of his endeavour.

Business Ethics: It concerns the rules and principles that define right and wrong, good and bad conduct. Ethics also deals with moral ability and obligations. It is viewed as a system of rules governing the ordering of values in society. Business ethics is sometimes called management ethics, and it is the application of ethical principles to business relationships and activities. The entrepreneurs and employees have ethical responsibilities or obligations, which are placed on them by virtue of the positions, they occupy in the organization. Business ethics is becoming a subject of intense concern for society, which is now demanding that organizations should operate responsibly and maintain very high ethical standards to improve the quality of life of the people. Managers are thus dealing with different publics. A recent review of entrepreneurial studies finds that the general lack of business ethics—lack of disciplined behaviour by entrepreneurs and officials charged with the execution of government entrepreneurial assistance programmes—was a major missing link in successful entrepreneurial development.

Social Responsibility: The establishment of every business venture is backed up by the profit motive. It is the profit that drives shareholders into buying shares and private capital owners into investing their capital. The profit motive leads to the production of goods and services. The business venture also has the responsibility to embark on certain projects within and outside its environment as part of its social responsibility. Business should not only be concerned about the quality of goods and services they produce to generate profit but also their contribution to the quality of life in their operational environment.

It is the obligation of businessmen to pursue those policies, to make those decisions or to follow those lines of action, which are desirable in terms of objectives and values of the society of their location. The business operators have a responsibility to protect and improve society, and their actions should not in anyhow endanger a community or society. They should display high degree of corporate responsiveness, which is the ability of an organization to relate its operations and policies to the environment in ways that are mutually beneficial to the organization and the society.

The entrepreneur in a small business venture still must effect some social responsibilities, even if not on a larger scale like those undertaken by corporate organizations. He needs to make contribution to community development, product safety, employment generation, ethical business practices, contribution towards educational activities like award of scholarships, and even creating opportunity for apprenticeship training, and so on. Undertaking some of these responsibilities may endear the entrepreneur to his host community; enhance his image and social standing, thus contributing significantly to his business success.

Leadership: Leadership is the most important single factor in determining business success or failure in our competitive, turbulent, fast moving global economy. The quality of leadership is the decisive strength or weakness of organizations and institutions. The ability to produce the necessary leadership is the key determinant of achievement in all-human activities. Successful entrepreneurs are successful leaders—they have power to motivate the entrepreneurial venture. In other words, for an entrepreneur to succeed, he/she must have the ability to direct the organization and persuade others to seek defined objective enthusiastically. Entrepreneurs are creative individuals with unique leadership qualities and personal styles. They seek opportunities, initiate projects, gather the physical, financial and human resources needed to carry out projects, set goals for themselves and others, and direct and guide others to accomplish goals. Effective leadership is a potent tool in the hands of the entrepreneur, which helps him to turn his business vision into reality.

Decision-making: Decision-making is at core of entrepreneurial activities. Making a decision is one thing and making the right decision given the circumstances is another. Many individuals have difficulty bringing their ideas to the market and creating a new venture. Yet entrepreneurship and the actual entrepreneurial decisions have resulted in several millions new businesses being started throughout the world. Dccision-making is the process of selecting among available alternatives. This selection process may be very difficult especially when the available alternatives are numerous. An entrepreneur makes decisions on daily basis and therefore has to acquire adequate knowledge and skills in decision making to enable him/her make the right decisions.

The decision taken at any point of time may either make or mar an enterprise completely. The ability to make good decision is one of the most important skills of the successful person. In studies where the careers of managers who were promoted rapidly were compared to those of managers who were passed over for promotion, researchers found that the one distinguishing behaviour of the more rapidly promoted managers is that they were more decisive in everything they did". Making a decision is as important as implementing the decision. Sometimes the right decisions are actually made but the courage to implement it is not there. An entrepreneur has to acquire adequate knowledge, skills and attitude to making the right decisions and implement it in order to achieve optimum result in a given situation. It follows therefore, that an entrepreneur can only succeed in his undertaking when he makes the right decisions and is also able to ensure that they are implemented and subject to change if necessary.

Financial Management: One of the characteristics of a successful entrepreneur is his/her ability to source for funds for his enterprise. These funds have to be properly managed to ensure that at any point in time, there will be adequate funds to cater for the day to day running of the enterprise. Financial management covers planning, organizing, directing and controlling of the firm's financial resources. An entrepreneur needs to acquire knowledge on financial management issues like anticipation of financial needs for the enterprise, acquisition of funds and allocation of funds in order to yield optimum result.

To achieve these goals he or she needs to maintain the correct proportion of the firm's finances in three key areas: savings, insurance and investments. Most entrepreneurial failure is due to the inability of the entrepreneurs to effectively manage funds which they source for their ventures. The acquisition of financial management knowledge is therefore a necessary factor in entrepreneurial success. The essence of financial management is, therefore, to ensure that there is adequate cash on hand to meet the necessary current and capital expenditures as well as to assist in maximizing growth and profits.

Entrepreneurial Competencies and Performance

There is a very strong link that strengthens entrepreneurial competency and performance. The competency of an entrepreneur in his business can be measured only by his performance. The various measures of business performance include, longevity of survival or more popularly age of the enterprise, sales growth, growth in market share, growth in market scope (local, national or international), growth in investment (in the same unit), additional units created via acquisition and diversification growth in number of employees, profits and so on.

Most of these are physical growth and financial growth parameters and have been the traditional measures of entrepreneurial performance. In the early 1980s, an entrepreneur is said to be competent only if he generates high profits. Of late, other measures of performance such as customers' satisfaction, employee satisfaction, image and credit rating are also becoming increasingly relevant. These measures are typically referred to as 'stakeholder-based' parameters. As the small firms grow into acquiring corporate identities, market based parameters such as stock price and EPS may also be the relevant measures of entrepreneurial performance. This new development has played a major role in breaking the myth that the competency of an entrepreneur is only measured in terms of his monetary performance.

Development of Entrepreneurial Competency: Competence can be acquired and developed (Baron and Ensley, 2006; Bird, 1995; DeTienne and Chandler, 2004). Baron and Ensley (2006) found that experienced entrepreneurs were able to recognize more seemingly unrelated patterns than novices and that these were more closely related to the actual business operations. This suggests that, with experience, entrepreneurs develop skills and acquire knowledge. But for an entrepreneur to be competent, he should have some attitudinal, managerial and behavioural competences along with the learned competencies.

In other words, the development of entrepreneurial competence is crucial for entrepreneurial success, but the acquisition of knowledge alone is insufficient and has to be followed by the ability to use it and the belief that one has access to it.

Common Entrepreneurial Competencies

In addition to defining competencies in terms of the possession of traits, skills, and knowledge, researchers have attempted to organize these entrepreneurial characteristics into key competency areas. Baum et al. (2001) distinguished between specific competency and general competency. Specific competency consists of industry skills and technical skills, while general competency includes organization skills and opportunity recognition skills.

Sony and Iman (2005) decomposed entrepreneurial competency into four dimensions: management skills, industry skills, opportunity skills and technical skills. In a meta-analysis of entrepreneurial competencies, Man et al., (2002) identified six areas of competencies associated with the firm's performance, i.e. opportunity competencies, relationships competencies, conceptual competencies, organizing competencies, strategic competencies, and commitment competencies. These competencies were derived from the studies carried out in developed economies. He defined entrepreneurial competencies as higher-level characteristics encompassing personality traits, skills and knowledge, which can be seen as the total ability of the entrepreneur to perform a job successfully. Six major competencies identified in his work are as follows.

Opportunity Competencies: The most important competency required for the entrepreneur is the opportunity related competency. Along with idea generation, an entrepreneur should also have the ability to recognize and envision taking advantage of opportunities. This category of competencies comprises of the entrepreneurial activities in spotting opportunities, actively seeking new opportunities, and developing the opportunities.

Organizing Competencies: Organizing competencies are

similar to the managerial competencies. These groups of competencies calls for the ability to lead, control, monitor, organize, and develop the external and internal resources towards the firm's capabilities through the entrepreneur's organizing competencies in different areas.

Strategic Competencies: Formulation and implementation of strategy is very important when an entrepreneur starts his business. Strategic competencies play a vital role as it requires the entrepreneur to have a vision or a big picture in their mind for their business, to have clear goals to achieve, or to formulate and implement strategies to achieve these vision and goals.

In essence, these competencies are related to setting, evaluating and implementing the strategies of the firm, while calling for abilities and skills from a broader and long-term perspective.

Relationship Competencies: The influence of an individual-to group and person-to-person interaction cannot be neglected in the present business scenario like building a context of cooperation and trust, using contacts and connections, persuasive ability, communication and interpersonal skill. To successfully do so, an entrepreneur needs to possess competencies in relationship building, communication, persuasive and interpersonal abilities (McClelland, 1987; Lau et al., 2000). Bird (1995) described this relationship building activities as entrepreneurial bonding, which includes not only the creation of relationship, but also the restructuring of relationships as the company grows or a partnership is dissolved.

Commitment Competencies: More than any other factors, total dedication to success as an entrepreneur can overcome obstacles and setbacks. Sheer determination and an unwavering commitment to succeed often win out against odds that many people would consider insurmountable. They also can compensate for personal shortcomings by being highly successful in the work they do.

In other words, an entrepreneur who possesses strong

competency in totally committing, determining and dedicating, as well as taking proactive actions towards their responsibilities and duties can succeed. Another aspect of this competency area is the initiative or proactive orientation, which calls for the entrepreneurs taking actions before being asked or forced to by events. To sum up, commitment competencies are those competencies that drive the entrepreneur to move ahead with the business.

Conceptual Competencies: Conceptual competencies represent a category of competencies which are not easily identifiable behaviours but are often considered to be important for entrepreneurial success. Prior research suggests that risk-taking, innovativeness, decision making skills are among the conceptual competencies of entrepreneurs (Man et al., 2002).The ability in making cognitive and analytical thinking, learning, decision-making and problem solving, sustaining temporal tension, innovating and in coping with uncertainty and risk, belong to this category (McClelland, 1987; Bird, 1995).

They have a stronger linkage with entrepreneurial traits and are less directly observable. They involve high level of conceptual activities and are reflected in the entrepreneur's behaviours when they conduct analysis, learn, make decisions and solve problems etc. They may also enhance the effectiveness of carrying a task in the present or in the future. Similar to strategic competencies, conceptual competencies require a more abstract level of abilities. However, unlike strategic competencies, conceptual competencies are concerned with a shorter-term perspective, resolving instant events, or requiring intuitive responses (Man et al., 2002).

Entrepreneurial Competencies in Attitudinal, Behavioural and Managerial Domains

Entrepreneurship scholars suggest that entrepreneurial competencies are vital to business growth and success. Different competencies are needed at different stages of the venture development (Churchill and Lewis, 1983). Man et al. (2002) suggested that entrepreneurial competencies are more important during the start-up phase, while managerial competencies are more significant at the growth stage. External stimuli (e.g., uncertainty (Autio et al., 2011); business environment (Man and Lau, 2005); social environment (Mitchelmore and Rowley, 2010), situation (Capaldo et al., 2006) and internal stimuli (e.g., the nature of education (Colombo and Grilli, 2005); family background in business (Basu and Goswami, 1999); and individual's characteristics (Brownell, 2006)) influence on emergence and development of entrepreneurial competencies.

Attitudinal Competency Attributes

An attitude is a mental or neural state of readiness organized through experience which exerts a directive or dynamic influence upon the individual's response to all objects and situations with which it is related (Allport, 1935). Hence, entrepreneurial attitude denotes the entrepreneur's dispositions that are constituted by one's beliefs, affects and behavioural tendencies. 'Attitudinal Competency' is the ability to select, maintain or adapt one's best attitudes for the present. Some attitudinal competencies are as follows:

Self-confidence: Self-confidence is an important trait for an entrepreneur because in order to succeed, he should have a realistic belief in himself and should have the ability to achieve the pre-determined goals. A successful entrepreneur has a strong belief in oneself and his own abilities. He expresses confidence in his own ability to complete a task or meet a challenge and sticks with own judgment in case of opposition or lack of success

Self-esteem: Self-esteem of an entrepreneur represents his ability to develop healthy confidence and respect for himself. He feels confident for being capable for life, able and worth or to feel right to achieve happiness. An entrepreneur respects himself and defends his own interest and needs.

Dealing with Failures: Entrepreneurship is about getting up whenever the business fails, and learning from that failure. An entrepreneur believes that failure is part of the entrepreneurial process, and often without it, success would not be possible. Further, he is able to make mistakes, learn from them, and quickly recovers and changes his direction and moves into the future.

Tolerance for Ambiguity: In the entrepreneurial process, tolerance for ambiguity refers to the ability of an entrepreneur to perceive ambiguous situation as desirable, challenging, and interesting and neither denies nor distorts their complexity of incongruity.

Performance: A successful entrepreneur perceives that his performance is different from others. He believes that it is his high performance which ultimately differentiates him from low performers.

Concern for High Quality: An entrepreneur should do things that will meet or beat existing standards of excellence. They have a desire to produce work with high quality and compare their own work with others to overcome their shortcomings. By doing this, an entrepreneur remains ahead of others in the market place.

Locus of Control (LoC): Locus of control indicates the degree to which an individual assumes or feels responsibility for success or failure in his life as opposed to feeling that external agents, like luck, is in control. The concept which was introduced by Rotter (1966) and expanded by Phares (1973) and Lefcourt (1976) is derived from social learning theory. They strongly believed that entrepreneurs can shape their own destiny.

Behavioural Competency Attributes

Behavioural competences are personal, learnable competences related to entrepreneurial or enterprising behaviour. They represent the answer to the question—how to behave in certain entrepreneurial situations. The behaviour an entrepreneur should highlight in particular competences are related to:

researching and realisation of entrepreneurial opportunities, production of creative ideas, taking responsibility for the execution of such ideas or other activities, handling the uncertainties and risks, creating favourable coalitions within an organisation, selling skills, initiative taking, problem solving and overcoming potential barriers (Jong and Wennekers, 2008). The attributes contributing to behavioural competency are as follows.

Initiative: Taking the initiative refers to his behaviour as a self-starter who sees problems and takes action to correct them without being told. An entrepreneur with high initiative searches for information needed to accomplish tasks or make decisions, develops new plans, procedures, or systems and takes an active role in critical situations and exhibits the pacesetter style of leadership when required. It further denotes that he is able and willing to do more than what is required or expected of him in a job.

Persistence: An entrepreneur is said to have persistence when an extraordinary effort is made to complete a task or overcome an obstacle. A persistent entrepreneur takes repeated action to overcome obstacles and ensure that the goals are met. Entrepreneurs seldom give up when things are not going well.

Assertiveness: Assertiveness of an entrepreneur is about confronting issues directly. Successful entrepreneurs do not become emotionally involved in stressful situations and address key issues and conflicts with confidence. It is his behavioural aspect that affirms his rights or point of view without either aggressively threatening the rights of others (assuming a position of dominance) or submissively permitting others to ignore.

Need for Achievement: Successful entrepreneurs are characterized by a need for achievement which motivates them to take up responsibilities for finding solutions to problems. Further, this quality helps them to set challenging goals for themselves, assume personal responsibility for the goal accomplishment and they are highly persistent in pursuit of these goals.

Need for Autonomy: A main driver of entrepreneurship is the need for autonomy. Stepping into self employment means becoming your own boss and the need for autonomy as a non-financial value becomes an important explanation when entrepreneurs take this career choice although their financial outcome might be lower when compared to other alternatives. The need for autonomy of an entrepreneur is characterized by one's strive to be independent and having control. Therefore, successful entrepreneurs should have high need for achievement and low need for power.

Risk-taking: Entrepreneurs are essentially persons who take decisions under uncertainty and therefore they are willing to bear risk. Entrepreneurs are usually moderate risk takers. However, successful entrepreneurs will always prefer to take on those risks that they can manage.

Drive and Energy: Entrepreneurs are driven to succeed and expand their business. They are always on the move, full of energy and highly motivated. They are driven to succeed and have abundance of self motivation.

Innovation: Innovation refers to the behaviour pattern of an individual who has interest and desire to seek changes in techniques and ready to introduce such changes into his operations practically and feasibly.

Creativity: An entrepreneur is said to be creative when he is able to identify a gap in the market and think up a product or service to meet that gap. Creativity of an entrepreneur also implies the ability to do old thinks in a new way or able to give new solutions.

Managerial Competency Attributes

Quinn et al. (1996) proposed eight managerial roles that have to be played by an entrepreneur: mentor, facilitator, monitor, coordinator, director, producer, broker, and innovator. Each role demands some specific competences—in most cases related to communication skills—for example, entrepreneurs as mentors should be able to communicate effectively with their subordinates and to develop them as well. LeBrasseur, Blanco and Dodge (2002) in their study of entrepreneurial competences, identified the top five competences required during the survival stage of a small firm: perseverance, effective communication, judgement, individual productivity, and creative thinking. If an entrepreneur has the ability to direct his staff and to get the work done efficiently and effectively, then he is said to possess managerial competency. Some vital managerial competency attributes are as follows.

Information Seeking: An entrepreneur should be capable to make an informed decision and take action on how to get information in order to help the business to achieve its objectives or to solve business problems. For example, conducting personal research on a product or service, consulting with experts or relevant authorities to get information, using contacts or information networks to obtain useful information or personally undertaking market research, analysis or investigation.

Systematic Planning: An entrepreneur is expected to develop logical, step-by-step plans to reach goals. He should develop plans that will anticipate the obstacles and also evaluate various alternatives.

Problem Solving: Entrepreneurs should identify new and potentially unique ideas to reach goals. They should be capable of generating new ideas or innovative solutions to solve problems and they take alternative strategies to solve the problems.

Persuasion: Entrepreneurs with this competency influence the environment comprising individuals and institutions for mobilizing resources, organizing production and selling goods and services to develop business contacts. They have an inherent ability to influence others and to present themselves in a convincing way to others. This helps them to create contacts and maintain good rapport.

Goal setting and Perseverance: Goal setting refers to the ability of an entrepreneur to set clear and specific goals and objectives. Successful entrepreneurs are able to achieve great things only by overcoming the obstacles that stand in their way. Therefore, they need to have perseverance which implies commitment, hard work, patience and endurance apart from being able to bear difficulties calmly and without complaint.

Communication Skill: Communication skill refers to the ability of an entrepreneur to transfer ideas, plans, policies and programmes to employees, debtors, creditors, customers and everyone who is connected with the business in order to inform, influence and to express his feelings.

Technical knowledge: An entrepreneur needs to address the rapid technical changes in the industry. Higher levels of technology must be introduced in the production methods in order to achieve productivity demands. Therefore, he must up date his technical knowledge in order to serve customers quickly and more effectively.

Social Skill: Social skill of entrepreneurs include social perception (the ability to perceive others accurately), expressiveness (the ability to express feelings and reactions clearly and openly), impression management (skill in making favourable first impressions on others), and social adaptability (proficiency in adapting one's actions to current social contexts) in the process of managing his business.

It may be concluded that the entrepreneur is an important agent of change, contributing significantly to the economic development of India in terms of wealth and employment creation, stimulation of indigenous entrepreneurship and so on. The government on its part recognizes the strategic and economic role of the entrepreneur and has continuously crafted policies that would enhance the development of entrepreneurship in the country. The government policy initiatives have tended to emphasize more of financial resources than other critical factors to entrepreneurial success.

The critical success factors—the entrepreneurial competencies—which have been neglected for long, should be considered as very essential and necessary variables in entrepreneurial development. The entrepreneur needs to acquire competencies in such areas as managing time effectively, communication, human resources management, business ethics and social responsibilities, developing effective leadership qualities, decision making skills, marketing and financial management. These entrepreneurial competencies, which are rooted in effective training and development, can serve the needed tonic for success in business.

References

Abraham, H. and Gurzynski, Z.S.A. (1987), The Entrepreneur as a Non-factor, *South African Journal of Economics*, Vol. 55, No. 2, pp. 115-118.

Barcelona, A.C. and Valida, A.C. (1994), Inter-relationships between Personal Variables and Entrepreneurial Potentials of Senior Students of University of Utara Malaysia, *Malaysian Management Review*, 29(4).

Burch, J.G. (1986), Entrepreneurship, John Wiley & Sons, New York, NY.

Brockhaus, R.H. (1982), The Psychology of the Entrepreneur.

Cunningham, J.B. and Lischeon, J. (1991), Defining Entrepreneurship, *Journal of Small Business Management*, Academic Research Library, p. 45.

Gartner, W. (1985), A Conceptual Framework for Describing the Phenomenon of New Venture Creation, *Academy of Management Review*, Vol. 10, pp. 696-706.

Gorman, G., Hanlon, D. and King, W. (1997), Some Research Perspective on Entrepreneurial Education, Enterprise Education and Education for Small Business Management: A Ten Year Review, *International Small Business Journal*, 15(3), pp. 56-87.

Herron, L. and Robinson, R.B. (1993), A Structural Model of the Effects of Entrepreneurial Characteristics on Venture Performance, *Journal of Business Venturing*, 8(3), pp. 281-294.

Mayer, F. and Sutton, K. (1996), Personality: An Integrative Approach, Prentice-Hall, Inc., New Jersey.

McClelland, D.C. (1967), The Achieving Society, The Free Press, New York, NY.

Olson, D.E. (2000), The Role of Entrepreneurial Personality Characteristics on Entry Decisions in a Stimulated Market,

Association of Small Business and Entrepreneurship (USASBE); United States;

Schumpeter, J.A. (1934), The Theory of Economic Development, Cambridge, MA: Harvard University Press, 1934.

Spencer, L.M. and Spencer, S.M. (1993), Competence at Work: Models for Superior Performance, John Wiley and Sons, New York, NY.

Warren, L. (2004), Negotiating Entrepreneurial Identity-Communities of Practice and Changing Discourses, *International Journal of Entrepreneurship and Innovation,* 5(2), pp. 25-37.

3

Digital Age in Banking and Finance

Rajagopalan P.

The business of banking, especially financial services/retail banking, is undergoing a sea change, as the business shifts increasingly to online environment. The increasing number of customers transacting online would move the "market place" to "market space", where banks would be forced to expand their product range to competitors' products, while rapidly innovating their own value-added products.

Technology, and more specifically, the internet, has evolved in to an essential access channel. The internet offers for banks, a cost effective means of innovating, publicizing and delivering services to the customers. It also helps to maintain customer relationships. For the customer, the internet has opened up enormous possibilities of convenience and choice. Today, most banks use internet as their global expansion platform, offering an increasing array of financial services online.

Electronic finance can be defined, as all which relates to the linking of business, finance and banking via electronic means, encompassing information gathering, processing, retrieval, and transmission of data as well as the transmission, purchase, and selling of goods and services. Franklin Allen, James McAndrews and Philip P. Strahan define e-finance as *the provision of financial services and markets using electronic communication and computation.* Financial services is concerned with the design and delivery of advice and financial products to individuals and businesses within the areas of banking and related institutions, personal financial planning, investment, real assets, insurance, and so on.

E-finance including investing, banking, mortgage lending and insurance has grown at a dazzling rate in the recent years. E-finance empowers both consumers and businesses, enabling them to reduce transaction costs, speedily process documents online, and have instantaneous access to information. For businesses, online finance can dramatically improve efficiency and decrease the costs of internal business functions such as expense reporting, contract labour management etc. The increasing importance of e-finance, in which the computer is playing a more central role in delivering financial services, is bringing tremendous changes to the structure of the banking industry.

Efficiency of a financial system depends upon the quality and variety of financial services provided by financial intermediaries. The term financial services can be defined as activities, benefits and satisfactions, connected with the sale of money, that offer to users and customers, financial related value.

Electronic financial services, especially online banking, and brokerage services, whether delivered online or through mobile phones or other remote mechanisms or through smart cards have spread quickly in the recent years. This e-finance revolution is dramatically changing the structure and nature of financial services around the world. E-finance penetration varies by type of service. Most affected have been brokerage markets where online trading is becoming a norm. Trading system for equities, fixed income, and foreign exchange are consolidating and going global.

Trading is moving toward electronic platform not tied to any location. Electronic trading and communication networks have lowered the costs of trading and allow for better price determination. The internet and other technological advances have shrunk economies of scale in the production of financial services. Lower scale economies have increased competition, particularly among financial services that can easily be unbundled and commoditized through automation including bill payment services, mortgage loans, insurance, and even trade technology.

Managing risks will become more important to protect consumers and investors. E-finance can increase long-standing risks such as theft and lack of privacy as well as create new ones. Thus, more emphasis is needed on better disclosure, education and information. The internet is starting to provide solutions, with firms acting as certification agents, aggregators, and vendors of security and privacy hardware and software on behalf of consumers, investors and financial service providers.

Benefits of Electronic Banking

The two important benefits of electronic banking as far as the customers are concerned are as follows:

- Systematically Important Payment System (SIPS): High value clearing and Real Time Gross Settlement (RTGS) are classified under this category since they benefit large corporate and high net worth customers.
- Financial markets clearing and other important retail payment facilities: Financial markets clearing is intended primarily for government securities and foreign exchange markets. Retail payment systems, such as e-banking, gives customers, the control over nearly every aspect of managing their bank accounts.

There are at least three benefits of electronic banking for the banks. They are:

- The internet allows banks to reach new markets and high net worth individuals, because there are no geographic boundaries with the internet. It also provides a level playing field for small banks who want to add to their customer base.
- The internet provides the bank with an almost paperless system. With better and faster options, a bank can create better customer relations and satisfaction.

- In the long-run, a bank can reduce expenses by not paying for tellers or for managing branches.

An essential element of an efficient and deep financial system is the ability of intermediaries to effect smooth and secure transfers of money and exchange financial claims embedded in financial instruments.

International Standards and Codes for Payment and Settlement Systems

The Committee on Payment and Settlement Systems (CPSS) was set up by the Bank for International Settlements as a standing committee, with the objective of strengthening financial market infrastructure through promoting sound and efficient payment and settlement systems. CPSS was formed by G-10 Central Banks in 2001 with the specific objective of formulating broad supervisory standards and guidelines for payment and settlement systems.

The membership of CPSS has widened beyond G-10 countries, to include 25 Central Banks in 2009. The RBI is a member CPSS. After formulating the "Core Principles of Systematically Important Payment Systems" in 2001, CPSS published in 2002, along with International Organization of Securities Commissions (IOSCO), its "Recommendations for Securities Settlement Systems (SSS)". This was followed up with CPSS-IOSCO "Recommendations for Central Counterparties" (CCP) in 2004.

Payment and Settlement Systems in India

The RBI has spearheaded a vast change in the use of technology for making banking in India safer, more secure, smoother, and more efficient. RBI was empowered in 2007 through the enactment of the Payment and Settlement Act, 2007 to regulate and supervise payment and settlement systems in India, formulate relevant policies and provide a legal basis for multinational netting and settlement finality. To operationalise the Act, RBI framed the "Board for Regulation and Supervision of Payment and Settlement Systems Regulations, 2008" and Payment and Settlement Systems Regulations, 2008".

Retail Payment Systems

Retail payment systems are required primarily for purposes such as payments for goods and services, bill payments, cash payments and so on. The paper based payment and settlement mechanisms in practice in India are as follows:

- Magnetic Ink Character Recognition (MICR) cheques and non-MICR cheques.
- High values clearing.
- Speed clearing of cheques drawn on outstation CBS branches of drawee bank processed in local clearing.
- Cheque truncation.

The electronic clearing and settlement system being operated are as follows:

- Electronic Clearing Service (ECS), National Electronic Clearing Service (NECS).
- Electronic Funds Transfer (EFT).
- National Electronic Funds Transfer (NEFT).

Paper-based Instruments in Retail Payment System

Cheques: The most common form of notational money is an account with cheque facility. A cheque is an order authorizing the transfer of money from one account to another.

Magnetic Ink Character Recognition (MICR): Magnetic ink character recognition is a character recognition system that uses special ink and character. The cheque, which contains this ink, needs to be read, and passed through a machine, which magnetizes the ink and then translates the magnetic information into characters. Banks use MICR technology on cheques, which provides secure, high speed method of scanning and processing information.

Speed Clearing: This new clearing arrangement was introduced in India in 2008 for collection of outstation cheques through local clearing, provided such cheques were drawn on "Core Banking Solution" (CBS) enabled branches of paying banks. Cheques drawn on outstation CBS branches of a bank can be processed in local clearing, thus reducing the time taken for realization of out station cheques, thus enabling payment on a (T+1) [1] or (T+2) [2] basis. Speed clearing has been introduced at 53 centres as of March 2009. As on June 30, 2012, there are 1,234 speed clearing centres.

High Value Clearing: This is a paper based clearing for large value payments, currently operational at 27 major cities in India. The clearing process is computed on the same day for cheques of ₹ 1 lakh and above payable in the same city.

Cheque Truncation: Truncation is the process of stopping the transit of a paper based cheque from the drawer to the drawee branch of a bank. The physical cheque will be truncated at some point enroute to the drawee branch, and would be replaced by an electronic image of the cheque. Cheque truncation is a more secure alternative to the actual movement of physical instruments from place to place.

Electronic Retail Payment Systems

Electronic Clearing Service (ECS): Bulk and repetitive payments like interest/dividend are mostly paper based involving printing of warrants in costly MICR format, dispatching them by post and reconciliation thereof after payment by the agency banks. ECS is a retail payment system that facilitates bulk payments (such as dividend payment) and bulk receipts (such as utility payments). These two aspects are handled by two components of the system-ECS (Credit) and ECS (Debit). *ECS (credit)* facilitates bulk payments, where an institution makes payment to several retail customers.

Examples are payment of dividend and interest warrants to investors, payment of salaries to employees etc. In *ECS (Debit),* many individuals/firms pay to one firm or utility. Thus, the accounts of various customers of the utility in different banks have to be debited and the amounts have to be credited to the utility company's account with designated banks. Using a specific mandate, the utility can also advice the customer's banks to debit payments on due dates.

ECS (Centralised): A third facility called the NECS is centralized and available at the RBI, Mumbai.

NECS-Credit, like ECS (Credit), facilitates multiple credits to beneficiary accounts at destination branches across the country against a single debit in the account of a user with the sponsor bank from a single central location at Mumbai.

Similarly, the NECS-Debit would facilitate multiple debits to destination account holders across the country against a single credit to the user account at Mumbai.

The NECS is a nationwide system leveraging on CBS of member banks. All CBS bank branches are participants in the system, irrespective of their location.

National Electronic Funds Transfer (NEFT): Electronic funds transfer system was introduced by RBI in 1997 as an inter-city, intra-city and inter-bank, intra-bank fund transfer mechanism by which funds can be transferred by any bank branch to any other bank branch from one city to another.

EFTs process pre-authorized debits or credits from one bank account to another within a 48-hour period.

It is similar to standing instructions maintained in customers' accounts, which are carried out automatically at pre-appointed dates.

The EFT system was replaced in November 2005 by the NEFT, an electronic message based payment system using Public Key Infrastructure Technology to ensure end-to-end security.

NEFT using the INFINET to connect bank branches for electronic transfer of funds.

Plastic Money and E-money

Plastic money refers to substitution of currency at the time when a payment is taking place by using a card normally made of plastic representing such substitution. The most important objective would be the need to postpone actual payment, or pre-purchase payment on the card that is issued. The most important advantage of plastic money is protection to the user from the risks of carrying cash. Since it is the exclusive property of the card holder, it means that it can be used only by him. The different types of plastic money are as follows:

Credit Cards: Credit cards started off as a type of payment cards issued by some merchants for the convenience of their customers. It is believed that the first such card was issued by SEARS in 1910. The popular DINER'S CLUB Card was introduced in 1949 to be used in multiple restaurants. Today, credit cards are synonymous with a form of short-term, revolving credit to the card holder.

Credit cards can be broadly classified into three types: Bank Cards, Travel and Entertainment Cards and, Company or Retail Store Cards. The *Bank Cards* are sponsored by individual banks and considered all purpose cards. Each bank decides credit limits, annual fees, terms and conditions. e.g., MasterCard, Visa.

The *Travel and Entertainment Cards* are used by people for travel and entertainment expenses. In many cases, card holders are expected to pay the balance outstanding in full every month, e.g. American Express, Diner's Club. Unlike credit cards, here, card holders are expected to pay the balance outstanding in full every month. The *Company or Retail Store Cards* are used in the retail store or gas station. These are issuer specific and cannot be used for all purposes, e.g., Wal-Mart, Reliance, BP.

According to the purpose for which the credit cards are used, they can be classified into three main categories: (i) credit card, (ii) charge card, and (iii) in-store card. A charge card is intended to serve as a convenient means of payment for goods purchased at member establishments rather than a credit facility. The in-store cards are issued by retailers or companies. In India, such cards are issued by five star hotels, resorts etc. The new types of credit cards are: (a) corporate credit cards, (b) business cards, and (c) smart cards. Corporate credit cards are issued to private and public limited companies.

Depending upon the requirements of each company, operative add-on cards will be issued to persons authorized by the company like directors, secretary etc. A business card is similar to a corporate credit card. It is meant for the use of proprietary concerns, firms, and firms of chartered accountants etc. A smart card is a new generation card. In the smart card, an embedded microchip will store a monetary value. When a transaction is made using the card, the value is debited and the balance comes down automatically. Once the monetary value comes down to nil, the balance is to be restored all over again for the card to become operational.

Debit Cards: Debit card is a product through which the customer's own account with the card issuer is debited immediately to the extent of the transaction value. Debit card does not allow the customer to borrow, nor does it provide revolving credit.

If credit card advocates 'pay later', debit cards signify 'pay now'. The most important benefit of debit card is that the customer does not have to carry a cheque book or large sums of cash.

Other Payment Channels/Products

Automated Teller Machines (ATMs): Consumer behaviour is changing rapidly due to the development of technology, and the use of banking services is characterized by individuality, mobility, independence of time and place, and flexibility. Cash delivery is increasingly being done on the huge base of automated teller machines (ATMs), which are being increasingly net worked together to permit customers to collect cash from different banks. The spread of ATMs has increased from about 35,000 in March 2008 to about 1,26,950 in August 2013. The wonders of modern computer technology have also enabled banks to lower the cost of bank transactions by having the customer interact with an electronic banking facility rather than with a human being. One important form of an e-banking facility is the automated teller machine (ATM), an electronic machine that allows customers to get cash, make deposits, transfer funds from one account to another, and check balances.

Virtual Card: A virtual card is a card that can be generated by anybody, at any time provided he has already registered his name in the bank's website. There is always a fear in the minds of credit card holders that their credit card numbers might get into the hands of some unscrupulous persons. So, for those who do not want to part with their credit card number to the merchant web site, the solution is to use a virtual card.

Mobile Banking: Mobile banking can be used for small value payments at relatively lower costs. Therefore, mobile banking is being used in many developing countries as a delivery channel to facilitate financial inclusion. Studies indicate that formal banking reaches 37 percent of the population, while mobile phones are owned by more than 50 percent of the population. There are two distinct models that can be operated: (i) the bank-led, and (ii) telecom company-led models. India has adopted the bank led model. RBI provided guidelines for mobile banking transactions in India in October 2008.

Pre-paid Payment Instruments: There are payment instruments, such as smart cards, magnetic strip cards, interest accounts, internet wallets, mobile accounts, mobile wallets etc. where value is stored in advance to be used when required. The value stored is the value paid by cash, debit or credit card by the instrument holder. Purchase of goods and services is made against the stored value in the pre paid instruments. Hence, these instruments serve as a convenient and relatively risk-free mode of payment in-lieu of cash, and for e-payments through internet/mobile.

The importance of sophisticated or high technology for improving customer service, productivity, and operational efficiency of banks is well recognized. As a part of their action plans, banks in India have introduced many new techniques and a considerable degree of mechanization and computerization in their operations. By the end of June 1996 itself, they had installed 13,522 advance ledger posting machines (ALPM) at 4,238 branches, and 895 minicomputers at their regional and zonal offices at 441 branches.

Electronic Cash: Electronic cash is also known as electronic money, electronic currency, digital money, digital cash, digital currency, cyber currency, e-currency, and e-money. It is money or scrip that is only exchanged electronically. This involves the use of computer networks, the internet and digital stored value systems. e.g., electronic funds transfer (EFT), direct deposit, digital gold currency, and virtual currency.

To date, the use of e-cash or e-money has been relatively on a low-scale. The only success story is that of Hong Kong's Octopus Card System. It was started as a transit payment system and has grown into a widely used electronic money system. Other examples are: London Transports' Oyster Card System, a contactless pre-paid travel card, Singapore's FeliCa, Netherland's Chipknip and Ov-chipkart. In Belgium, a payment service company, Proton, owned by 60 Belgian banks issuing stored value cards, was developed in 1995.

It is concluded that during the last twenty years, technology has assumed the vital role of not only a facilitator, but also a source of competitive advantage for banks. The business of financial services shifts increasingly to the online environment. The increasing number of customers transacting online would move the 'market place' to 'market space'. The internet offers a cost-effective means of innovating, publicizing, and delivering services to the customer, as well as maintaining customer relationship.

As far as the customers are concerned, the Internet has opened up enormous possibilities of convenience and choice. Online banking began in the mid-1990s and is steadily becoming more important. In contrast to banks, insurance companies have used the internet a relatively small amount. Electronic brokerage services have been an important development in recent years. To sum up, the increasing importance of e-finance, in which the computer is playing a more central role in delivering financial services, is bringing tremendous changes to the structure of the banking industry in India.

End Notes

1. T+1 means that the party will receive money the very next day after the trade day.
2. T+2 means the second day after the trade day.

References

Allen, Franklin, McAndrews, James and, Strahan, Philip, *E-Finance-An Introduction,* Working Paper, Wharton Financial Institutions Centre, pp. 1, 4 and 34.

Claessens, Stign et al., *Electronic Finance-A New Approach to Financial Sector*, World Bank Discussion Paper No. 431, p. 5.

Suresh, Padmalatha and Paul, Justin (2010), *Management of Banking and Financial Services,* Dorling Kindersley (India) Pvt. Ltd., New Delhi, pp. 480-487.

Mishkin, Frederic S. and Stanley G. Eakins, *Financial Markets and Institutions*, Pearson Education Inc., New Delhi, pp. 45, 474.

Khan, M.Y. (2010), *Financial Services,* Tata McGraw Hill Education Pvt. Ltd., New Delhi, pp. 11-18.

Bhole, L.M. and Mahakud, Jitendra (2010), *Financial Institutions and Markets*, Tata McGraw Hill Education. Pvt. Ltd., New Delhi, p. 310.

4

Electronic Payment Systems and Liquidity Flow in Indian Business

M. Sarngadharan

Electronic payment is the financial exchange that takes place online between buyers and sellers in a business house. The content of this exchange is usually some form of digital financial instrument—such as encrypted card numbers, electronic cheques or digital cash—that is backed by a bank or an intermediary, or by a legal tender. The major factors that have forced the financial institutions to make use of electronic payments are many. The technology used in the networks is decreasing day by day, which is evident from the fact that computers are now dirt-cheap and internet is becoming free almost everywhere in the world. Due to reduced technology cost, the processing cost of various commerce activities becomes very less. The very simple factor that has favourably contributed to the popularity of electronic payment is that in electronic transactions, it is possible to save both paper and time.

Traditionally, a customer sees a product, examines it, and then pays for it by cash, cheque, or credit card. In the e-commerce world, in most cases the customer does not actually see the concrete product at the time of transaction, and the method of payment is performed electronically. Issues of trust and acceptance play a more significant role in the modern business world than in traditional businesses as far as payment systems are concerned. The state of e-financing has been on a growing stage in India. The transition to a full-scaled digital economy would depend on speedier deregulation which will follow once the macro-economic reforms process matures further.

The gradual acceptance of e-finance models is precisely the indicator of this inter-connectedness of e-financing structures with parallel developments and advances in the legal, regulatory spheres as well as the modernization of business and industrial markets. Corporate enterprises have, however, taken up modernization like implementing ERP systems which permit the use of advanced management techniques like CRM and data mining with enthusiasm and are, thus, more and more prepared to bring their entire supply chains onto e-financing structures.

There are at present three major statutes/guidelines governing e-finance in India, namely:

- Information Technology Act, 2000.
- Information Technology (Certifying Authorities) Rules, 2000.
- Central Bank [Reserve Bank of India (RBI)] guidelines on internet banking.

The RBI guidelines lay down the operational framework on Internet Banking and focuses on security issues. While RBI has mandated that the commonly used public key infrastructure (PKI) technology standard should be followed, no mandatory time-frame has been set. The guidelines detail the organisational, operational, and supervisory structures to be implemented by all banks offering Internet Banking. The IT Act, 2000 and the IT Rules for Certifying Authorities have been enacted and they lay down the framework for appointment of digital certifying authorities and acceptance of digital signatures. These regulations would thus enable the orderly development of cyber business.

Banking in India has been undergoing a paradigm shift in the way banks are doing their business and retaining and increasing their customer base. The basic underlying current that runs through this changing landscape is the ever increasing reliance on technology to cater to the needs of customers and process vast number of transactions including payment transactions. In fact, payment and settlement systems form the backbone of any economy. They are the conduits or the arteries for conducting trade, commerce and other forms of economic activities including remittances in any country.

An efficient payments system can be envisaged as the lubricant which speeds up the liquidity flow in the economy, thereby creating the necessary impetus and momentum for economic growth. The payments process is a vital aspect of financial intermediation; it enables the creation and transfer of liquidity among different economic agents. A smooth, well functioning and regulated payments system thus not only ensures efficient utilization of scarce resources but also eliminates systemic risks. The payments and settlement system is, therefore, a crucial component of the financial infrastructure of any country and more so of a country like India.

In India, almost half of the population remains outside the purview of banking. In fact, India has the highest number of households among the other countries in the world, who have not come under the banking fold. Financial inclusion should be seen not only as a social responsibility but also as a potential business model because of the huge untapped market that it seeks to bring into the fold of banking services. The huge section of the Indian population remaining outside banking, presents a large untapped market with a tremendous business potential. Therefore, the banks in India need to devise appropriate strategies for tapping the banking value that is represented by these large numbers of households at *the bottom of the pyramid.*

The spectacular growth in financial transactions in the economy of India has necessitated certain radical changes in the payments and settlement systems, whether it is in the area of wholesale payments or retail payments. While the changes in the wholesale payments are devoted to providing an efficient channel for transmission of monetary policy signals, and for the smooth functioning of various markets, the changes in the retail payments are aimed at providing efficient and timely payment mechanisms to the citizens of this country.

The payment system also assumes importance in the context of domestic financial sector reforms and global financial integration that the Indian economy has been undergoing since 1991. Foreign investments (direct and portfolio) are encouraged by the availability of an efficient payments system, as also the need for a low cost remittance facility for migrants to send money to their family members. Improved, faster and cheaper domestic money transfers through the payments system is also a part of the emerging scenario.

It is high time that we pay more attention to the EPS emphasizing five As of payment system—*availability, accessibility, acceptability, affordability and awareness* of the system and the products. Availability combines the notion of a level playing field for the service providers along with the availability of choice of products for the consumers. Accessibility as a concept should be the cornerstone to expand the reach of the banking systems and the various payment products to all the sections of the society including the financial inclusion plan and efforts. Acceptability is the thought process which enables the customers to embrace the newer products and technology such that these become ubiquitous in nature just as mobile telephony has become in the country.

Affordability is a key corner stone which should guide the product offering as being value for money for the customers with technology and innovation being the important drivers for providing cost effective and quality services by the service providers. Awareness creation through financial literacy campaigns is necessary to increase the volumes in the payments business and to generate the necessary network effects for the successful operationalisation and implementation of newer technologically cost effective sound payment products. It is also imperative to simultaneously create awareness for inculcating security consciousness among the users of the various payment products to prevent instances of fraud and misuse.

It is against this background, that an attempt is made here to review the components of existing e-payment systems in India from a global perspective.

Payment Systems in India

EPS enables a customer in India to pay for the goods and services online by using integrated hardware and software systems. The main objectives of EPS are to increase efficiency, improve security, and enhance customer convenience and ease of use. Although these systems are in their immaturity, significant changes and development have taken place. There are several methods and tools that can be used to enable EPS implementation. While customers pay for goods/services by cash, cheque, or credit cards in conventional businesses, online buyers may use one of the following electronic payment systems to pay for products/services purchased online:

- Payment cards containing stored financial value that can be transferred from the customer's computer to the businessman's computer.
- Credit cards, the most popular method used in EPSs, are used by charging against the customer credit.
- Smart cards including stored financial value and other important personal and financial information are used for online payments.
- Electronic funds transfer (EFT) involving electronic transfer of money is widely used by financial institutions.
- Electronic money (e-money/e-cash) converting standard money into an electronic format is used to pay for online purchases (this device is yet to gain popularity in India).
- Online payment is used for monthly payment for internet, phone bills, etc.
- Electronic wallets (e-wallets), similar to smart cards as they include stored financial value, are used for online payments.

- Micro-payment systems, similar to e-wallets in that they include stored financial value are used for online payments (used for small payments).
- Electronic gifts are used for sending electronic currency or gift certificates from one individual to another. The receiver can spend these gifts in their favourite online stores provided they accept this type of currency.

Although these groups appear to be separate, there is some overlap among them. When the industry matures, this duplication in naming and functioning ought to be renamed. For example, e-wallets can be classified as payment cards when they are used to store credit card information or as e-cash when they store electronic currency. The standardization of payment mechanisms on the Internet is essential to the success of EPS. Businesses offering domestic and international services must have assurance that payment will be received, that it is secure and that it is valid. Addressing security issues is crucial to the acceptance of online payment standards—consumers and merchants must be able to trust that their information is kept intact and remains secure during transmission.

However, electronic payment system accounts for more than 40 percent of the total volume of transactions, while it represents 90 percent of the total value of transactions. Introduction of electronic payment products, such as electronic clearing service and electronic funds transfer, which over the years have metamorphosed into National ECS and National EFT and RTGS have ushered in new ways of payment processing. Now, let us discuss the components in the EPS individually, under different heads based on the above mentioned grouping.

Payment Cards

The most commonly used payment cards are credit cards, debit cards, charge cards, and smart cards.

Credit Cards: Credit card is the payment card issued to

users as a system of payment. It allows the cardholder to pay for goods and services based on the holder's promise to pay for them. The issuer of the card creates a revolving account and grants a line of credit to the consumer (or the user) from which the user can borrow money for payment to a merchant or as a cash advance to the user. A credit card is different from a charge card—a charge card requires the balance to be paid in full each month. In contrast, credit cards allow the consumers a continuing balance of debt, subject to interest being charged. It also differs from a cash card, which can be used like currency by the owner of the card. It differs from a charge card that a credit card typically involves a third-party entity that pays the seller and is reimbursed by the buyer, whereas a charge card simply defers payment by the buyer until a later date.

Credit cards are issued by a credit card issuer, such as a bank or credit union, after an account has been approved by the credit provider, after which cardholders can use it to make purchases at merchants accepting that card. When a purchase is made, the credit card user agrees to pay the card issuer. The cardholder indicates consent to pay by signing a receipt with a record of the card details and indicating the amount to be paid or by entering a personal identification number (PIN).

Also, many merchants now accept verbal authorizations via telephone and electronic authorization using the Internet, known as a card not present transaction. Electronic verification systems allow merchants to verify in a few seconds that the card is valid and the credit card customer has sufficient credit to cover the purchase, allowing the verification to happen at time of purchase. The verification is performed using a credit card payment terminal or point-of-sale (POS) system with a communications link to the merchant's acquiring bank. Data from the card is obtained from a magnetic stripe or chip on the card—the latter system is called Chip and PIN.

For *card not present transactions* where the card is not shown (e.g. e-commerce, mail order, and telephone sales), merchants additionally verify that the customer is in physical possession of the card and is the authorized user by asking for additional information such as the security code printed on the back of the card, date of expiry, and billing address. Each month, the credit card user is sent a statement indicating the purchases undertaken with the card, any outstanding fees, and the total amount owed.

After receiving the statement, the cardholder may dispute any charges that he or she thinks are incorrect .The cardholder must pay a defined minimum portion of the amount owed by a due date, or may choose to pay a higher amount up to the entire amount owed which may be greater than the amount billed. The credit issuer charges interest on the unpaid balance if the billed amount is not paid in full (typically at a much higher rate than most other forms of debt). In addition, if the credit card user fails to make at least the minimum payment by the due date, the issuer may impose a late fee and/or other penalties on the user. To help mitigate this, some financial institutions can arrange for automatic payments to be deducted from the user's bank accounts, thus avoiding such penalties altogether as long as the cardholder has sufficient funds.

Many banks now also offer the option of electronic statements, either in lieu of or in addition to physical statements, which can be viewed at any time by the cardholder via the issuer's online banking website. Notification of the availability of a new statement is generally sent to the cardholder's email address. If the card issuer has chosen to allow it, the cardholder may have other options for payment besides a physical check, such as an electronic transfer of funds from a bank account. Depending on the issuer, the cardholder may also be able to make multiple payments during a single statement period, possibly enabling him or her to utilize the credit limit on the card several times over.

The main benefit of credit card to each customer is convenience. The credit card allows small short-term loans to be quickly made to a customer who need not calculate a balance remaining before every transaction, provided the total charges do not exceed the maximum credit line for the card. Many credit cards offer rewards and benefits packages, such as enhanced product warranties at no cost, free loss/damage coverage on new purchases, various insurance protections, for example, rental car insurance, common carrier accident protection, and travel medical insurance.

Credit cards can also offer reward points which may be redeemed for cash, products, or airline tickets. Researches in the global scenario have examined whether competition among card networks may potentially make payment rewards too generous, causing higher prices among merchants, thus actually deteriorating social welfare and its distribution, a situation potentially warranting public policy interventions.

Merchants, who accept credit cards, must pay interchange fees and discount fees on all credit-card transactions. In some cases, merchants are barred by their credit agreements from passing these fees directly to credit card customers, or from setting a minimum transaction amount. The result is that merchants may charge all customers (including those who do not use credit cards) higher prices to cover the fees on credit card transactions. Researches show that a substantial fraction of consumers (about 40 percent) choose a sub-optimal credit card agreement, with some incurring huge amount of avoidable interest costs.

Several studies have shown that consumers are likely to spend more money when they pay by credit card. Researchers suggest that when people pay using credit cards, they do not experience the abstract pain of payment. Furthermore, researchers have found that using credit cards can increase consumption of unhealthy food.

For merchants, the credit card transaction are often more secure than other forms of payment, such as cheques, because the issuing bank commits to pay the merchant the moment the transaction is authorized, regardless of whether the consumer defaults on the credit card payment (except for legitimate disputes). In most cases, cards are even more secure than cash, because they discourage theft by the merchant's employees and reduce the amount of cash on the premises. Credit cards reduce the back office expense of processing cheques/cash and transporting them to the bank.

Prior to credit cards, each merchant had to evaluate each customer's credit history before extending credit. That task is now performed by the banks which assume the credit risk. Credit cards can also aid in securing a sale, especially if the customer does not have enough cash. Extra turnover is generated by the fact that the customer can purchase goods and/or services immediately and is less inhibited by the amount of cash in his pocket and the immediate state of his bank balance.

Parties involved in credit cards are cardholder, card-issuing bank, merchant, acquiring bank (the financial institution accepting payment for the products or services on behalf of the merchant), independent sales organization (but in general is the organization that the merchant deals with), credit card association (an association of card-issuing banks such as Discover, Visa, MasterCard, and American Express), transaction network and affinity partner, and insurance providers. The flow of information and money between these parties—always through the card associations—is known as the interchange, and it consists of a few steps.

Debit Cards: Debit card is electronic plastic card that is used as a substitute for cash. Bank debit card helps reduce the need for carrying cash and cheque. Debit card is directly linked to a cardholder's bank account. Whenever a card holder withdraws money from an ATM or uses the debit card for making payments, his account balance is automatically reduced. The number of debit cards is projected to cross 34.4 million by 2016 in India. The history of debit cards shows that they have largely been used to pay for food and drinks. The same financial institutions offer both debit cards and credit cards. Both the cards have been offering special rewards, such as points and cash back on purchases made through the card.

Debit cards and credit cards can be used to make online payments with the help of the PIN assigned to them. They can be used to withdraw money from ATMs, depending on the cash limit available on these cards.

Debit cards and credit cards differ in some significant ways. In the case of a credit card, the issuer offers credit and overdraft facilities. This facility is not available with a debit card, which will only debit payments from existing and available funds within the cardholders account. A credit cardholder therefore has a monthly bill to pay in every month that the card is used. If they do not pay that bill, high interest charges are applied. A debit card holder is free from the hassle of paying those bills, and from the risk of building up large debts to credit card companies.

Debit cards are offered by banks in the following forms: online card; prepaid card; offline card; electronic purse debit card; debit cards for telephone, mail and internet transactions. Debit cards offer the benefits such as they help people to be disciplined financially, since one cannot splurge with the limited amount of funds deposited for the card and person with poor credit can obtain a debit card without too much trouble. Debit cards can be used to make online purchases and payments and they provide freedom from carrying cash and cheques, while travelling, thereby offering more safety. Debit cards do not charge high interest rates or fees on card transactions.

However, there are limitations for debit cards, such as they come with lesser fraud protection facilities than credit cards. Some transactions cannot be carried out with a debit card, for instance, renting a car in a foreign country. In case of an emergency where credit is urgently needed beyond the account balance, a debit card may not be enough to meet the needs. Debit cards are becoming more popular because they use the funds from the cardholder's savings account, offering convenience and safety. Find an overview on the debit card companies which have been acting as a substitute for cash while travelling or buying things from the market. Debit card has been used as an alternative mode of payment these days.

Charge Cards: Charge cards are similar to credit cards except they have no revolving credit line, so the balance must be paid off every month. Credit, debit, and charge card methods of payments have been successfully utilized in the pre-internet period, and they are often used in the e-commerce world as well. Some of the reasons for their popularity in the e-commerce world are their availability (most customers own one of these cards), ease of use, and acceptance. To use these cards as an online payment system, a well-defined process is followed.

The procedures are: To accept cards payments, a merchant must have a merchant account with a bank. The buyer will be required to submit his credit-card number, expiration date and shipping and billing information when making a purchase online using a payment card. A customer using his browser clicks on a product on the merchant's website and adds it to an electronic shopping cart. The customer provides the shipping instructions and payment card information. This information is sent securely over the internet to the merchant's commerce site. The server software adds the merchant identification to the information transmitted. The merchant then submits this information to the acquiring bank with which the merchant holds an account.

The merchant bank transmits this information to the customer's bank for authorization. Then, the buyer's account information is verified. This involves the issuing bank from which the buyer obtained the credit card, and the credit-card association. Verification is received by the acquiring bank and is passed on to the merchant who then ships the product. Payment cannot be issued to the merchant until the product has been shipped. This entire process (not including shipment) takes only a few seconds. The relative merit of charge card is that the customer need not pay immediately but only at the end of the monthly period, if he has a bank account, it is debited automatically. Otherwise, he needs to transfer money directly to the card association.

Smart Cards: Most people have an image of smart cards as rectangular pieces of plastic that resemble credit cards. Although this is often the case, smart cards can take several forms, including Credit cards, Key-shaped tokens; and SIM chips in GSM cellular phones. Smart cards contain a built-in processor and are programmable. Smart cards have secure storage for data, including private keys and public key certificates. While the card has processing capability, it must be connected to a PC device to be useful for purposes such as smart card logon to a domain. This connection is achieved by placing the card in a smart card reader that is connected to the computer.

There is another type of smart card, called a contactless card that transfers data over radio waves. At this time, however, this type of card is not covered by the specification that defines smart cards and readers. Smart cards run embedded operating systems and in many cases a form of file system in which data can be stored. Smart cards must support authentication and authorization: the card holder is authenticated through a personal identification number (PIN) or other mechanism, and can be authorized to access only particular data on the card, or carry out a particular range of activities with the card.

Smart cards can be disposable or rechargeable. A popular example of a disposable smart card is the one issued by telephone companies. After using the pre-specified amount, the card can be discarded. Smart cards have been extensively used in the telecommunications industry for years. Smart-card technology can be used to hold information on health care, transportation, identification, retail, loyalty programs and banking, to name a few. Smart cards enable information for different purposes to be stored in one location. The microprocessor chip can process different types of information, and therefore, various industries use them in different ways. Due to their multipurpose functions, their popularity in India is also on the rise.

Smart cards are broadly classified into two groups: contact type of smart card must be inserted into a special card reader to be read and updated. A contact smart card contains a microprocessor chip that makes contact with electrical connectors to transfer the data. Contact-less type of smart card can be read from a short distance using radio frequency. A contact-less smart card also contains a microprocessor chip and an antenna that allows data to be transmitted to a special card reader without any physical contact.

This type of smart card is useful for people who are moving in vehicles or on foot. They are used extensively in developed countries for collecting payment for highway tolls, train fares, parking, bus fares, and admission fees to movies, theatres, plays, and so forth. Some of the advantages of smart cards include the points: that they store many types of information; are not easily duplicated; do not occupy much space; portable, are of low cost to issuers and users; and have high security. There are a few limitations for smart cards like lack of universal standards for their design and utilization. On the other hand, smart card applications are expected to increase as a result of the resolution of these limitations in the near future.

Electronic Funds Transfer (EFT)

Electronic funds transfer is one of the oldest electronic payment systems. EFT is the groundwork of the cash-less and cheque-less culture where and paper bills, cheques, envelopes, stamps are eliminated. EFT is used for transferring money from one bank account directly to another without any paper money changing hands. The most popular application of EFT is that instead of getting a pay check and putting it into a bank account, the money is deposited to an account electronically. EFT is considered to be a safe, reliable, and a convenient way to conduct business. The benefits of EFT contain Simplified accounting; improved efficiency; reduced administrative costs;

and improved security.

EFT is actually a computer-based system which is utilized to carry out financial transactions electronically—basically through ecommerce websites. It is a revolutionary concept that is included in the ecommerce website mainly for monetary transactions which enables flow of cash for free as well as without taking much of time. This is important for website marketing. The best thing about this concept of the e-commerce website is that it requires no paper work as well as no personal checks for the procedure is to be completed as the entire procedure is done through networks.

This procedure becomes quite easy due to the availability of information. EFT through an ecommerce system is a very good way of transferring funds as the location of the provider as well as the recipient does not matter at all. Corporate business, large industry and multinational firm use EFT as a very important aspect for directly depositing all payments to their respective bank accounts of the company. There are certain formalities to be performed to make easy and smooth use of EFT through ecommerce website as a way of financial transaction.

EFT is of a great solution for those that want to get their money very quickly. It is always observed that there is some risk involved when any kind of transaction is carried out which is related in terms of money, most importantly when the two parties are far away from each other. However, this will no more be a problem with EFT and with ecommerce websites as due to its fast transaction feature it would not lead to any delay in money transfer.

Another thing that is very essential to know about EFT through ecommerce website is that there is no aspect of risk in handling transactional functions. EFT with marketing online can be used for number of concepts like cardholder, direct deposit, direct debit, online payment through e-commerce websites, wire transfer and many more.

Automated Teller Machines (ATMs)

ATMs are electronic machines, which are operated by a customer himself to deposit or to withdraw cash from bank. For using an ATM, a customer has to obtain an ATM card from his bank. The ATM card is a plastic card, which is magnetically coded. It can be easily read by the machine. To operate an ATM card, the customer has to inset the card in the machine. He has to enter the password (number). If the authentication or password (number) is correct, the ATM permits a customer to make entries for withdrawal or for deposit.

On completion of the transaction, the customer's card is ejected from the ATM. ATMs provide service round the clock. The customer can withdraw cash up to a certain a limit during any time of the day or night. ATMs provide convenience to the customers. Now-a-days, ATMs are located at convenient places, such as at the airports, railway stations, etc. and not necessarily at the bank's premises. It is to be noted that ATMs are installed off-site (away from bank premises) as well as on-site (installed within bank's premises). ATMs provide mobility in banking services for withdrawal.

There are two primary types of automated teller machines, or ATMs. The basic units allow the customer to only withdraw cash and receive a report of the account's balance. The more complex machines will accept deposits, facilitate credit card payments and report account information. To access the advanced features of the complex units, you will usually need to be a member of the bank that operates the machine. ATMs are scattered throughout cities, allowing customers easier access to their accounts.

Anyone with a debit or credit card will be able to access most ATMs. Using a machine operated by your bank is usually free, but accessing funds through a unit owned by a competing bank will usually incur a small fee. ATMs are of great help to travellers. They need not carry large amount of cash with them. They can withdraw cash from any city or state, across the country and even from outside the country with the help of ATM. The customer also gets brand new currency notes from ATMs. In other words, customers do not get soiled notes from ATMs.

Cheque Truncation System (CTS)

Truncation is the process of stopping the flow of the physical cheque issued by a drawer at some point with the presenting bank en-route to the drawee bank branch. In its place an electronic image of the cheque is transmitted to the drawee branch by the clearing house, along with relevant information like data on the MICR band, date of presentation, presenting bank, etc. Cheque truncation thus obviates the need to move the physical instruments across branches, other than in exceptional circumstances for clearing purposes.

This effectively eliminates the associated cost of movement of the physical cheques, reduces the time required for their collection and brings elegance to the entire activity of cheque processing. Cheque truncation speeds up the process of collection of cheques resulting in better service to customers, reduces the scope for clearing-related frauds or loss of instruments in transit, lowers the cost of collection of cheques, and removes reconciliation-related and logistics-related problems, thus benefiting the system as a whole.

With the other major products being offered in the form of RTGS and NEFT, the Reserve Bank has created the capability to enable inter-bank and customer payments online and in near-real time. However, as cheques are still a prominent mode of payments in the country and Reserve Bank of India has decided to focus on improving the efficiency of the cheque clearing cycle, offering cheque truncation system (CTS) as an alternative. CTS is a more secure system *vis-à-vis* the exchange of physical documents. In addition to operational efficiency, CTS offers several benefits to banks and customers, including human resource rationalisation, cost effectiveness, business process re-engineering, better service, and adoption of latest technology. CTS, thus, has emerged as an important efficiency enhancement initiative undertaken by Reserve Bank in the Payments Systems area. The Reserve Bank has implemented CTS in the National Capital Region (NCR), New Delhi and Chennai with effect from February 2008.

The new approach envisioned as part of the national roll-out is the grid-based approach. The concept of grid-CTS clearing is being envisaged as part of roll-out of CTS at Chennai. Under the grid clearing, cheques drawn on centres included in the grid will be cleared as part of local clearing. There is no change in the clearing process for customers. Customers continue to use cheques as at present, except to ensure the use of image-friendly-coloured-inks while writing the cheques.

Of course, such of those customers, who are used to receiving the paid instruments (like government departments) would also receive the cheque images. Cheques with alterations in material fields (explained in detail later) are not allowed to be processed under the CTS environment. The benefits are many. With the introduction of imaging and truncation, the physical movement of instruments is stopped. The electronic movement of images of cheques speeds up the process of settlement and can facilitate reduction in the clearing cycles as well.

Moreover, there is no fear of loss of instruments in transit. Further, limitations of the existing clearing system in terms of geography or jurisdiction can be removed, thus enabling consolidation and integration of multiple clearing locations managed by different banks with varying service levels into a nation-wide standard clearing system with uniform processes and practices. CTS brings elegance to the entire activity of cheque processing and clearing. Cheque frauds can be greatly reduced with introduction of minimum security features prescribed under CTS Standards 2010, such as embedded verifiable features such as bar-codes, encrypted codes, logos, watermarks, holograms, etc., for early interception of altered/ forged instruments. Obviating the need to move the physical cheques is extremely beneficial in terms of cost and time savings.

The benefits from CTS include shorter clearing cycle; superior verification and reconciliation process; no geographical restrictions are there as to jurisdiction; operational efficiency for banks and customers alike; and reduction in operational risk and risks associated with paper clearing. Under CTS, the physical cheques are retained at the presenting bank level and do not move to the paying banks. In case a customer desires, banks can provide images of cheques duly authenticated. In case, however, a customer desires to see/get the physical cheque, it would need to be sourced from the presenting bank, for which a request should be made to his/her bank. An element of cost/charge may also be involved for the purpose. To meet legal requirements, the presenting banks which truncate the cheques need to preserve the physical instruments for a period of 10 years.

CTS in India mandates the use of prescribed image specifications only. Images that do not meet the specifications are rejected. As the payments are made on the basis of the images, it is essential to ensure the quality of the images. To ensure only images of requisite quality move in the CTS processing cycle, there is a rigorous quality check process at the level of the capture systems and the clearing house interface (of the presenting bank). The solution encompasses image quality assessment (IQA) at different levels. The presenting bank is required to perform the IQA during the capture itself. Further, IQA is done at the gateway before onward transmission to clearing house.

The images are captured with digital signatures of the presenting bank and thereafter transmitted to the clearing house and then to the paying banks. Further, the paying banks, if not satisfied with the image quality or for any other reason, can ask for the physical instrument to facilitate payment processing. Further, the new cheque standard CTS-2010 prescribes certain mandatory and optional security features to be available on cheques, which will also add to the uniqueness of the images.

Banks/Customers should use "CTS 2010" cheques which are not only image friendly but also have more security features. Customers may request/insist their banks for cheque forms that are compliant with the "CTS 2010" standards. They should preferably use dark coloured ink while writing cheques and avoid any alterations/corrections thereon. Preferably, a new cheque leaf may be used in the event of any alterations/ corrections as the cheque may be cleared through image based clearing system as enumerated above. Banks should exercise care while stamping the cheque forms, so that it does not interfere with the material portions such as date, payee's name, amount and signature.

The use of rubber stamps, etc., should not overshadow the clear appearance of these basic features in image. It is necessary to ensure that all essential elements of a cheque are captured in an image during the scanning process and banks/customers have to exercise appropriate care in this regard. There are two modes in which banks may participate in CTS i.e. Direct membership wherein banks may participate as direct member provided they have a settlement account with the settlement bank and have put in place necessary infrastructure for participating in CTS and indirect/sub-membership wherein banks may become sub-members/ indirect members of the direct members by using the infrastructure and/or settlement services of the direct members. The settlement for such indirect/sub-member could be done either directly (if such banks have settlement accounts with the settlement bank) or through the direct member through whom they are participating. With amendments in the Sections 6 and 1(4), coupled with the introduction of 81 A to the Negotiable Instruments Act, 1881, truncation of cheques is now legalized.

Mobile Banking

Mobile banking is an electronic system that provides most of the basic services available in daily, traditional banking, but does so using a mobile communication device, usually a smart phone. In some cases, a well developed mobile banking system can actually provide point-of-sale ability similar to an ATM or credit card, except the purchaser buys by using their phone instead. Mobile banking as a financial tool has been seeing its time of acceptance occur very much thanks to increasing mobility offered by smart phones. Phones essentially pack the capability of a basic computer and internet access into a communication device.

The technological push for increased mobility and function via a phone has begun to take shape with increased capital investment into networks and systems that can support these features. Furthermore, young generations expect an increasing amount of automation to occur and meet their expectations of how the world should work. Banks, keen on increasing their portfolios and customer base, are redesigning how they market their services. The capability of mobile banking to offer to customers is seen as a niche advantage that can be offered by the more technologically capable market players. By attracting new customers with these features for daily banking, the banking industry then has new consumers—it can market other products to that make more profits, such as loans and investing services.

Today, more than half the population in India has a mobile phone. However, less than one percent of them use mobile phone as a medium for banking. Though mobile banking is synonymous with the word convenience banking, its usage is not anywhere close to its potential. With the advent of smart phones and ever growing usage of internet on mobile handsets, application based banking has emerged as a new concept within this space. Other than SMS banking, banks are now offering banking services on mobile handsets through WAP-based internet websites and application based mobile banking services.

With the RBI relaxing the limit on the value of mobile-based transactions and allowing non- banks to offer banking services as business correspondents appointed by banks, the focus is to drive banking services in rural areas where a large population is still devoid of banking facilities. This will also allow banks and non-banks to offer payment solutions using a mobile phone with the development of near field communication, barcode and sound wave technologies.

This will help to reach the goal of financial inclusion in India. With these technologies in place, banking on mobile handsets should lead to more transactions on the move as increased reach and last mile connectivity is better achieved via mobiles compared to traditional banking channels like branches and ATMs. Mobile-based payments and the commerce eco-system is still at a nascent stage and hence, acceptance among merchants and customers is currently low but is bound to increase over a period of time.

Internet Banking

Internet banking is a term used to describe banking transactions that are performed via a secured internet application. Web banking transactions include such things as paying bills, transferring funds, viewing account statements and paying down loans and mortgages. Although web banking has been popular among young internet-savvy people for many years, its popularity is expected to grow rapidly as Internet usage grows internationally and people discover the many advantages that it provides. Web-banking.org provides an overview of internet banking. It discusses conventional and virtual banks, e-banking services, internet security and the cost/benefit considerations.

Almost all the banks in the world are providing the online facility that includes from day to day transactions to account opening, issuing credit cards paying and getting the loans and debts and providing customers facilities to shop online. Some banks are also providing the facilities to draw cash from their bank accounts online and they can pay their bills individuals to perform banking activities at home, via the internet. Some online banks are traditional banks which also offer online banking, while others are online only and have no physical presence.

Online banking through traditional banks enable customers to perform all routine transactions, such as account transfers, balance inquiries, bill payments, and stop-payment requests, and some even offer online loan and credit card applications. Account information can be accessed anytime, day or night, and can be done from anywhere. A few online banks update information in real-time, while others do it daily. Once information has been entered, it does not need to be re-entered for similar subsequent checks, and future payments can be scheduled to occur automatically.

Many banks allow for file transfer between their program and popular accounting software packages, to simplify record keeping. Despite the advantages, there are a few drawbacks. It does take some time to set up and get used to an online account.

Also, some banks only offer online banking in a limited area. In addition, when an account holder pays online, he/she may have to put in a cheque request as much as two weeks before the payment is due, but the bank may withdraw the money from the account the day that request is received, meaning the person has lost up to two weeks of interest on that payment.

Online-only banks have a few additional drawbacks: an account holder has to mail in deposits (other than direct deposits), and some services that traditional banks offer are difficult or impossible for online-only banks to offer, such as traveller's checks and cashier's checks. The internet is rapidly turning out to be a tool of world wide communication. The increasing use of internet earlier promoted producers and entrepreneurs to sell their products online. It has also become an important source of information and knowledge. Due to this, many banking and finance organizations have come up with the idea of Internet banking or online banking.

Telephone Banking

The concept of telephone banking has been around for several decades. Initially, the process required manual intervention by a bank employee. Customers would call into the bank, answer questions to verify their identities, and submit queries to the service representative. While somewhat labour intensive, this approach did make it possible to conduct a number of banking transactions from the comfort of home. With the advent of touch-tone services, the idea of telephone banking took on a new direction. Instead of connected with a live bank representative, customers could use the keypad on a touch-tone phone to enter an automated system and obtain information on bank accounts as of the latest posting day.

One advantage of this newer approach is that bank customers could call any time of the day or night and check the status of their accounts. As technology continued to progress, the scope of functions that could be performed with the automated system expanded, making the service even more valuable to customers. There are several ways that a telephone banking service may be configured. Some function of a validation process that includes voice recognition before access to the customer accounts is granted.

Other systems make use of login credentials such as user names and pass codes that must be entered using the telephone keypad. Once the customer enters the correct data, the automated system makes it possible to perform a wide range of functions in relation to the accounts connected with the login credentials. The typical bank telephone customer can access his or her accounts to perform a variety of functions. Balances can be checked and the latest activity can be reviewed. The customer can also transfer funds between accounts using telephone banking, as well as order more cheques, make loan payments, or request information on other services the bank offers.

Electronic Cheque (E-cheque)

The electronic cheques are modelled on paper cheques,

except that they are initiated electronically. They use digital signatures for signing and endorsing and require the use of digital certificates to authenticate the payer, the payer's bank and bank account. They are delivered either by direct transmission using telephone lines or by public networks such as the internet—well suited for clearing micro payments. Conventional cryptography of e-cheques makes them easier to process than systems based on public key cryptography (like digital cash). They can serve corporate markets. Firms can use them in more cost-effective manner. They create float and the availability of float is an important requirement of commerce.

E-cheque is the result of cooperation among several banks, government entities, technology companies, and e-commerce organizations. An e-cheque uses the same legal and business protocols associated with traditional paper checks. It is a new payment instrument that combines high-security, speed, convenience, and processing efficiencies for online transactions. It shares the speed and processing efficiencies of all-electronic payments. An e-cheque can be used by large and small organizations, even where other electronic payment solutions are too risky or not appropriate. The key benefits of e-cheque are that it possesses qualities such as secure and quick settlement of financial obligations; fast check processing; and low transaction cost. E-cheque is being considered for many online transactions.

Electronic Cash

Similar to regular cash, e-cash enables transactions between customers without the need for banks or other third parties. When used, e-cash is transferred directly and immediately to the participating merchants and vending machines. Electronic cash is a secure and convenient alternative to bills and coins. This payment system complements credit, debit, and charge cards and adds additional convenience and control to everyday customer cash transactions. E-cash usually operates on a smart card, which includes an embedded microprocessor chip. The microprocessor chip stores cash value and the security features that make electronic transactions secure. The electronic payment systems are gradually used after the electronic commerce was in fashion.

However, the electronic cash (e-cash) in every electronic payment system cannot be circulated to other e-cash systems. In addition, the e-cash usually presents a fixed amount of money and should be used the whole amount in a trade. It is difficult to have the change back when the purchase price is lower than the amount of the e-cash. Herein, an e-mint system based on the Song-Korba's scheme which offered the anonymity and no-repudiation properties, is proposed. The proposed scheme not only can circulate all e-cash systems but also allows exchanging a large amount of the e-cash into some small amounts of e-cash. Therefore, anyone can keep the remainder money if he does not spend the whole amount of the e-cash in a trade.

Assume that there is an electronic cash-issuing bank (e-mint) that generates electronic cash. The e-mint signs the electronic cash as the issuer. It may use a digital signature algorithm. The e-mint issues the electronic cash based on the funds provided to it by the customer. The payer (customer) can use this electronic cash to purchase items over the Internet. The e-mint may typically issue electronic money in denominations of one cent to US$ 100, although other denominations (in various currencies) are also possible. Electronic cash transactions take place in three distinct and independent phases:

Phase 1: Obtaining e-cash: The consumer requests his/her bank to transfer money to the e-mint to obtain electronic cash. The consumer bank transfers money from the consumer's account to the e-mint. The e-mint sends electronic cash to the consumer, who saves the electronic cash on a hard drive or a smart card.

Phase 2: Buying with e-cash: This phase is executed whenever the consumer desires to make a purchase with electronic cash. It can take place at any time after the consumer has obtained electronic cash from the e-mint. A consumer can make purchases more than once as long as he/she does not run out of electronic cash. The consumer selects the goods and transfers the electronic cash to the merchant. The merchant provides the goods to the consumer.

Phase 3: Redeeming Cash: This phase occurs whenever the merchant is ready to redeem the electronic cash. The merchant should be capable of converting this electronic cash to money for the merchant's bank account. The merchant transfers the electronic cash to the e-mint. Alternatively, the merchant may send the electronic cash to his/her bank and the bank in turn redeems the money from the e-mint. The e-mint transfers money to the merchant's bank for crediting the merchant's account.

A similar scheme can be devised to transfer money between two individuals or institutions such as banks, universities or other businesses. E-cash is yet to gain popularity in India.

Electronic Wallets (E-wallets)

Electronic wallets being very useful for frequent online shoppers are commercially available for pocket, palm-sized, handheld, and desktop PCs. They offer a secure, convenient, and portable tool for online shopping. They store personal and financial information such as credit cards, passwords, PINs, and much more. To facilitate the credit-card order process, many companies are introducing clectronic wallet services. E-wallets allow you to keep track of your billing and shipping information so that it can be entered with one click at participating merchants' sites. E-wallets can also store e cheque, e-cash and your credit-card information for multiple cards

Micro Payments

Merchants must pay a fee for each credit-card transaction that they process; this can become costly when customers purchase inexpensive items. The cost of some items could actually be lower than the standard transaction fees, causing merchants to incur losses. Micro payments are used for small payments on the web. The process is similar to e-wallet technology where the customer transfers some money into the wallet on his or her desktop and then pays for digital products by using this wallet. Using micro payment, one will be able to pay for one article from a professional journal, a chapter from a scientific book, or one song from a CD on the web.

The micro payment system can be used for billing by banks and financial institutions, internet service providers (ISPs), content providers (offering games, entertainment, archives, etc.), telecommunications, service providers (offering fax, e-mail, or phone services over the web), and by premium search engines and specialized databases. Many developers have tried to push micro payment solutions to the Internet, but only very few have succeeded. The difficulty was never the technical implementation but the Internet itself. Every company on the internet gives away small pieces of information for free. Thus, it is hard to validate the need to pay for small bits of information. The other issue is a psychological difficulty. It makes financial calculations more difficult as you do not know in advance how much money the service will cost and spending money means always thinking about it for a while.

Peer to Peer Payments

A peer-to-peer payment service allows the transfer of digital cash (e-cash) via e-mail between two people who have accounts at e-cash-enabled banks. Peer-to-peer transactions allow online financial transfers between consumers. One example of peer-to-peer payment service is PayPal. Transactions through PayPal are immediate, the service is free for individuals sending money to one another and the payee is not required to enter any credit-card information. Businesses pay a small transaction fee. It allows a user to send money to anyone with an e-mail address, regardless of what bank either person uses, or whether or not the recipient is pre-registered with the service. That amount is hilled to the person's credit card, payment notification is sent to the recipient, and an account is established in the recipient's name.

When the person to whom the payment is sent, receives the e-mail notification, he simply registers with service provider and has access to an account containing the payment. The funds in this account can he transferred to the recipient's bank account by direct deposit or mailed by cheque. The transaction begins processing immediately after it is initiated, reducing the risk of fraud or overdrawn accounts. The buyer or the seller can initiate the service.

National Electronic Fund Transfer (NEFT)

National Electronic Fund Transfer (NEFT), introduced in November 2005, offers eleven hourly near real-time settlements on week days and five settlements on Saturdays. One of the unique features of the system is a mandatory *Positive Confirmation* to the originator confirming successful credit to the beneficiary's account. Since its inception, the system has witnessed a surge in the volume and value of transactions settling on a single day.

Real Time Gross Settlement (RTGS)

Real Time Gross Settlement (RTGS), introduced in March 2004, settles gross inter-bank and customer transactions. Steps have been initiated to replace the existing RTGS system with the Next Generation Real Time Gross Settlement (NG-RTGS) by adopting the latest technology and emerging business processes. Some of the new features proposed to be implemented in the NG-RTGS system are advanced liquidity management facility; extensible mark up language (XML) based messaging system conforming to ISO 20022; and real time information and transaction monitoring and control systems.

Other Retail Payment Channels

The National Financial Switch (NFS) as its name indicates

is a national infrastructure with pan-Indian presence provides a switching service for connectivity across ATMs of banks. The NFS enables customers to perform their transactions (both financial and non-financial) using ATMs under the NFS network without reference to the card issuing banks.

Core banking solution (CBS) in Reserve Bank of India will bring significant benefits to all the key stakeholders like government, banks, primary dealers, financial institutions and the common citizens. It will enable anywhere banking (especially payments) to government departments, treasuries, sub-treasuries through online access and use of e-payment modes/delivery channels. In other words, it would facilitate government to use RTGS, NEFT, NECS and other electronic delivery channels for making all its payments through a single bank resulting in reconciliation being that much easier. Banks and financial institutions will benefit from system of having a centralised account for funds and securities and an online transaction tracking mechanism linking funds and security legs. CBS is also intended to provide limited functionality of RTGS in case the RTGS services are not available for any reason.

In conclusion it may be stated that electronic payment is highly convenient to business as well as the consumers. Electronic payment lowers costs for businesses. The more payments they can process electronically, the less they spend on paper and postage. Offering electronic payment can also help businesses improve customer retention. A customer is more likely to return to the same e-commerce site where his information has already been entered and stored. The payment system today is vibrant, robust and technologically superior with multiple payment instruments, multiple access points and delivery channels to choose from.

However, the benefit of modern payment system is yet to fully percolate to all segments of the society. As a result, a substantial portion of the population is still outside the realm of the formal and modern payment system. In this endeavour, educating customers on the security comfort afforded by the payment products and the measures required to be taken by the customers for minimizing fraud and misuse should also be an integral part. It may be reiterated at this juncture that awareness creation through financial literacy campaigns is inevitable to enhance the volumes in the payments business and implementation of newer technologically would be cost effective for sound payment products.

References

Approach Paper for Rationalisation of Service Charges Levied by Banks on Electronic Payment Products (RTGS/NEFT/ECS) and Outstation Cheque Collection, RBI, September 11, 2008.

Daniel D. Garcia-Swartz, Robert W. Hahn, and Anne Layne-Farrar (2006), A Move Toward a Cashless Society: A Closer Look at Payment Instrument Economics, *Review of Network Economics,* 5(2): 175-198.

Das, Ashish and Rakhi Agarwal (2010), "Cashless Payment System in India: A Roadmap", Indian Institute of Technology Bombay.

Reserve Bank of India (2010), Annual Report of the RBI for the Year 2009-10, August 24.

Reserve Bank of India, Customer Charges for Use of ATMs for Cash Withdrawal and Balance Enquiry, RBI/2007-2008/260 DPSS No. 1405/02.10.02/2007-2008, March 10, 2008.

Reserve Bank of India, Report of the Working Group on Regulatory Mechanism for Cards (2005), RBI Report, April.

Vageesh, N.S. (2010), Shift to Card Payments to Save on Cash Printing Cost: Study, thehindubusinessline.com., September.

5

Ethical Dilemmas in the Digitized Era

Usha P.M.

Information has evolved as an imperative resource for any organization. The accessibility of information at fingertips has made information systems an inevitable component of business concerns. Bill Gates, Chairman of Microsoft, remarked that "Information technology and business are becoming inextricably interwoven. I don't think anybody can talk meaningfully about one without talking about the other".

But information systems can act as a double edged weapon because there are scores of ethical and social issues allied with the exploitation of information systems. These issues have taken a new face with internet becoming very popular and all organizations doing majority of their operations online.

Ethics generally relate to the socially accepted behaviour. This applies very well for behaviour in the digital world also. Unethical behaviour is usually caused because of the ignorance about what is ethical and what is not ethical, or it could be just an accident. But in most of the cases, it is clearly done with a proper intention.

Ethical dilemmas crop up in three major areas. Ethical issues of information systems crop up when there is a *threat to personal privacy*. Another major area of concern is the *threat to protection of intellectual property. Insider threats* by employees who know the trick of systems is also a major issue.

Transformation through Digitization

Digitization unfolds a world of opportunities for business. Businesses are positively impacted through automation, integration, business intelligence tools and the like.

Automation made the management of communication, inventory, customer relations, finance and other allied functions simple. Information technology has provided an assortment of tools for business facilitating and enhancement of quality in business operations. And also, integration of heterogeneous activities through information systems has fostered quality decision-making. Construction of simulation models with the aid of business intelligence tools like data mining promoted forecasting the future trends also. Thus, there was a paradigm shift in the role of information technology from record manager to strategy designer.

Some Moral Issues of Information Systems

Technological advancements through the availability of intelligent tools and electronic exchange of information inspired businesses to exploit these tools to the maximum advantage neglecting the ethical facet resulting in hordes of threats. Information generated for business advantage of organizations turns out to be a threat to personal privacy of individuals. Opportunities of malpractice with the aid of technology have increased manifold.

Threat to Personal Privacy: Personal privacy is challenged with the advent of mass digitization. Any action indulging the privacy of an individual will be an annoyance for them. The inception of networks and internet posed serious threats to the maintenance of privacy of personal information. Technologies including web mining, cookies and RFID have been instrumental for this.

Threat to Personal Privacy with Web Mining: Web mining is the process by which information is retrieved from web documents with the help of analytical techniques like data mining. Web mining is categorized as 'content and structure mining' and 'usage mining'. Content and structure mining derives information, based on the contents entered in websites. In the contrary, usage mining derives the required information by studying the pattern of web usage by individuals.

Online entry of personal information for registration in job sites or online purchase can be clubbed with additional online information in websites like social networks to create personal profiles. Personal profiling can be instrumental for segmentation and targeting of customers. Personal information is unveiled without the consent or knowledge of the user concerned, which may disturb individuals.

In usage mining, the web behaviour of users is scanned by verifying the IP address. The name of the person will not be revealed, but the details of his/her web behaviour like the duration of usage, time of the day and the type of browser used for logging can be identified. Market intelligence systems analyze this information allowing the marketer to design a customized approach of marketing. This again is an intrusion to privacy.

Threat to Personal Privacy with Cookies: Cookie [1] profiling is yet another breach to maintenance of personal privacy Cookies are sent by the web server to the web browser. The user's activities are packaged in a cookie and saved. Cookies keep track of the sites the user has visited and record the activities. Next time when the user visits the same page, the cookies are activated. This facilitates the websites to provide customized service and personalized contents to the users by giving them stuff of their interest. Cookie profiling helps marketers to identify their potential customers.

Cookies are not a virus, nor are they considered as malware. But cookies can act as a threat to the privacy of individuals. Even though users cannot be identified by name, the cookies stored in the system can identify the browsing habits of the users. Marketers enhance their advertising with this collated data. Apart from companies using it for own advantage, profit making is accomplished through sale of this mined information to other marketers.

While browsing through websites, a user may occasionally click on certain advertisements which trigger some interest in him/her. Cookies can store these details which will help to determine the kind of advertisements to be displayed while the user is surfing the websites.

When a user registers in some websites by giving their personal details this can be extracted with the help of cookies which is again a threat to privacy.

Personal privacy can be protected by blocking or deleting the cookies. Internet browsers can be configured for protecting from cookies. An option for deleting cookies is present in all internet browsers.

Yet another hitch can be generated by technology called as spyware which is actually malicious software which gets installed in the computer. It keeps track of the user's behaviour on web. This makes the user, the target of uncalled for sales offers and advertisements made by companies. Spyware can also affect the normal functioning of your system.

Threat to Personal Privacy with RFID: RFID is the acronym for Radio Frequency Identification. RFID technology functions by using radio waves for identifying objects or people who are having an RFID tag attached. Unlike barcodes, this identification is done without real contact with the object/person. RFID tags are used on consumer products with the objective of reducing shoplifting and also for inventory management. But this technology can lead to many ethical issues associated by the use of these tags. RFID tags can track the movement of people. The shopping paths of individuals can be tracked this way.

This information will be utilized by the marketing professionals for efficiently identifying the target group. This may be a violation to the maintenance of privacy of individuals. RFID tags are incorporated on credit cards also which is again a threat to privacy of an individual. RFID chips are embedded in passports also which will reveal details of travel to the reader. These tribulations can be eradicated by various courses of action like killing the RFID tag when the consumer is leaving the shop, using blocker tag for blocking reading etc. (Ari Juels, Ronald L. Rivest and Michael Szydlo,

The Blocker Tag: Selective Blocking of RFID Tags for Consumer Privacy).

Threat to Personal Privacy with Employee Monitoring Systems: Human resource is the most imperative resource for an organization. Employee productivity can be enhanced by instilling in them an ownership attitude towards organization. Sense of ownership will be present only in the mind of a satisfied employee. Treatment of employers is a major contributor of job satisfaction. Generation Y prefers freedom at workplace. In the current environment of stress filled and highly demanding work hours, employees feel relieved by engaging themselves with some non official activities like "cyber loafing". Cyber loafing is described as the usage of internet for non-work related activities during working hours. Temptation for cyber loafing is a dangerous threat on productivity. Tangible and intangible loss associated with cyber loafing bothers the organization. The impact is more on Generation Y than on Generation X.

Cyber loafing can be for entertainment like gaming. Matter turns out to be more unethical and grave when employees engage themselves in on line businesses and trading. Permitting personal mails during work hours opens the door for unethical transfer of confidential information pertaining to the organization to strangers. Company resources are utilized for pure unproductive and unsafe activities.

Organizations implement various methods to thwart cyber loafing and manage internet usage. Websites are blocked selectively. Employee monitoring software can be installed in the organization which can monitor the activities performed by employees in the network. This software can monitor the internet usage, sites visited, mails opened, software and document usage etc. It can even monitor the keystrokes done. Work Time Corporate Employee monitoring software, Net Vizor are some examples. Software like Web Watcher captures screenshots of computer screens used by employees.

When you consider from an employee's point of view,

cyber loafing is not a very severe issue, rather employee monitoring is in fact much more unethical. From their point of view, management needs to be bothered only about completion of work on time. Employees privacy is questioned when they are kept under observation. Employees feel offended when even their personal mails are made available to the employers by employee monitoring systems. The trust that employers keep on employees is an essential ingredient of employee satisfaction. When this is violated, the attitude of employees might also be subjected to change.

Many insurance companies, banks and other organizations are interested in acquiring employee data to be loaded to the data warehouse which forms input for their business intelligence software. Manufacturing and service organizations are no exemption from this. Transfer of employee's personal information by employer is at times done without the consent of employees.

Cyber loafing is not considered unproductive by certain organizations. According to a study conducted by corporate wellness site Keas.com, it is revealed that when employees were allowed to use Facebook, they turned out to be 40 percent more productive than the control group which was not allowed any breaks. They claim that browsing through social network for a short while is a psychologically refreshing activity.

Threat to Protection of Intellectual Property Rights: Intellectual property rights are framed for protecting creative and original work. It includes copyrights, patents, trademarks, protection of trade secrets, and, increasingly, personal identity rights.

Infringement of intellectual property right is violation of the intellectual property rights. For example, copyright infringement is unauthorized use of work done by another person without the permission of the copyright holder. The copyright holder of the software developed by the in-house development team of the organization will be the organization itself. Individual members of the team cannot reproduce the work for his personal advantage. An incident of copyright infringement that had happened in a reputed software firm in the town was narrated by a leading software developer in Calicut. While resigning from the organization, a team member of the development team unethically copied the source code of copyrighted software developed by the organization.

On inception of a new software firm, the aforementioned employee started offering the software for a much lower price than what was quoted by the organization. Customers opted for this product owing to financial advantage. This matter is pending at district court as a case of *copyright infringement*.

Trademark Infringement: Another concern is about trademark of products. A trademark is a "distinctive sign, which identifies certain goods or services as those produced or provided by a specific person or enterprise". Occasionally, same trademark might be used by two different organizations. But in this case the organizations might be located in geographically far off places. But now, with the advent of internet, world has become like a small village. Geographical distance is not a matter of concern at all. Search engine might end up detecting names of two organizations while searching for a trademark. But this is not an intentional case of infringement.

Ethical Implications of Piracy: Piracy [2] is undeniably an illegal activity. Nasscom had remarked about software piracy as, "Software piracy involves the use, reproduction or distribution without having received the expressed permission of the software author". Piracy is widespread among individuals as well as in business organizations. Monetary advantage is one of the key influencing factors. Timely availability can be another persuading cause. Nevertheless, pirated copies result in heavy repercussions. Pirated software may not respond to software fixes incorporated at later stages and will eventually lead to a disastrous data loss.

According to the study conducted by Harrison Group

based on 1,580 interviews with both business decision makers and IT Professionals, mid-market companies having 25-499 PC's in the US, UK, China, and Brazil, the following observations were made.

1. Companies using unlicensed software were 73 percent more likely to have loss/damage of sensitive/valuable data and 43 percent more likely to have critical system failures lasting 24 hours or more than those using fully licensed software.
2. Companies using unlicensed software were 28 percent more likely to lose a customer's personal information and 24 percent more likely to have a significant system failure with at least one group down for 4-23 hours than those using fully licensed software.
3. Companies using unlicensed software had:

- 81 percent more critical system failures that led to downtime of 24+ hours.
- 63 percent more experiences of losing sensitive internal data.
- 42 percent more occasions where significant system failures occurred for 4-23 hours.
- 21 percent more minor system failures.

The study also found that the impact of these failures on customers and employees were very high.

According to 2011 BSA Global Software Piracy Study, the piracy rate in India is 63 percent.

Insider Threats

Insider threats happen when the threat is originated by an employee of the organization or a former employee. The digitization had increased the vulnerability of information to attacks. Insider threat can happen in many ways. Introduction of viruses to systems, information theft and deletion of data in the databases are some of them which question the integrity of the systems.

In conversation with a leading advocate who deals with

cyber crimes, a recent incident of corruption was narrated by him, which was reported in Chemmannur Jewellers, which is a well-known Jewellers group having branches inside and outside India. The front office accountant was behind this scam. Chemmannur Jewellers offers gold schemes where payment is done monthly and purchases happen once in three years. The accountant successfully convinced the customers by giving printed receipt on payment. The receipt was not generated by the information system, but was only a printed document which was not recorded in the database.

Information on the working of information systems makes the insider capable of modifying the data to suit his requirements. Monetary advantages persuade such actions.

To quote an incident in a bank, the interest for savings bank account is usually calculated on a specific date in a month. A wrong entry of deposit is made by the employee prior to the interest calculation. By default, calculated interest is credited to the employee's bank account. The reverse entry is performed to regain status. The threat was done by securing his higher authorities' password.

The custodian of the data warehouse of companies can also act as intermediaries in selling mass volume of information about employees which can add value to the market intelligence operations.

A Solution for Insider Threats: The loop holes in the information systems make it more vulnerable for attacks by insiders. In order to avoid this and have a better control a maker checker arrangement is done. In maker checker arrangement for any transaction, at least two individuals are given the charge of validating the transaction. Like the name of the concept there will be a maker of the transaction and a checker of the transaction. This will reduce the insider threats unless the maker and checker are frauds which are less likely to happen.

Ethical Issues in Online Banking

Introduction of online banking has changed the way a

common man carries out his banking transactions. Even though the developers claim that the transactions are highly secured, certain loopholes prevail which prevents a common man from being completely free of hassles while transacting online. Malicious software like spyware can steal your username and password by understanding your web movements. The online banking users of Singapore were subjected to attack from a spyware called "Spy Eye" which can steal your confidential information like password.

Man in the Middle Attacks

Yet another problem is man in the middle attacks. Man in the middle, as the literal meaning of the word, is actually an attack where the attacker captures a connection between the server and the customer. Attacker intercepts the messages sent by customer and also answers the messages pretending as the server. An attacker can gain access to messages, modify the messages and also insert it back to the network.

Usually banking communications between members of online banking happens in encrypted manner. A pair of public key and private key is used for encryption and decryption. Documents encrypted by private key can be decrypted only by its corresponding public key and vice versa.

When X is requesting Y for an encrypted transfer of information, the hacker will interrupt and pretends as Y. Hacker sends his public key to X. It also sends the message send by X to Y pretending as X. Y will send all the messages using the key received which is actually that of the hacker. Now the hacker can decrypt the message, modify according to his requirement and send to X pretending as Y.

Man in the middle attack has affected Citibank customers in the year of 2006. A fake log-in site was created by the attacker. Log in details of the customers were captured by these websites. Customer interacts with the fake website and this website communicates with the bank.

Hacking with Pattern Recognition

During on line transactions, hackers get hold of confidential information by identifying certain patterns generated by the software during the transactions. To avoid the above mentioned situation, different algorithms are generated for carrying out same function. When these methods are changed and applied at regular intervals, the hackers will not be able to study and identify a peculiar pattern. Hacking can be reduced to an extent by such practices.

Figure 5.1: Man in the Middle Attack

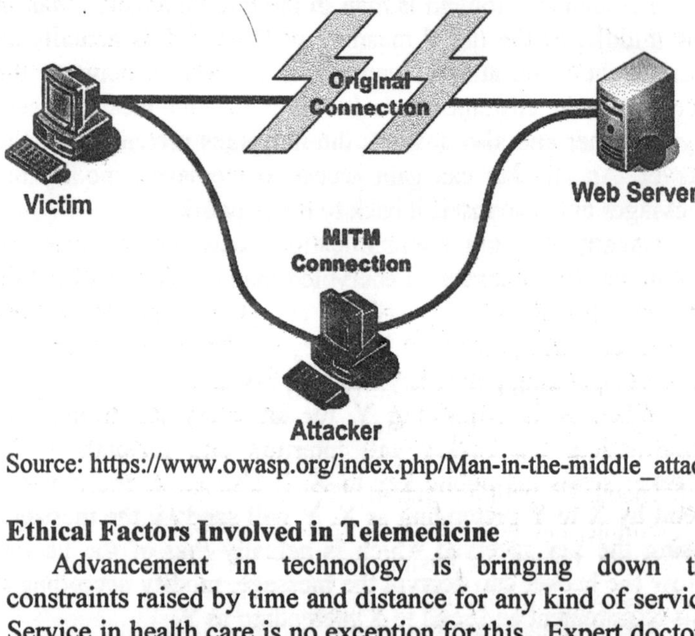

Source: https://www.owasp.org/index.php/Man-in-the-middle_attack

Ethical Factors Involved in Telemedicine

Advancement in technology is bringing down the constraints raised by time and distance for any kind of service. Service in health care is no exception for this. Expert doctors, who are geographically located away from the location of request of service, can provide health care interactively being online at the same time or offline also. Telemedicine should follow ethical practices during the process. Maintaining the confidentiality of client information is of utmost importance. When the medical records of the patient are transmitted online, it should be done only with proper consent of the patient maintaining the privacy and confidentiality of the records. Access privileges should be assigned appropriately. Even when human beings are examined by a doctor through telecommunication facilities like video conferencing, the patient should be informed about the presence of others in the video conferencing room with the doctor for discussion. When clinical information about the patient is send online for observation, assurance should be there regarding the accuracy, compatibility and timely availability of information.

Tarnishing the Public Image through Websites

Organizations sometimes become the victim of digital abuse by competitors. Websites are a medium of publicity. Most of the advertisements end with a footer message "For more details visit www.xxx.yyy". For enhancing customer satisfaction generally these websites are made interactive. Certain incidents had occurred where this facility was taken as an opportunity by competitors to tarnish the image of the organization.

For example, in a construction company located in Kochi, in Kerala, a similar incident took place. This organization had a website where there was a provision included for posting grievances by customers. This facility was misutilized by some forged customers. With the intention of tarnishing the image of the above mentioned organization, their competitors entered some fake complaints about non-fulfilment of promises given by organization. This would naturally affect the public image of the organization. Prospective customers will naturally think twice before making a deal. Finally, the organization had to block their website.

Nigerian Scam

Several unethical issues of information systems in business are explored now. There exists a category of people for whom these unethical practices are their business. Nigerian scam is one among them. Nigerian scam is involved in money transfers. Usually the victim gets an email which offers a huge amount of money picturing the person as a lottery winner or a person selected by someone abroad as successor of their unlimited property.

A leading advocate explained a case of similar nature dealt by him. This case was presented in the Court of Chief Judicial Magistrate in Manjeri, a small town in Malappuram district in Kerala. An Ayurvedic doctor conducting a Psoriasis clinic at Valluvamburam in Malappuram received a message in the email address of the hospital that a millionaire who died of Psoriasis had set apart 15 million dollars in his will for conducting charity hospital for the treatment of psoriasis. The people behind this scam managed to fraudulently obtain thirty lakh from the doctor. For this he had send many forged messages of even Reserve Bank of India. Finally, the culprits were convicted and they were sentenced to undergo rigorous imprisonment for 5 years and fine of ₹ 50,000.

Ethical Hacking

When organizations operate online, we very often come across terms like hacking, cracking etc. which is the process of gaining unauthorized access over information systems. When it becomes malicious, you refer to it as cracking.

The website of Tamil Nadu police was hacked by "Anonymous" an activist group on July 10, 2012. Complaints posted by individuals in the Tamil Nadu police website and the follow up actions were hacked by the group and the same was published in social networking site. This incident created distress for people who had launched such online complaints. This case is looked upon by cyber crime cell.

Unethical hacking can create havoc in any information system. Organizations take precautions to avoid such suicidal conditions. As technology advances, capabilities of information systems are also advancing. At the same time, the chance of security breaching is also moving at an increasing rate. Even if the latest and most powerful mechanisms are used any system is said to be "as weak as its weakest link" and the weakest link among the components of information system is usually the "people or person" component. A crime can be conducted only if favourable opportunities arise. When systems are designed, it can be done in such a way as to reduce opportunities. Organizations depute trained ethical hackers in order to test out the loopholes with regard to the security of the system. Ethical hackers try to penetrate into the systems and identify these loopholes so that precautions can be taken to prevent cracking.

Conclusion

In the current era of globalization and development, information systems are the most powerful tool used by organizations to efficiently progress to success. Nevertheless, in the process of profit making, ethical values are neglected at times by organizations while transacting using information systems. When organizations are incorporating digital approaches for recognizing the customers, like web mining, RFID and cookies, they are actually invading into the privacy of individuals. Insider threats are increasing with the advent of information systems. Vulnerability of systems to attacks questions the integrity and confidentiality of information. Loop holes in the systems are paving the way for invention of new digital methodologies to wrestle against such atrocities created.

End Notes

1. Cookies are small files stored in the user's computer hard disk when they visit websites.
2. Piracy is unauthorized copying or duplication of software having copyright and distributing it to other individuals or organizations.

References

David Gielbman (2011), *Impact of Unlicensed Software on Mid-Market Companies*, Harrison Group, Ninth Annual BSA Global

Software Journal.

Kennet, C. Laudon and Jane P. Laudon (2007), *Management Information systems-Managing the digital firm*, Pearson, p. 46.

New Spyware Threat for Singapore Internet Banking Users, International Business Times, 2011 September 30.

Cyber Crime Cell to Probe Hacking of Website, *The Hindu,* 2012, July 11, Chennai.

http://geiselmed.dartmouth.edu/cfm/resources/ethics/chapter-14.pdf.

http://mozilla.gunnars.net/firefox_help_firefox_cookie_tutorial.html.

http://www.rfidtown.com/privacy.html.

http://www.rsa.com/rsalabs/staff/bios/ajuels/publications/blocker/blocker.pdf.

6

Value Stream Costing for Effective Lean Management

Leena George

In the path towards efficiency, corporate houses have moved towards lean management processes. Lean management derives its values from 2-key principles of lean; respect for people and continuous improvement. Lean is all about customer focus. Value is defined by the customer and we develop and maintain processes to provide this value. Processes are run by people. Only through support and proper leadership and guidance you can drive your people to continuously improve the processes that add value to the customer. The management system that helps you to achieve this is a lean management system. Lean companies face a problem in choosing the right method of costing.

Standard cost accounting which is often used by all companies presents a problem for lean companies. Its measurements motivate behaviours that are harmful to lean, and it does not provide reliable cost information for decision-making in a lean environment. Standard costing is driven by labour efficiency, machine utilization, and absorption of overhead. The standard cost techniques were traditionally used by managers to build excessive inventories and generate positive variances to improve profitability leading to higher management incentive bonuses.

Rationale for Value Stream Costing

The economic recession has created a need for lean accounting. However, since most accountants have not used lean tools, the application has been unused. Lean accounting deals with tracking revenue and the associated variable costs required to generate those sales. An understanding that lean contribution from sales directly improves the bottom line, motivates one not to spend funds unless they are associated with generating revenue. Since lean accounting provides better information for decision-making it has a positive impact on sales. In a slower economy, companies need tools like value stream costing and similar lean-decision making applications for effective cost control.

The reason why standard costing does not work in a lean company is that it is based upon a contrary model of how companies make money in manufacturing. The model which traditional costing is designed to support is the traditional mass production model that seeks economies of scale to create the lowest unit cost for items produced. Using this model, we want to encourage a highly automated factory capable of producing large production, amortize the cost of these expensive resources. Companies make money by reducing the per unit cost. Lean on the other hand, seeks to make products one at a time promoting the flow through the production process. Companies make money by flowing greater volumes of production through the same resources.

Limitations of Standard Costing

- Standard costing allocates all overhead to products and relates the overhead to direct labour hours.
- Standard costing encourages non-lean behaviour by focusing on utilization of resources, people's individual efficiencies, and overhead allocations.
- Standard costing calls for elaborate and wasteful data collection systems; the opposite of lean thinking.
- Standard costing does not provide the data needed to support and encourage lean manufacturing.

Most standard costing systems measure the efficiency of the use of machinery and people using what is known as a volume variance. A volume variance simply compares the cost of the labour or machines actually incurred by a production operation to make a given number of items with the amount of cost that would have been incurred at the standard or planned volumes. If fewer items are made than planned, then the actual cost per item will exceed the planned for the period and the amount of labour and overhead consumed are less than the amount that was planned.

The so-called "negative" variance indicates that the production process produced at less than full capacity during the period, usually a month. Negative volume variances are very undesirable in a mass production environment as the goal of this philosophy is to achieve economies of scale and lowest per unit cost by using machines and people to the optimum. The mass production mentality to achieve economies of scale is completely contrary to lean. When companies begin the lean journey, they normally reduce the volumes produced as they work down inventories and seek to produce only the amounts demanded. These lower volumes create significant negative variances and lower profits as these variances increase expenses. In addition, lower volumes cause higher per unit overhead cost allocations.

Implementing Value Stream Costing

Value stream costing is a process of identifying and establishing costs for all the process steps required to provide value to the customer. It is a function of determining how much value is created by each process step. Value stream costing uses activity-based process modelling techniques to capture cost, time and other operational data along any given value stream. It offers a unique view, across the functional silos or departments which enable any business system to:

- Fully understand what it costs to provide valuable services to customers.
- Measure resource capacities and utilizations.
- Identify process bottlenecks.
- Perform what-if scenarios based on changing market

volumes and demographics.

Characteristics of Value Stream Costing

- Value stream costs are typically calculated weekly.
- No distinction is made between direct or indirect costs. All costs of the value stream are considered direct costs.
- Costs included in the value stream are production labour, production materials, production support, machines and equipment, operation support, facilities and maintenance, and all other value stream costs (Table 6.1).
- Value stream costing includes a simpler cost collection method and reduces the number of cost centres.
- Value stream costing provides a "real" income statement due to the elimination of unnecessary costs outside the control of value stream managers.
- Costs outside of the value stream are referred to as "sustaining costs" of the business and are not allocated to the value stream.
- Emphasis is placed on maximizing the flow of product through the value stream, not on production.

The behavioural consequences of applying standard costing measurements or lean measurement systems in a factory reflect the differing assumptions regarding how money is made.

Table 6.1: Standard Costing versus Lean Management

Standard Costing World	Lean World
• Make more product • Build inventory • Utilize resources to the maximum • Optimize department efficiencies • Track direct labour • Allocate other costs	• Eliminate barriers to flow • Focus on value stream rather than departments • Continuous improvement and team work • Eliminate waste, inventory and over production

From the aforesaid, it should be clear that performance measures created to support the traditional manufacturing motivates behaviour that is contrary to lean. Trying to manage a lean plant using these measures will have serious negative consequences for the lean program. So for a lean company, it is necessary to create a system of performance measures and cost accounting that is compatible with a lean business model. Thus, it is imperative to have costs to measure the efficiency of the value stream process, for understanding product costs and for making management decisions in a lean organization—lean value stream is the set of processes through which a group of products pass. It extends from the receipt of the customer order to the delivery of the product and possesses unique characteristics compared with a traditional product routing as shown in Table 6.2.

Table 6.2: Comparison of Value Stream and Traditional Routing

Lean Value Stream Process	Traditional Product Routing
• All Products pass through the same processes, they have a common routing • The processes are located adjacent to one another to maximize flow • Products pass through the processes quickly–in a matter of days • Inventories are low and level	• Each product has its own separate routing • Product routings move all over the factory • Products pass through the process slowly–in a matter of weeks or months • Inventorics are high and fluctuate

In the traditional routing, calculating a product cost entails adding up the unit costs of production at each of the operating steps through which the product passes. In the lean value stream this is not necessary inasmuch as all products passing through the value stream have the same routing. Since products flow through the value stream very rapidly, very much like liquid through a pipeline, the costing process can be treated in a manner similar to other flow operations. In this "flow" model, the cost of the product equates to the total cost of operating the process (a value stream in this case) divided by the number of items shipped from the process.

Value Stream Costing Process

The value stream cost is typically calculated weekly (bi-weekly or monthly) and it takes account of all the costs in the value stream. It makes no distinction between direct costs and indirect costs; all the costs within the value stream are considered direct. Costs outside of the value stream should be eliminated.

Costs that make up the total value stream cost include all labour costs; both traditionally direct costs and traditionally indirect costs. If the people work in the value stream then they are included irrespective of whether they make the product, move materials, design the product, maintain machines, plan production, make sales, or do the accounting.

The production material costs are generally calculated from how much material has been purchased for the value stream during a particular week. Every time material is brought into the plant its cost is assigned to the value stream. The total value stream material cost is the sum of everything purchased during that week. For this material cost to be valid there needs to be low raw materials and work-in-process inventories; and these inventories must be under good control. If inventories are low, then the materials brought during that week will be used quickly and will accurately reflect the material cost of the product manufactured that week.

Support costs like spare parts and soft tooling are purchased for the value stream (often using a purchase credit card assigned to the value stream so the costs are directly posted to the value stream cost/profit centre) and the costs of consumables, supplies, and other day-to-day expenses are assigned to the value stream.

All in all, value stream costing is an effective method as it provides relevant and timely information. The costing method determines how much value is added in each step of the process. Value stream costing offers a unique view across functions and departments which enables a business to understand the costs that provide value to the customers, to measure resource capacities and utilizations, to identify process bottlenecks and to perform what-if scenarios based on changing market volumes and demographics. The value stream costing method provides better information and contains the real cost of the value stream which can be readily and reliably used for day-to-day decision-making.

References

Baggily, B. and Maskel (2003), *Value Stream Management for Lean Companies*, Part II, *Journal of Cost Management* (May/June), Volume 24(30).

Bill, Waddell (2009), *Lean Accounting is the Key*, retrieved from http://www.evolvingexcellence.com/blog/2009/07/lean-accounting-is-the-key.html.

Bruce, L. (2003), Costing by Value Stream, *The Journal of Cost Management,* (May/June), Volume 17(3).

Strothmann, David (2009), *Value Stream Cost and Profitability Management for the Lean Enterprise.*

7

Customer Relationship Management (CRM) through Data Mining

Suresh Chandra Bihari

CRM can be defined as the process of predicting customer behaviour and selecting actions to influence that behaviour to benefit the company (Jenkins, 1999), usually leveraging on information technology and database-related tools. CRM initiatives usually seek to fulfil several objectives. One of the objectives is to get closer to the customer by utilizing the data "hidden" in scattered enterprise databases. Examining and analyzing the data can turn raw data into valuable information about customer's needs. By predicting customer needs in advance, businesses can then market the right products to the right segments at the right time through the right delivery channels. Customer satisfaction can also be improved through more effective marketing.

Another objective of the CRM initiative is to transform the company into customer-centric organizations with a greater focus on customer profitability as compared to line profitability. The insights gained from CRM enable companies to calculate or estimate the profitability of individual accounts. Other CRM objectives include increased cross-selling possibilities, better lead management, better customer response and improved customer loyalty (Chin, 2000).

CRM is a business model that aligns product and sales strategies with customer requirements and preferences. Services are then provided in a timely manner using the channels that are preferred by the customers. Effective CRM starts by focusing on the development of business strategies and by aligning an organization to serve customers. These business strategies are then executed using CRM technology solutions. The most successful business strategies are developed only after an organization learns about customers' behaviour patterns and attitudes. Behaviour studies show what products or services have been purchased in the past and what products or services are currently being bought. Attitudes studies show what customers are thinking and feeling about future buying decisions.

Uncovering customers' behaviour patterns and attitudes involve collecting relevant transactional and survey data, placing the data into a data repository, and then applying analytical techniques. After the information is collected from the data, an actionable business plan can be developed to create the multi-channel customer contact strategies that offer the optimal products or services.

Approaches to CRM

The effective use of CRM principles requires a three-pronged approach. First, all CRM efforts should begin with a well-defined strategy. Second, an infrastructure must be developed to achieve appropriate objectives. Specifically, the infrastructure should align product and sales goals to meet customer needs, according to their preferences, in the most cost-efficient manner. Third, continuous analytic intelligence should be used to determine and modify customer interaction. In addition to the above approach, implementing CRM involves collecting and reviewing the most relevant customer data. Relevant customer data can uncover needed information about behaviour patterns and attitudes.

Once identified, the customer data should be incorporated into the infrastructure so that effective marketing plans can be developed. The execution of marketing plans is driven both by analytic insights obtained about customers and by any existing marketing communication plans. These 'drivers' can be used to place customers in pre-identified groups or to support triggers and scores that identify specific individual behaviour patterns. After appropriate customer data analysis and marketing plan development is complete, the multi-channel customer contact strategies can be implemented within the CRM technology infrastructure.

There is an evolutionary approach to CRM that focuses heavily on "customer equity" assets management. This approach begins with business strategy development. Next, a data infrastructure is created that supports customer interactions. Then, a technology infrastructure is designed to produce CRM results. Finally, customer communication channel strategies are created, and strategy execution technology is used to create an on-going dialog with the customers.

Customer-focused organizations can benefit most from CRM. These organizations develop business strategies that use CRM to identify the needs and the "hurt points" of existing customers. It is not that customer-focused organizations ignore potential customers, but they do understand the importance of keeping existing customers, especially during difficult economic times. For example, a customer-focused organization might use CRM to help create incentives that produce more business from existing customers, such as offering priority service, free delivery, and so on. Managing customer relationships promotes cheap growth by selling products and services to those customers who are most likely to buy, while wasting less time and resources trying to sell to those customers who are less likely to buy. Customers will pay more for a product or service if they have a long-standing relationship with a provider that they believe is responsive to their needs.

Successful customer initiatives often include one or more of the following characteristics: they are affordable, they help companies generate return on investment (ROI) through higher profit margins, they produce greater wallet share, and they improve operational and administrative efficiency.

Investments in CRM process changes can be made incrementally. In some ways, the move toward an incremental or a modular rollout of customer initiatives is part of the natural maturation of CRM. For example, emergent pilot programs (programs designed to address problems or capture "low-hanging ROI") require a piecemeal approach.

Whether modular or not, to be effective, a customer initiative must have enterprise-wide impact.

Customer Equity during Different Economic Cycles

Customer relationships are an important company asset. A firm can use this customer equity to improve its growth and profitability prospects during economic downturns and upturns. Just as a squirrel buries nuts in anticipation of winter, a smart business will build customer equity during good times in order to produce more business during bad times.

Companies should know who their most valuable customers (MVCs) are. More resources should be used to market relevant products and services to these MVCs while fewer resources should be expended on unprofitable customers. The goal is to make the right offer to the right customer at the right time. Such customer knowledge can immediately and significantly reduce total cost while, at the same time, increase sales with individual customers. This strategy enables an organization to anticipate greater returns from its campaigns, a reduction in costs, an increase in conversion rates, and more one-to-one communication initiatives (which will gradually replace the organization's previous dependence on mass marketing tactics).

The "Picket Fence" strategy can be used to isolate the firm's MVCs from the broader customer base. For each customer behind the picket fence, there is a particular objective and a strategy for achieving that objective by the management team. In an upturn economy, business strategies should involve growth. This includes acquiring new customers and increasing the number of current customers. In a downturn economy, business strategies should involve harvesting. Harvesting implies that an organization gets the most from every existing relationship by selling more to current customers. The concept of harvesting is sometimes referred to as cheap growth.

Product versus Customer-centric Business Strategy

Traditionally, banking and financial organizations are organized around product-cantered and function-cantered models rather than a customer-cantered model. By becoming truly customer-cantered, a bank or financial organization can achieve the following benefits:

- Higher returns on invested capital.
- More profitable customers.
- Lower capital costs (due to the consistency of financial results that comes from those long-term, carefully managed customer relationships).
- Larger investment opportunities (due to their understanding of customer finances and unmet needs).

Many components play a pivotal role in the management of the customer asset base, especially now, with complex business environments and fierce global competition. Two of the most important components include effectively serving the existing MVC base and growing the MVC base.

Customer Information Systems

Almost every major bank or financial organization that has been in business for the last a few decades has typical account servicing legacy systems. These systems facilitate account opening, balance maintenance, and support a monthly or periodic statement-generating process.

However, these legacy systems lack the capabilities to manage and grow MVCs because their sole objective is to service the transaction activity of an account. Building an intelligent customer information system (CIS) is the fundamental first step required to manage customer equity in this scenario. The focus of the CIS should be to collect, store, and maintain the following types of information on the customers in a data warehouse:

- Customer or household identification (name, phone, address, title, company name).
- Rating (size, value level, or profitability contribution).
- Background (demographic, lifestyle characteristics).
- Communication record (contact with company, participation in marketing programs, types of information or services required, channels of contact, requests for information, complaint frequency).
- Purchase behaviour (frequency, monetary value).
- Credit-worthiness.
- Performance ratings or credit scoring, and history (performance evaluation, loyalty, and likelihood to refer the company to others).
- Customer survey data collection.

The next generation of advanced CIS is called a knowledge discovery database (KDD). Instead of mining layers upon layers of customer transactional and lifestyle data for knowledge nuggets, KDDs establish a set of flexible knowledge-required algorithms. The available data is then searched to find any exceptions.

Any good CIS or KDD must be able to provide the launching pad to evaluate, classify, acquire, grow, and support the efficient servicing capabilities of customer equity asset management activities.

Challenges to Customer Equity Asset Management

The following key challenges face those that try to implement customer equity asset management:

Limited Scope: Many existing CIS tools are very limited in scope, and do not support customer equity management.

Complex Technology: Technology solutions sold by vendors have become very complex to use, expensive to maintain, and contain irrelevant information for data mining.

No Pertinent Data: Most of the existing data warehouses lack information on recency, frequency, and monetary values. They also offer information that is insufficient for supporting predictive modelling and predictive scoring.

Extended Time to Market: The addition of new capabilities to existing data warehouses is cost prohibitive and takes a long time to bring into production stage capabilities (or even to catch up with the fast-changing dynamic nature of the market place).

Multi-vendor Tools and Capabilities: Over the years, many major financial organizations have developed data warehouses by purchasing diverse sets of software tools and then building data warehouses in-house. For example, Data quality and cleansing tools, extract transform load (ETL) tools, database management and storage tools, data mining, and campaign management solutions from various vendors.

Overburdened Internal Information Technology Organization: Information technology organizations have had to employ individuals who have specialized vendor product skill sets to support multi-vendor tools. This can increase organizational expenses significantly.

Lack of Integrated Capabilities: The focus of many CIS systems has shifted to service only ad hoc reporting and to provide simple querying capabilities rather than becoming an infrastructure for efficient customer equity management or for enabling some sort of KDD.

CRM in New Age Banking

In the era of cut throat competition globally as well as locally, data mining is used by almost all the proactive corporations and organizations to build and manage customer relationships. The saying in Marketing, 'Customer is the King' has now been made possible by using the data mining applications by not only maintaining a good relationship with the customers; but also by effectively utilizing the data warehouses to add new customers.

Data mining helps to retain the customers by understanding and fulfilling their needs proactively and thus delighting them in the long run. Earlier, it was very difficult to understand and manage the data. But now with the usage of CRM Software from companies like SAP, Siebel, Oracle, Amdocs and others; many companies are utilizing the benefits of enhancing customer loyalty through customer relationship management.

In the banking sector in India, new age private banks like ICICI Bank, HDFC Bank, Axis Bank are at the forefront of utilizing the data mining techniques to enhance the customer relationship.

Data Mining

Data mining is defined as exploration and analysis of large quantities of data by automatic or semi-automatic means to discover meaningful patterns and rules and these patterns allow a company to better understand its customers, improve its marketing, sales, and customer support operations (Berry and Linoff, 1997). The process of extracting hidden key information from a large pool of available data is called data mining. Data mining is often done to analyze data in order to gain knowledge about the behaviour patterns of customers and to identify key relationships that may help in decision making.

Data mining is the principle of sorting through large amounts of data and picking out relevant information. It is usually used by business intelligence organizations, and financial analysts, but it is increasingly used in the sciences to extract information from the enormous data sets generated by modern experimental and observational methods. The internet and technology opens up a wealth of information 24 hours a day, seven days a week, thereby heightening the transparency of the markets. Customers use the internet to quickly shop around and see what competitors can provide. As a consequence, the attention span of customers has decreased, and customer loyalty is subject to new laws.

Customers are looking beyond products to assess whether the overall solution you provide addresses their individual needs and priorities. Customers and knowledge about customers is one of most important assets of today's organization. The period of time between a new customer request and its fulfilment is decreasing. This means that, if one doesn't react quickly enough, the customers will find someone else. Technology has also paved the way for a new dimension of customer relationship management. The falling costs for computing power and the arrival of new software tools for capturing and analyzing mass data have provided the main thrust behind the increase in importance of analytical solutions in general.

Powerful hardware and software give better ways than ever before to understand and leverage customer relationships. Data mining is one of the technologies which provide analytical ability to the organizations for leveraging on customer relationships and thus customer loyalty and this paper analyzes the potential of data mining for building and managing better relationships (META, 2007).

Data mining uses a variety of techniques to find hidden patterns and relationships in large pools of data and infer rules from them that can be used to predict future behaviour and guide decision making (Fayyad et al., 2002; Hirji, 2001). To use data mining effectively for managing customer relationships the data must be categorized in some manner if it is to be accessed, re-used, organized, or synthesized to build a picture of the organization's competitive environment or solve a specific business problem (Pearlson, 2001, p. 196). In recent years, the need to extract knowledge automatically from very large databases has grown.

Customer relationship management form a learning relationship with the customers by noticing their needs with the use of online transaction processing i.e. operational CRM, remember their preferences with the use of decision support data warehouses and learn how to serve them with the use of data mining. There may be number of channels by which company interfaces with its customers for example direct mail, email, telemarketing etc. And key data for customer analytics come from these channels only and CRM is about serving customers through all these channels. Analytical CRM (Laudon, 2006) includes applications that analyze customer data generated by operational CRM applications to provide information for improving business performance management. For example, developing customer profiles, analyzing customer profitability etc.

Advanced statistical tools are used in data mining to understand current behaviour and to predict future behavioural patterns. Mathematics, genetics, cybernetics and other fields of research make extensive use of data mining. In CRM, web mining (pertaining to web-related information) is used to gain insights into customer behaviour. Interesting little poll over on KD Nuggets today, readers were asked where they had applied data mining in the last 12 months. The top 5 were CRM (26.1 percent of respondents), banking (23.9 percent), direct marketing/fundraising (20.3 percent), science (18.8 percent) and fraud detection (18.8 percent).

Role of Data Mining in Customer Relationship: To widen your customer relationships, data mining can answer questions like:

- Which kind of customers would you like to acquire?
- Which kind of customers will drive your growth in future?
- Which new customers are likely to be interested in your products?

Customer acquisition is the prime issue for small company marketers. As corporations increase budgets to attract and obtain new customers, data mining becomes a critical tool for profiling good customers, performing market segmentation, and improving the results of direct-marketing campaigns. The number of campaigns that can be managed in a given time period is often much lower than what the business demands. Data mining solves these problems by putting tools in the hands of the marketers driving these campaigns—it keeps control where the need is. As a result, marketers can be much more responsive to creating new campaigns and can implement a direct feedback loop to improve their efforts on a regular basis. To lengthen the customer relationships, data mining can answer these questions:

- Which customers in particular do you want to keep?
- Which customers will drive most of your profits?
- Which customers might switch to your competitors and why?
- Which customers are dissatisfied with your services and products?

Customer Retention: This retention is also a major issue for all businesses. One Harvard study suggests, "Reducing customer attrition by 5 percent can double a company's profits". Given the high cost of finding new customers, a key issue for many organisations is customer retention. Often referred to as chum, customer turnover is a difficult problem to manage because it usually occurs without warning. For example, when a customer calls their long-distance carrier to have their account closed in favour of a competitor, the telecommunications provider knows only at that moment that their valued customer is churning. Once they are predisposed to leave, it is unlikely that the customer can be convinced to stay.

Data mining introduces a major paradigm shift to churn management by adding predictive capabilities. Data mining tools can be used to model the patterns of past churning customers by examining billing histories, demographic information, and other customer data. Then, the same model can be used to predict other good customers who are likely to leave in the near future. Armed with this information, the marketer can proactively instigate campaigns to keep their customer, rather than fighting to get them back later

Transforming Minor Customers to Profitable Ones: Intensifying and deepening customer relationships also require data mining tools to answer essential questions, such as:

- With which customers can you increase the share of wallet?

- Which products and services interest a particular customer?
- Which products are typically bought together? Which cross selling opportunities should you consider?

Cross-selling: Growing a customer's value is yet another critical marketing function. The notion of increasing customer share is key to most organisations. Unlike increasing market share, which focuses on obtaining a greater number of customers, increasing customer share refers to getting more of the dollars each individual customer has to spend. Two common methods for this are customer-based product—launch campaigns, and cross-selling. Riddled with as much guesswork and gut instinct as they are today, these methods are often not as effective as they could be.

Data mining tools improve product launches to an installed base, as well as cross-selling activities by helping marketers understand which customers are most likely to purchase new products, and which products are typically purchased together. This results in a more focused effort to customers ready to spend additional dollars.

Personalization provides relevant and specific recommendations for individuals, taking into account personal preferences, demographics and behaviour. Personalization permits delivering recommendations with the touch and timing of someone who knows you well. Personalization uses data mining technology to analyze the large amounts of data gathered from web sites and other applications to find patterns within purchase, demographic, ratings, and navigational data.

Personalization makes recommendations using data mining technology without the need to explicitly define manual rules. Personalization automatically deduces the customer's interests from the customer's behaviour. Personalization collects customer profile data and uses them to build predictive models that support personalized recommendations. The underlying rules derived through data mining can be more sophisticated and thus yield better results than the other techniques noted above. For example, "a person who has clicked links *x* and *y* and who has demographic characteristics *a* and *b* is likely to buy *z*".

Data Mining as a Tool for CRM

The first analytical step in data mining data description—for example, summary of statistical attributes (such as means and standard deviations), may represented by using charts and graphs, and look at the distribution of values of the fields in your data. One needs to build a predictive model based on patterns determined from known results, and then test that model on results outside the original sample. A good model should never be confused with reality, but it can be a useful guide to understanding the business.

Data mining can be used for both classification and regression problems. In classification problems you're predicting what category something will fall into, for example, whether a person will be a good credit risk or not, or which of several offers someone is most likely to accept. In regression, problems are like predicting a number such as the probability that a person will respond to an offer.

In CRM, data mining is frequently used to assign a score to a particular customer or prospect indicating the likelihood that the individual will behave in the way organization wants. For example, a score could measure the propensity to respond to a particular offer or to switch to a competitor's product. It is also frequently used to identify a set of attributes (called a profile) that segments customers into groups with similar behaviours, such as buying a particular product. A special type of classification can recommend items based on similar interests held by groups of customers. This is sometimes called collaborative filtering. There are some basic steps of data mining for CRM analytics.

Building a Marketing Database

To build the marketing database, the data cleaning up process is required for building good models. The data needed may reside in multiple data resources such as the customer database, product database, and usage databases. This means integrate and consolidate the data into a single marketing database and reconcile differences in data values from the heterogeneous sources. There are often large differences in the way data is defined and used in different databases. Some inconsistencies may be easy to uncover, such as different addresses for the same customer. Making it more difficult to resolve these problems is that they are often subtle. For example, the same customer may have different names or multiple customer identification numbers may exist.

Exploring the Data: Before building good predictive models, one must understand the consolidated data. Graphing and visualization tools are a vital aid in data preparation, and their importance to effective data analysis cannot be overemphasized. Data visualization most often provides good insights. Some of the common and very useful graphical displays of data are histograms or box plots that display distributions of values. Some may also want to look at scatter plots in two or three dimensions of different pairs of variables. The ability to add a third, overlay variable greatly increases the usefulness of some types of graphs.

Preparing Data for Modelling: This is the final data preparation step before building models and the step where the most "art" comes in. There are four main parts to this step:

1. First, select the variables on which to build the model. Ideally, take all the variables, feed them to the data mining tool and let it find those which are the best predictors.
2. Second step is to construct new predictors derived from the raw data. For example, forecasting credit risk using a debt-to-income ratio rather than just debt and income as predictor variables may yield more accurate results that are also easier to understand.
3. Thirdly, decide to select a subset or sample of data to build predictive models. If there is lot of data, however, using all data may take too long or require buying a bigger

computer than you would like. Working with a properly selected random sample usually results in no loss of information for most CRM problems. Given a choice of either investigating a few models built on all the data or investigating more models built on a sample, the latter approach will usually help to develop a more accurate and robust model of the problem. *Last,* transform variables in accordance with the requirements of the algorithm for building the model.

Building Data Mining Model: The most important thing to remember about model building is that it is an iterative process. Explore alternative models to find the one that is most useful in solving business problem. Most CRM applications are based on a protocol called supervised learning. Start with customer information for which the desired outcome is already known. For example, use historical data because previously mailed to a list very similar to the contemporary one. Or conduct a test mailing to determine how people will respond to an offer. Then split this data into two groups. On the first group train or estimate the model. Then test it on the remainder of the data. A model is built when the cycle of training and testing is completed.

To conclude, CRM is essential to compete effectively in today's marketplace. The more effectively you can use the information about your customers to meet their needs the more profitable you will be. Operational CRM with the help of analytical CRM with predictive data mining models as its core provides the business a cutting edge to maintain and enhance relationship. The path of a successful business like ICICI Bank and innumerable other corporations and organizations is built on data mining as the guiding factor.

References

Berry M.J.A. and Linoff G. (1999), *Mastering Data Mining: The Art and Science of Customer Relationship Management,* John Wiley and Sons, Inc. Fayyad U. Grinstein G.E. and Wierse A. (2002), *Information Visualization in Data Mining and*

Knowledge Discovery, Morgan Kaufmann Publishers, Academic Press.

Jenkins, D. (1999), *Customer Relationship Management and the Data Warehouse*, Call Centre Solutions, 18(2): pp. 88-92.

Laudon, K.C. and Laudon, J.P. (2006), *Management Information System: Managing the Digital Firm*, Pearson.

Pearson, K.E. (2007), *Managing and Using Information Systems: A Strategic Approach.* New York, Wiley, 2001: John Wiley and Sons, Inc.; META Group, *To CRM and Beyond,* Research Note ADS 805.

8

Human Resources Management (HRM) and Practices

Pankaj M. Madhani

The term 'resource' refers to the use of available materials, including natural, physical and human resources. The amount of natural and physical resources is limited, but the creative value of human resources is without limits. In the present environment of globalization and increased competition, most organizations consider their employees, often called human resource (HR), to be their most valuable strategic assets. It is well recognized that one of the sources of sustainable competitive advantage resides in non-tradable, difficult to imitate, firm-specific human resources of the organization (Sirmon, Hitt and Ireland, 2007). For a business organization to develop successfully, it must have a strong talent pool in addition to having adequate plant, equipment, technology and capital.

In this era of knowledge economy and information revolution, the knowledge people possess is being viewed as the new factor of production. HR is the basis of competitive advantage. Hence, virtually every organization spends heavily to acquire and retain its human resource—its employees and their skills—than any other resource.

Usually, an organization uses a set of performance measures that involve the return on the capital (or investment) they employ. However, few organizations employ a measure of the return on the amount of compensation and benefits they provide to employees, despite the fact that usually the amount spent in this way is usually quite a few times larger than the amount invested. In many cases, an organization's people cost more than all other resources combined. Employee wages and benefits make up close to half of many organizations' operating expenses and can be even higher in some sectors such as financial services, information technology (IT) and IT-enabled services (ITES).

Because of the importance of knowledge and intellectual capital as a competitive advantage, HR evaluation is becoming a very important measurement issue. Yet there are not enough revealing and readily available metrics of HR measurement and evaluation. In this scenario, return on human resource (ROHR) is being emphasized as an important business tool that can be used to assess an organization's performance in terms of human asset use.

HRM: Assessment and Evaluation

As worldwide economic uncertainties continue to concern business leaders, their attention turns to the various organizational levers that can foster success in uncertain times. Hence, the contribution of the workforce to organization success is perhaps the most important lever to competitive advantage. With globalization of world economy, the structure of traditional organizations has quickly transformed from being labour-intensive to being knowledge-intensive.

In the globalized economy, organizations realize that they can no longer use labour cost reduction methods to enhance the competitiveness of their products in the international market. Instead, competitiveness is enhanced through innovations related to products, production processes, customers and the market. All of these innovations originate from human talent. Therefore, in addition to the pursuit of market share, global enterprises must enhance their strengths and capabilities of human talent.

Human resources have received growing attention in business, and human resources planning, staff recruitment and allocation, salaries and benefits, labour relations and other HR activities have gradually become important elements of business management.

The management of people, also called as human resource management (HRM) involves HR planning as well as practices in such a way that HR can in itself be a source of competitive advantage for the organization. With the development of HRM, organizations have an increasing need for a comprehensive, systematic evaluation of HR performance. According to Tsui and Gomez (1988), the assessment of HRM performance has the following aims:

- **To provide information ensuring the effectiveness of HRM:** This is accomplished by comparing plans with actual results and using this as a basis for planning, implementation and oversight of HRM activities. This information will help ensure that the human resources available are sufficient to meet the long-term goals.
- **To take advantage of opportunities provided and predict the symptoms of poor HRM:** The assessment results should be used to predict adverse changes in HR and solve these problems before they become too severe.
- **To assess financial impact and increase cost-consciousness:** Such assessment requires calculating the financial benefits and costs of HR programs and allowing the HR manager to be cost-conscious and plan investment in HR activities using a profit-cantered approach. Hence, it ultimately strengthens the HR functions.

HR Investment: Key Concepts

Buy 'low' and sell 'high' is the adage in investment world, but what about the labour market? Organizations don't literally buy and sell people like stock transactions in stock market; however they do hire human resources with some expectation of a payback on the deal. Adopting return on investment (ROI) approach for human resource means viewing employees as an investment. It means considering money spent on recruiting, selection, training, developing, motivating and retaining employees like investments in plant and machinery (capital expenditure) or plant expansion—as expenditures with an expected future pay back within a certain time period.

Investment and returns in the area of HR differ significantly from those in the accounting and financial world in several aspects; hence, ROI measurement for HR is more than simply an accounting issue.

- HR investment is not an investment in fixed assets, as apart from investment it involves a learning process with subsequent behaviour change and performance improvement (McLagan, 1989). Also, how much one can learn and how successfully one may deploy the learned skills on the job in the organization depends on many variables such as past learning experience, education background, work experience etc.
- The impact of learning outcome on final business output often interacts with various organizational and environmental factors, such as organization culture and market conditions (Wang, 2000).
- The benefit of HR investment may take on a value other than monetary or intangible.

Managing HR investment involves following key questions:

- How much organizations need to invest in HR?
- What is the desired payback?
- How soon to break even?

Proactive organizations are viewing HR as in investment to be optimized rather than a cost to be minimized. Hence, they see money spend on recruitment, training and development, motivating and retaining employees as investments similar to investments in plant, equipment or plant expansion as expenditure with an expected future payback. HR investment in organizations is optimized when there is significant progress in 'knowledge', 'motivation', and 'opportunity' to perform, as explained below:

Knowledge: It involves investment in growing the base of talent which involves recruiting, training and developing men-power. When managed correctly, this investment adds required skills, knowledge and abilities to the organization. Knowledge investment by organizations generates organizational capabilities.

Motivation: This investment can increase effort level of individual employee. HR practices of hiring and layoff will have major impact on motivation level of employees. Other motivational drivers include compensation and benefits, such as salary, variable pay, incentives, employee stock options, health and welfare plans. Motivational investment by organizations creates sustainability of organizational capabilities.

Opportunity: It involves investment in HR practices that provides flexibility. The value of organization increases with level of organizational flexibility. Fundamental basis of sustainable superior performance of a firm is its organizational capability to exploit current assets and dynamically match its future resources and capabilities with its surrounding environments. Hence, organizations must simultaneously focus on the exploitation of existing assets/opportunities and the exploration of new opportunities thrown up by environmental uncertainties (March 1991).

Investments in human assets can be designed and managed to protect the firm's human assets from uncertainties such as downside risks (e.g. obsolescence) and to exploit upside opportunities created by uncertainties (e.g. development of new products) (Sanyal and Sett, 2011a). Firms cannot easily adjust the organizational capabilities to the emergence of market opportunities. Therefore, the firms that have made investments in capabilities appropriate to these opportunities are likely to gain advantage over those who have made sub-optimum choices (Kogut and Kulatilaka, 2001).

Thus, organizations must broaden their focus from the simple pursuit of capital productivity to the accumulation, training, development and motivation of human resources, which can advance organizations and create competitive advantage. Human resources must be based on the needs of the organizations and should be seen as highly valuable assets.

After an organization commits to HR investment, its overall outcome is measured in terms of the achievement of organizational capabilities, sustainability and flexibility.

HR Investment and Strategic Outcomes

The organizations do not achieve and sustain a competitive advantage simply by possessing knowledge-based resources. Thus, if organizations are seeking competitive advantage through HR, they should design HR practices in ways that allow it to leverage and exploit these resources and enable employees to use the knowledge for competitive edge. HR practices are defined as "a set of distinct but interrelated activities, functions and processes that are directed at attracting, developing and maintaining (or disposing of) a firm's human resources" (Lado and Wilson, 1994).

HR practices represent organization's capabilities that create value for the organization by developing enabling human skills and behaviour (Sanyal and Sett, 2011). The use of strategic HR practices and processes for managing human capital can give a clear performance advantage through cost savings from increased utilization, lower turnover, and higher productivity of human resources. Investments in HR practices by organizations will increase employee commitment and that increased employee commitment is a lead indicator of customer commitment, which is a lead indicator of organizational profitability (Rucci et al., 1998). Organizations that invest in some HR practices are more likely to have financial returns than firms that do not invest in these HR practices (Pfau and Kay, 2001). As explained below, major drivers of HR investment are *organizational capability, sustainability* and *flexibility.*

Organizational Capability and Sustainability: Human resources are valuable for the organizations because of their ability to create, use and share knowledge. Hence, developing a critical mass of employees who are knowledgeable or skilled may constitute a potential source of competitive advantage for the organizations. HR planning is the process of analyzing, diagnosing and identifying the needs for and availability of human resources so that the organization can reach its objectives. By avoiding unnecessary employment variability, organizations can reduce the substantial transaction costs associated with activities related to adding and cutting employees. In a period of recession or economic downturn the demand for the goods and services of the organization and, in turn, the demand for the workforce will go down (Madhani, 2010). Hence, many organizations resort to downsizing and lay-off of employees.

However, lay-off will reduce overheads in the short term; it may result in much heavier long-term costs. In the next economic boom, the organizations will lose time and money on hiring and training new employees. Such reactive HR planning policy and practices will lose competitiveness of the organization in the long run. Downsizing or employees lay-off produces an immediate and significant reduction in the organization's payroll expenses, which makes the bottom line look better in the short run. However, downsizing of the organization is much like radical life saving surgery—the patient may survive from critical condition, but is in a weakened state. When business conditions later improve and significant hiring is required, the organizations will incur all the costs associated with hiring, such as screening, selecting and training employees with the necessary skills.

Downsizings and layoffs of the organization have unintended negative consequences for individuals as well as the organizations, such as reduced job performance, organizational commitment and trust and loyalty. Such practices by the organization break the implicit psychological contract between employer and employee—a contract that implies long-term employment in return for hard work and loyalty. The organization is expected to provide stable employment and opportunities for individual development and promotion of work force.

Employees' perceptions of a layoff as a violation of the psychological contract, may lead to several organizational problems such as low morale, low trust and low productivity and correspondingly a negative impact on the financial performance of the organization. Any downsizing initiative by organizations also leaves the organization's survivors (the employees left behind) overloaded, and often with work they have not been trained to do. Workforce reductions by layoff may produce feelings of insecurity and stress among the surviving employees.

Consequently, morale and productivity of employees often declines and some may leave, which can have a significant impact on the top and bottom line of the organization. Employees may begin to feel that they are less valued or respected in the organization and cultivate feelings of mistrust toward their employers, with a subsequent decline in morale. Lay-offs create a serious disruption within an organization's culture that can affect all stakeholders, including customers and suppliers. For these reasons, downsizing often causes more problems than it solves.

Spending on HR should not be considered simply as costs, but rather as investment. Human resources are a factor for differentiation and a source of competitiveness. Hence, proactive organizations are continuing HR investment even during period of recession. In recession or down cycle of economy, cost considerations will dominate the HR practices and strategies. But HR practices should consider the long term prospects as well. Many organizations are using proactive HR planning and practices and hence use the recession as an opportunity to hire skilled and competent personnel from potentially larger applicant pool at considerable low cost.

Right HR planning, recruitment practices and retention strategies will take advantage of the recession and arm the organization with the best of the newly available talent. Lay-offs caused by economic downturns typically produce large supplies of highly qualified and experienced individuals in the employment market. Such downturns or recession also provide surpluses of high-quality fresher or inexperienced job applicants graduating from colleges and universities, available at relatively cheaper cost. This means that, during economic downturn the bargaining power is with the organizations. This will also be an opportunity to shed the deadwoods in the organization by replacing the poor performers. Organizations that hire during downturns can replace underperforming employees. This will enable the organization to better position itself when the economic climate becomes favourable again.

Through opportunistic hiring during economic downturns, bargains in quality human capital can be obtained without incurring the premium salaries of a seller's market as it happens during economic upturn (Madhani, 2011). Thus, organizations can invest in human capital during economic downturns by stockpiling high-quality key personnel critical to strategic initiatives. Such hiring practice will also increase retention rate of workforce as workers hired during a recession may not switch jobs after the recovery starts because of the preference for the status quo in decision-making.

Satisfied employees stay at their jobs and do not search for information on other employment because of the increased loyalty effect and organizational commitment effect. Lower turnover among employees hired during economic downturns is also a result of their increased risk avoidance. By such HR practices of hiring in down cycle of the economy also called as countercyclical hiring by the organization, will decrease investment in people and ultimately increases ROHR.

Similarly, avoiding work force lay off during down cycle of economy will also increase ROHR in long run through decrease in employee investment and increase in return derived from enhanced morale and productivity of employees. However, countercyclical hiring depends on size, characteristics as well as performance of the organization (Madhani, 2011).

Organizational Flexibility: It is important to understand that strategic HR planning and practices will take a long term view of things. Most of the traditional methods for evaluating HR practices, have failed to take into consideration the uncertainties inherent in human resources and the projects in which they are engaged. Therefore, these evaluation methods have performed poorly in evaluating the effects of HR practices on the ability to properly manage future opportunities as they lack the ability to measure either the current value of human assets or their flexibility (Sanyal and Sett, 2011b). The ability of an organization to use the flexibilities of its firm specific resources effectively and efficiently over a range of operating conditions leads to superior outcomes (Sanchez, 2004).

According to Bhattacharya and Gibson (2005), flexibility of employee skills, employee behaviours and HR practices represent critical sub dimensions of HR flexibility and are related to superior performance. The contribution of HR practices to organizational flexibility should thus also be included in measurements to provide a sound foundation for understanding the value-creation and decision-making processes. The organizations with flexible workforce can react efficiently to any environmental changes. Flexibility is valuable to organizations as it provides them with the ability to adapt to changing environment when faced with uncertainty (Kulatilaka and Marks, 1988). Flexibility is created by those organizational capabilities that manage uncertainties proactively.

Flexibility in strategic decision-making is a critical factor for organizations facing ever- increasing market competition in the current era of globalization (Madhani, 2008). Boyer et al., (2003) go to the extent of describing strategic planning as 'an exercise in managing flexibility'. Human resource are considered as a strategic asset and accordingly Bhattacharya and Wright (2005) framed the conceptual model to consider HR practices as creating real options in terms of reducing the uncertainties of return, volume, and costs. Specifically, they defined HR options as "investments in the human capital pool of an organization that provides the capability to respond to future contingent events". Following are the major types of organizational flexibility.

A. Co-ordination Flexibility: Co-ordination flexibility is the extent to which the firm can reconfigure the chain of resources and redeploy the resources. These flexibilities are choices that firms make with respect to the dynamic environment. Variety of skills in the workforce and ability to acquire diverse skills from contingent workforces are the indicators of co-ordination flexibility (Wright and Snell, 1998).

B. Functional and Numerical Flexibility: It is critical that the core employees of an organization are functionally flexible so that in a changing environment, they can take over other jobs through job rotation. Organizations should also strive for functional flexibility of employees through job enrichment (vertical) and enlargement (horizontal). Organizations facing uncertainties due to rapid fluctuations in product mix and output volume are expected to have greater strategic flexibilities and are likely to show superior long-term performance if they are able to create the requisite functional as well as numerical flexibilities in their workforce (Atkinson, 1984).

Such flexibility involves, adjusting the workforce itself to changes in demand, hiring to bring in new skills as needed and presumably implementing layoffs to eliminate redundant or obsolete skills, as well as relying more on "contingent" work. Such flexibilities may be achieved in a number of ways such as multi-skilling, systematic job rotation and constitution of temporary project teams. Toyota is an example of an organization with cross-trained and multi-functional workforce that allows Toyota to adapt to the ups and downs of market without workforce lay-off or downsizing.

C. Locational Flexibility: Locational flexibility of the employees will lower the expenses for the organization. Non-core activities of the organizations can be outsourced. Dell and many other computer hardware, software as well as financial services organizations in US have outsourced back-end customer services functions to India. Many organizations now use IT and web-based solutions to create virtual conferences or tele-conferences where the employees are at different parts of the world, but attend meetings virtually. This can save the organization on travel and other organizational overhead costs.

D. Resource Flexibility: Resource flexibility is the extent to which a resource can be applied to a larger range of alternative uses, the costs and difficulty of switching the use of a resource from one alternative use to another and the time required to switch. Individual skill breadth and ability to acquire new skills are strategic HR indicators of resource flexibility (Wright and Snell, 1998).

E. Reward Flexibility: Reward flexibility will mean that the workforce of the organization will be rewarded for their excellent performance which will finally lead to better performance for the organization. Many organizations offer its employees some sort of reward for excellent performance.

In this way, certain HR practices are valuable to the organizations because they increase its flexibility, add to the effectiveness of the workforce and ultimately enhance ROHR.

Measurement and Evaluation of HR Practices

Recent research on best HR practices has shown that the HR function is a source of competitive advantage and as such it is indeed an important success factor of the organizations. Along with the development of HR practices, organizations increasingly require a comprehensive assessment of the contribution of human resources. Research on HR measurement and evaluation practices has focused on developing procedures that resemble acceptable corporate approaches such as behavioural accounting, human resource accounting, human resource costing, human resource audits, investment returns or balanced scorecards. Historically, a variety of HR measurement and evaluation methods are developed and used to demonstrate the effectiveness of HR practices.

Flamholtz (1985) has proposed HR accounting system to measure HR contribution. McConnell (1989) has identified 16 categories to be measured in the human resource auditing. Pauly (1993) has proposed converting HR function to profit centre concept. Kaplan and Norton (1996) have developed Balanced Score Card (BSC), a measurement and evaluation framework that helps in translating strategic goals into operational objectives. Ulrich (1997) has emphasized how HR practices relate to BSC through productivity, people and process indicators. Becker, Huselid and Ulrich (2001) have outlined HR Score Card model, which aims at managing HR as a strategic partner, and demonstrating HR's contribution to the financial success.

Phillips (1999) has identified 12 approaches that have been used to evaluate the HR function such as survey approach, HR reputation approach, HR accounting, HR auditing, HR case studies, HR cost monitoring, competitive benchmarking, key indicators, HR effectiveness index, HR management by objectives, HR profit centres, and return on investment (ROI). Cascio and Boundrenau (2008) has proposed a behavioural costing methodology to measure the financial impact of HR functions, which measures the economic consequences of employees' behaviour such as absenteeism, turnover, employee attitudes and employee training. For HR evaluation process to be effective, it must balance many issues, including simplicity, feasibility, credibility, and soundness as explained below.

Simplicity: The HR evaluation methodology must be simple, void of complex formulas, lengthy equations, and complicated methodologies.

Economical: The HR evaluation methodology must be economical, with the ability to be implemented easily. The process should have the capability to become a routine part of HR without requiring significant additional resources.

Credibility: The assumptions, methodology, and

outcomes of evaluation must be credible. Logical, methodical steps are needed to earn the respect of HR practitioners, top managers, and researchers. This requires a very practical approach to the HR evaluation process.

Theoretically Sound: From a research perspective, the HR evaluation methodology must be theoretically sound and based on generally accepted practices. The HR evaluation process must strike a balance between maintaining a practical and sensible approach and a sound and theoretical basis for the procedures.

Organizations have started believing that HR improvements are the best ways to enhance organisational efficiency in the ever increasing competitive environment of the organisations. According to Pfeffer (1998), organizations would build profits by putting people first. The success of organizations in the present competitive environment largely depends upon the calibre of their human resources and innovative HR practices. High level of organizational performance requires having the right people with right skills in the right place within the organization within the purview of HR practices.

The most HR measures today focus on how the HR function is using and deploying its resources, and whether they are used efficiently, even when their connection to organization effectiveness is unknown. If there is any analysis of the HR, the tendency is to focus almost exclusively on controlling wage and benefit costs rather than measuring and enhancing the meaningful output of human capital.

There are many reasons for this, but the primary one is this: the organizational system isn't in place to measure the current return on HR, to determine the impact of investment in these HR or to make informed decisions about how to maximize these impacts. Hence, HR measurement and evaluation methods need to extend its traditional focus on the HR function, and increase its capability to support key decisions about human capital that drive organizational effectiveness (Boudreau and Ramstad, 2006).

Top management wants HR measurement systems that enhance their decisions about human capital; however, HR measures largely focus on the traditional paradigm of delivering HR services quickly, and cheaply. This is important but incomplete (Boudreau and Ramstad 2003).

Two underlying premises often underlie these measurement attempts: (i) measures will lead decision makers to make more rational and productive choices about how people are managed; or (ii) measures will help convince management to support and invest in HRM programs (Boudreau, 1991). The biggest challenge facing HR managers today lies in developing an effective measurement system to evaluate their ability to cultivate high quality human resource to improve organizational performance and their ability to manage human resources as effectively as possible.

An organization's capabilities are the deliverables from HR investment. These capabilities give investors' confidence (or lack thereof) in future earnings and increase (or decrease) market capitalization of firm. HR managers who link their activities to organizational capabilities and who then find ways to communicate those capabilities to investors deliver better shareholder value. A research framework for HR measurement by classifying diverse HR measures into five distinct types typically includes the following:

- Measures of HR practices reflecting measures of efficiency, such as cost per hire, time to fill vacancies, hours of training per employee etc.
- Measures of HR outcomes and include organizational capabilities, sustainability and flexibility that HR practices should develop such as measures of employee behaviour, attitude, and skills etc.
- Measures of the impact of HR practices on organizational capabilities.
- Measures of the impact of organizational capabilities, sustainability and flexibility on strategic outcomes such as financial results or customer satisfaction.

- Direct measures of the impact of HR practices on strategic outcomes.

Return on Human Resources (ROHR)

Normally, at the end of the diagnosis phase of HR practices, a clear picture of organization's workforce effectiveness emerges. It is expressed in terms of ROHR and defined as:

ROHR (percent) = R/I x 100

Where,

R = return on HR investment

I = HR investment

The ROHR methodology is a balanced approach to measuring the bottom-line impact of HR practices and holds the most promise for showing the contribution of specific HR programs. Although the interest in ROHR has heightened and progress is being made, it is still an issue that challenges even the most sophisticated and progressive organizations. Some argue that it is not possible to calculate the ROI in HR programs while other proceeds to develop measures for ROHR calculations.

Although, the overall interest in ROHR has heightened and progress is being made, it is still an issue that challenges even the most proactive organizations. The concept of ROHR suggests that decisions about allocating monetary resources on people should consider:

- The inflow of returns produced by that resource allocation.
- The offsetting outflows of resources required to make the HR or people investment.
- How the inflows and outflows occur in each future time period?
- With what discount factor it should be "discounted" to reflect uncertainty and riskiness of cash flow.

Illustration: The first step in understanding ROHR involves calculating the 'I' or investment in HR. In other words, how much organization invests in employees or people? It is a simple calculation that includes compensation, incentives, benefits, training, and the administration overhead costs. The return on HR investment is also affected by employee turnover. The output part of the 'employee turnover' issue may also mean a loss of relationships with important customers and suppliers.

Then, consider the input part of the 'employee turnover' problem, which is the cost of recruiting, hiring and training a new employee. Each time an employee leaves an organization, he or she takes always a significant amount of the organization's priceless skills, knowledge and know-how as well as the time and money spent training them. Hence, by reducing turnover of employees, return on human resource will be increased while investment in people got decreased. As ROHR is ratio of return and investment, it finally enhances ROHR.

Benefits: The ROHR provides organizations with quantitative information of return in monetary terms. As ROHR approach uses the currency of business and compatible with business processes, it is aligned with the business objectives and, therefore, often with its strategies. This is the approach that's most familiar to functional managers and hence improves communications about the business benefits of HR. In fact, the ROHR methodology directly involves top management in the computation process, thus actively involves them with HR. It also becomes difficult for management to argue with their own numbers. Finally, in this process the focus is on HR as an investment or asset, not as an expense, thus influencing how money invested in HR is viewed.

Limitations: ROHR methodology has frequently lacked the persuasive power of basic numerical evidence that is common to some other functional areas of the organization such as production, finance and marketing. ROHR could be politically sensitive, overstating benefits that actually occur from other functions and over assigning costs to other functions. The ROHR framework can be expensive to implement because of the need for active involvement of management and other personnel in the process (McLean, 2005).

In a rapidly changing world, ROHR takes too long to implement. The ROHR attempts to convert all inputs and outputs into financial terms and then determine how much the HR function has contributed to the organization. This provides opportunities to compare human capital investment to investment in other types of capital. However, such valuation is challenging because of problematic data gathering, the intangible nature of HR assets and the lagged effects of HR practices.

The ROHR components are not readily available for most HR decisions, as not all intangible return or benefits are financial, e.g. employee satisfaction, ethical organizational culture, etc. Similarly, investment or costs often omit important factors, e.g., depreciation, overheads, lost productivity. Hence, the ROHR approach requires thorough understanding of HR investments.

HR Measurement and Evaluation Practices in India

Until business organizations adopt a systematic and disciplined methodology for quantifying not just the costs but also benefits of investment in human resources, important decisions affecting this increasingly critical business variable will continue to be driven by opinions such as whether managers like an HR program or employees are satisfied with training program. When organizations use ROHR approach effectively, it will result in fact-based decisions about human resources.

Current status of HR measurement and evaluation practices carried out by organizations in India was studied by Srimannarayana (2010). The research study, first of its kind in India was conducted among 114 HR professionals covering the manufacturing and service organizations in both public and private sectors across India. The questionnaire developed by

Phillips (1999) was used for the purpose of the study. The research study found that ITES has stood first in HR measurement and evaluation practices, followed by manufacturing and IT. Following are major highlights of the research study.

- New HR programmes are occasionally implemented in organisations without some formal methods of measurement and evaluation (46 percent of the respondents).
- The return on investment in HR (or ROHR) is measured primarily by intuition and perception of senior executives in organisations (40 percent of the respondents).
- The observations by managers and reactions from the participants and users are primary methods of measuring return on investment (47 percent of the respondents). However, only few organisations measure return on HR investment primarily by improvements in productivity, cost savings and quality, etc. (13 percent of the respondents).
- Majority organisations have never developed cost and benefit comparisons of HR programmes (47 percent of the respondents). However, 42 percent of the respondents have asserted that their organisations have occasionally developed cost and benefit comparisons.
- The costs of specific HR programmes are estimated only by one-third of organizations when the programmes are implemented (32 percent of the respondents). However, some organisations never calculate the cost of HR programmes (11 percent of the respondents).
- In some organizations, pay-for-performance programmes exist only for a few key employees (21 percent of the respondents). While according to 48 percent of the respondents, it exists for most employees (line and staff).

Managerial Implications

There is pressure on HR function to measure its

contribution in the increasingly competitive and cost effective environment. HR departments are evolving from playing a merely administrative role to becoming "strategic partners" responsible for contributing to the achievement of organizational objectives. HR is moving away from the transactional, hiring/firing support function to a bottom line business decision maker (Caudron, 1994). HR evaluation is often simply not conducted because of its inherent difficulties.

However, the concern for measuring HR contribution is gradually increasing. Changing focus of HR also requires that new ways of defining and assessing HR success be developed. Measuring and evaluating HR practices makes good economic sense to a HR practice's contribution by providing convincing evidence. ROHR is a logical approach for identifying the important elements and critical variables of HR or people investments and integrating them in a way that enhances HR decisions.

To improve ROHR, organizations should also focus on the kinds of day-to-day issues and frustrations that drain productivity from the organization and reduce the "R" (Return) perceived from ROHR formula. Employee turnover, low productivity, low morale and absenteeism are big drags on returns derived from people investment. By reducing turnover or attrition rate and increasing employee morale and productivity, ROHR can be increased considerably.

To sum up, there is unparalleled consensus among business managers throughout the globe that people make the difference. Whether human resources can be effectively utilized through the full development of their creative potential is currently considered one of the key factors that determine the success or failure of a business. Among all resources in an organization, human resources are especially important because they are related to the survival and development of the business. HR practices are expected to create and sustain a competitive advantage for the organizations.

Better HR practices in terms of HR planning, flexibility,

recruitment and retention strategies will effectively respond to external environment. It is imperative for HR managers to develop methodology for measuring efficiency and effectiveness of HR practices. The problem of measuring and evaluating HR practices in order to manage them, however, is not new and relates to the broader issue of valuing intangibles. By making the committed efforts now to set a real and measurable value on ROHR, and putting in place HR practices and programmes for making the situation better, the sooner the organization will start to reap the benefits of HR capital. ROHR is a powerful, comprehensive assessment tool that can evaluate the value and contributions of HR activities.

References

Atkinson, J. (1984), Manpower Strategies for Flexible Organizations, *Personnel Management,* 16, 28-31.

Becker, B.E., Huselid, M.A. and Ulrich, D. (2001), *The HR Scorecard: Linking People, Strategy and Performance.* Boston. MA: Harvard Business School Press.

Bhattacharya, M. and Gibson, D.E. (2005), The Effects of Flexibility in Employee Skills, Employee Behaviours, and Human Resource Practices on Firm Performance, *Journal of Management,* 31(4), 622-640.

Bhattacharya, M. and Wright, P.M. (2005), Managing Human Assets in an Uncertain World: Applying Real Options Theory to HRM, *International Journal of Human Resource Management*, 16(6), 929-948.

Boudreau, J.W. and Ramstad, P.M. (2006), Talent Ship and Human Resource Measurement and Analysis: From ROI to Strategic Organizational Change, *Human Resource Planning,* 29(1), 25-33.

Boudreau, J.W. and Ramstad, P.M. (2003), Strategic HRM Measurement in the 21st Century: From Justifying HR to Strategic Talent Leadership in HRM in the 21st Century.

Boyer, M., Christoffersen, P., Lasserre P. and Pavlov, A. (2003), *Value Creation, Risk Management and Real Options,* CIRANO Burgundy Reports.

Cascio, W.F. and Boudrenau, J. (2008), *Investing in People: Financial Impact of Human Resource Initiatives,* New Jersey, NJ: Pearson Education Inc.

Caudron, S. (1994), HR Leaders Brainstorm the Profession's Future. *Personnel Journal*, 74(7), 54-61.

Dunnette, M. and L. Hough (eds.), Handbook of Industrial and Organizational Psychology, 2nd ed., 621-745.

Dyer, L. (ed.) Human Resource Management: Evolving Roles and Responsibilities, Washington, DC: BNA.

Fitz-Enz, J. (2000), The ROI of Human Capital: Measuring the Economic Value of Employee Performance, New York, NY: AMACOM.

Flamholtz, E.G. (1985), Human Resource Accounting, San Francisco, CA: Jossey Bass.

Kaplan, R. and Norton, D. (1996), Balanced Scorecard: Translating Strategy into Action, Boston, MA: Harvard Business School Press.

Kogut, B. and Kulatilaka, N. (2001), Capabilities as Real Options, *Organization Science*, 12(6), 744-758.

Kulatilaka, N. and Marks, S.G. (1988), The Strategic Value of Flexibility: Reducing the Ability to Compromise, *American Economic Review*, 78(3), 574-580.

Madhani, P.M. (2011), Managing Sales Employees' Compensation: A Countercyclical Investment Approach, *Compensation and Benefits Review*, 43(2), 109-122.

Madhani, P.M. (2010), Rebalancing Fixed and Variable Pay in a Sales Organization: A Business Cycle Perspective, *Compensation and Benefits Review*, 42(3), 179-189.

Madhani, P.M. (2008), RO-Based Capital Budgeting: A Dynamic Approach in New Economy, *The ICFAI Journal of Applied Finance*, 14(11), 48-67.

March, J. (1991), Exploration and Exploitation in Organizational Learning, *Organization Science*, 2, 71-87.

McConnell, J.H. (1989), How Are You Doing? Designing an Audit of the HR Function, *Human Resources Professional*, March/April, 61-64.

McLean, G.N. (2005), Examining Approaches to HR Evaluation: The Strengths and Weaknesses of Popular Measurement Methods, *Strategic Human Resources*, 4(2), 24-27.

Pauly, D. (1993), HR: The New Profit Centre, *Human Resource Executive*, (August), 36-41.

Pfau, B. and Kay, I. (2001), Human Capital Edge: 21 Practices Your Company Must Implement (or Avoid) to Maximize Shareholder

Value, New York, NY: McGraw Hill.

Pfeffer, J. (1998), *The Human Equation: Building Profits by Putting People First,* Boston, MA: Harvard Business School Press.

Phillips, J.J., Stone, R.D. and Phillips, P.P. (2001), *The Human Resources Scorecard: Measuring the Return on Investment,* Boston, MA: Butterworth Heinemann.

Phillips, J.J. (1999), *Accountability in Human Resource Management,* Boston, MA: Butterworth Heinemann.

Rucci, A., Kirn, S. and Quinn, R. (1998), The Employee-Customer-Profit Chain At Sears, *Harvard Business Review*, 76(1), 82-97.

Sanchez, R. (2004), Understanding Competence-based Management: Identifying and Managing Five Modes of Competence, *Journal of Business Research*, 57, 518-532.

Sanyal, S. and Sett, P.K. (2011a), Applying Real Options Theory to HRM: An Empirical Study of IT Software Firms in India, *The International Journal of Human Resource Management*, 22(1), 72-102.

9

From Mass Production to Mass Customization

Sona Padman

Mass production thrived in the bygone era of stable demand and little product variety. But in today's turbulent environment, mass production no longer works; in fact, it has become a major curse for a country's declining competitiveness. Virtually all executives recognize the need to provide outstanding service to the customer. Focusing on the customer is however an imperative as well as a potential curse. Many companies strive to invent new programs and products to cater to every customers request and thereby gain the recognition of being customer driven. Kotler pronounced that the concept of 'mass market' is dead and we have progressed to an era of mass customisation through effective market segmentation. In the current competitive landscape, it is highly impossible to produce standardized products or services for the homogenous market and still command superior returns.

Today's most innovative companies are embracing mass customisation as it provides them their space of freedom to have a signature of individuality and create greater assortment of products at desirable prices. Therefore, it paves way for managing new technology and variety seeking customers with attractive *tailor-made* benefits. But as Maslow opined, customer's needs are unlimited and increasingly diverse. Therefore, in order to meet their demands a customized product which meets the customer expectations has to be developed. This can be done if it is examined thoroughly as to what kind of customisation their customers want before they plunge ahead with a new built-to-order product.

Mass Production

Mass production is based on the principles of specialization and division of labour as described by Adam Smith in *The Wealth of Nations* in 1776 and it was popularized by Henry Ford in the early twentieth century in his Ford Model 'T'. Hence it is also known as *"Fordism"*. The path to mass production led from artisans responsible for producing an entire product by their own means and at their own pace in *Craft Production*. As the word specifies, mass production means manufacturing things in masses and for the masses. It is a system for manufacturing products in large amounts through effective combination of employees with specialized skills, mechanization and standardisation. With products being manufactured in mass production, probability of human error is decreased and the quality of goods is increased. It also reduces labour costs and non-productive effort of the work force. Mass production is the direct descendant of the American system.

The American system of mass production dictates eight principles for successful mass production viz:

- Interchangeable parts.
- Specialized machines.
- Reliance on suppliers.
- Focus on production process.
- Division of labour.
- Flexibility.
- Continuous technological improvement.

The American system was an extremely successful method of production from middle to late nineteenth century. But as the American system moved to the twentieth century, these factors were not enough to meet the increasing demands of a geographically dispersed economy and support large enterprises. Mass production was taken into new heights when focus was given on operational efficiency, flow, low cost and low prices, economies of scale, product standardization, degree of specialization and vertical integration. Therefore, mass producers were not only concerned with production, but also with the entire flow of raw materials from their raw state through production and distribution. The mass producers thus became mass suppliers as well as mass distributors. The reinforcing principles of this dynamic system of mass production are as follows:

- A company must make profit to stay in business. Therefore, selling more products at lower cost generates more profit. More products can be sold in large, homogenous markets than in others.
- Manufacturing cost can be reduced drastically through high product volumes achieving economies of scale.
- Demand is elastic; hence lowering prices as costs decrease brings even higher volume and greater revenue.
- Niche market represents different customer desires and support only relatively lower volumes. Therefore ignore them.
- To realize the lowest possible costs, the production process should be as automated as possible.
- It is very important to maintain efficiency of production process which can be achieved by stabilizing inputs, process and outputs.
- Research and development should focus upon new product breakthroughs that can be mass-produced. Sales should focus on pushing current production out of the door.

Thus, the entire system becomes a feedback loop through which new products can be mass-produced. The feedback loop of reinforcing factors is shown in Figure 9.1.

R indicates the reinforcing loop which overtime yields products of higher volumes with lower costs for large markets using the most efficient manufacturing processes at most stable demand levels. This entire process can be simplified in words as, "new product manufactured by a mass production process yield low cost, consistent quality and standardized goods for large, homogenous markets which eventually results in stable demand causing long product cycles which allow for long product development cycles from which new products are created".

Figure 9.1: The Paradigm of Mass Production as a Dynamic System of Reinforcing Factors

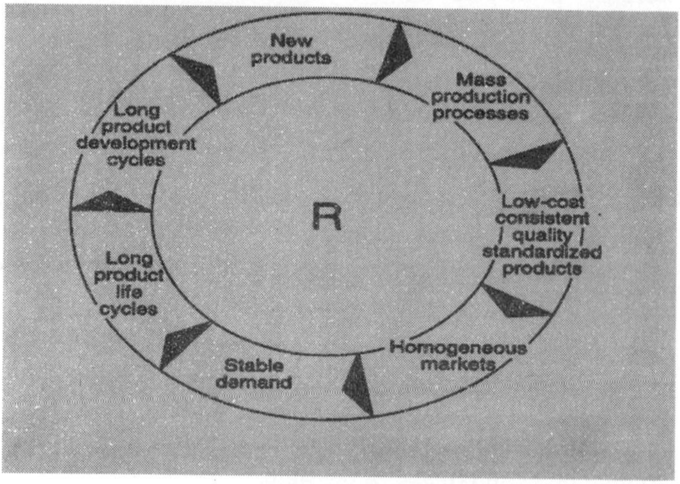

The mass production thinking says that the more and faster one produces, it is cheaper to produce. But this is true only from a direct cost per item perspective and it totally ignores the other real costs associated with overproduction and wastage. During mass production, it is harder to change the design of the product or to make the products slightly different from each other. Because of this, a manufacturer cannot cater to what each of their customers would like in a product.

With the growing competition on increasing diversity of the demands of customers and product costs, the manufacturing industry has been under tremendous pressure to meet the conflicting goals of efficiency and product variety. This manifests the idea of satisfying individual customer's needs with mass production efficiency, namely mass customisation which draws a lot of attention recently. In the *mass production* paradigm, the marketing department forecasts demand and these forecasts drove complex MRP systems to order the required parts and materials far enough ahead of time so that they would, hopefully, all arrive at the factory before the production run was scheduled. Assuming this was successful, equipment would be set up and a batch of products was built to satisfy the forecast. In order to make a batch of products, batches of parts would wait in *queues* before each operation—hence mass production is more aptly described by the less glamorous phrase, *batches and queues.*

Mass Production to Mass Marketing

The concept of mass marketing, it can be said, first emerged as a workable strategy during 1880s. It evolved along with mass production and involves selling the same product to everybody. It is also known as undifferentiated marketing which treats the entire market as a homogeneous entity, focusing on what is common instead of pursuing differences. Its monolithic mass-communication campaigns are usually focused on a narrow product range. Undifferentiated marketing campaigns tend to use a limited number of key messages designed to appeal to a broad number of consumers.

In mass marketing, the seller engages in the mass production, mass distribution and mass promotion of one product for all buyers. It allowed marketers to follow a product-and-sales oriented approach than a customer-driven approach. An understanding of consumer behaviour was less important in this environment. The marketing strategy was a total product-centric approach that is a sell what we make marketing philosophy. Mass marketing reflected a one-to-many model with producers offering a single standardized brand for everyone and leveraging economies of scale to control costs.

You can think of mass marketing as a shotgun approach: you blast out as many marketing messages as possible on every medium available as often as you can afford (*Jr., Robert Spellings. The Direct Marketing Voice.* Chicago: s.n., March

20, 2009). From 1880 to 1920, early innovators in many different industries stepped forward to seize this opportunity. Two of the most widely recognized examples are Ford and Coca-Cola. Automaker Henry Ford was very successful at both mass production and mass marketing. Ford pioneered the modern-day assembly line early in the twentieth century, which helped him cost-effectively pump out huge numbers of identical Model T automobiles. They came in only one colour: black.

"Any customer can have a car painted any colour he wants, so long as it is black," Ford used to joke. He also advertised in every major newspaper and persuaded all kinds of publications to carry stories about the new, inexpensive cars. By 1918, half of all cars on America's roads were Model Ts. His Model T was conceived and marketed as a "universal" car—one that would meet the needs of all buyers. By adopting mass production techniques and eliminating optional features, he was able to reduce costs and sell his product at an affordable price. The combination catapulted the Model T to the top of the market.

Coca-Cola was equally successful at using mass marketing in the soft-drink industry. Like Ford, it also viewed the product as being the only one that consumers needed and sold only one kind of coke in a 6.5 ounce bottle. No product in history has ever matched Coca-Cola's total sales until then. Coke simply did not have the competition that it faces today. However, the story is now much different. Coca-Cola has a wide range of products in multiple sizes and packages designed to meet the specific needs of unique market segments within the overall soft drink market.

Benefit of Mass Marketing

The main benefit of mass marketing is that it does not require as much focus on research identifying the tastes of individual market sections. It can also mean the company can be confident that it will not miss out any potential consumers in its marketing. This strategy makes sure marketing reaches people who do not fall into the supposed target market but would still be interested in buying. The other advantages of mass marketing are by focusing all the available resources in a single campaign and a limited line of products, a very large market is reached and significant economies of scale can be achieved, leading to cost leadership.

Because there is a very definite message and a much focused branding effort, the brand image is reinforced in the mind of the public. The conjunction of cost leadership and a strong image can create a large barrier to market entry, which ultimately discourages competitors to enter into their market. Mass marketing can also be suitable for a product or service that is intended to be profitable based on quantity of sales rather than high mark-ups or a high price. This often applies to products that meet common needs such as food, clothing or transport. If carried out successfully, undifferentiated marketing can lead to a product being so well-established that it dominates a market and even becomes synonymous with that market.

Demise of Mass Markets

Mass marketing slowly started to lose its glamour in the mid-1990s. It had to incur heavy advertisement costs to establish the brand and keep them in the public eye. The cost of distributing promotional literature was also very high as a large geographical area had to be covered. These costs could be affordable if mass marketing would have been effective and generated a huge response rate. But the average response rate to mass marketing promotion was only 0.1 percent. This was due to the inefficiency of the mass produced product to meet their needs. Another threat to mass marketing was that when a firm used a mass marketing strategy, consumers got tired of the product. If competitors offer different products or even same products with better service, it was easy for competitors to convince those segments. Another major drawback is that mass marketing never satisfied all the needs of any customer segment, it only satisfied all the segments partially. This provoked the marketers to think of a new product where they could meet the customer demands and also mint money.

Evolution of Mass Customisation (MC)

For many companies in many industries, the breakdown of mass production began in the 1960s, accelerated in the 1970s, and finally burst fully into management consciousness in the 1980s. During the late 1990s, things started to take a new turn. Now the landscape was completely different from the old world of mass production, in which standardized products, homogenous markets and long product development cycles were the rule.

A new paradigm of management was emerging, one in which variety and customisation supplant standardized products, heterogeneous and fragmented markets and product life cycles and development cycles spiral downward. Companies and industries had started making a *paradigm shift.* All the firms have thrown away the old paradigm of mass production, where focus was on efficiency through stability and control. Through the application of technology and new management methods, they have found their way to a new paradigm by creating *variety and customisation through flexibility and quick responsiveness*. This is the controlling focus of a new paradigm, *mass customisation.*

Mass customisation can be defined either very broadly or narrowly. The broad, visionary concept was first coined by Stan Davis in his book *Future Perfect* (1989) and promotes it as the ability to provide individually-designed products and services to every customer through high process agility, flexibility and integration (Pine et al., 1993; Eastwood, 1996). The main objective of MC systems is to deliver products and services that best translate the actual choices of individual customers.

While the practitioners of mass production shared the common goal of developing, producing, marketing and delivering goods and services at lower prices so that nearly *everyone can afford them*, practitioners of mass customisation shared the goal of developing, producing, marketing and delivering affordable goods and services with enough variety and customisation that nearly *everyone finds exactly what they want*.

Mass customisation is also known as *build-to-order, assemble-to-order, configure-to-order* and *engineer-to-order*. The logical tenets of this emerging system of management are as follows:

- Demand for individual products has become highly unstable. The large demand of standard mass market products has *fragmented* into demand for different variety or flavours.
- Since demand has fragmented, the large homogenous market became heterogeneous. The niches started becoming the market and the demand was for higher-quality goods that match closely with their individual desires.
- Since creating high levels of variety cannot be accomplished through mass production, it called for flexibility in manufacturing process, the anti-thesis of mass production.
- Since these new products closely meet customer desires, a premium price can be charged and this extra profit margin offsets any loss of efficiency due to lower volumes.
- Because the new niche markets are relatively smaller and constantly shifting, success can be achieved only if greater variety is produced more quickly and to achieve this, product development cycles should be reduced dramatically.
- The result is less demand for each individual product—demand fragmentation—but increasingly stable demand for the company and its products relative to the old system and to its competitors.

This progression can be viewed as a positive feedback,

creating a reinforcing loop of greater variety through increasing flexibility and more quickly-the exact opposite of mass production. At its heart, mass customisation has a dynamic system feedback loop that generates the demand for a multitude of products and services at an ever increasing frequency.

Technological innovation plays an important role in mass customisation. The application of new product technology like microprocessors increases the adaptability of products and results in greater variety and shorter product development lifecycles. Similarly, the application of process technologies like flexible manufacturing systems makes it increasingly economical to produce such variety. It is very important to notice that in this new paradigm, companies that can produce at lower costs and charge lower prices still have a competitive advantage; they will be more successful if they can retain the low prices and still cater to large variety demanded by the customers.

Mass customisation is an extension of product differentiation. The traditional form of product differentiation involves changes to be made in the product characteristics so that one firms product can be distinguished from other firms'. The goal of differentiation was to strike a chord of difference with its competitor's products, fit the products to the customers' needs and thereby gain a better competitive edge over the other firms. In mass customisation, the ultimate goal is to fit the products benefits to the customers' needs perfectly. It aspires to provide exactly what customer wants including the appropriate time of delivery and place (*Hart, 1995 cited in Bardakci and Whitelock, 2003*). Therefore, a company that chooses mass customisation should predict possible choices and preferences of the customer and introduce a set of limited options to them. For this purpose, it is essential to segment your potential customers effectively.

Nike iD is a service provided by the sportswear company Nike allowing customers to customize clothing purchased from Nike. The customer becomes the designer as they change and add a personal look and feel to a selected item. The service can be accessed both online from their homepage and in selected physical branches. The service was launched initially in 1999 and could only be accessed through their website. It provided customers the ability to choose from a limited range of different material and colours to develop their own style of tennis shoe.

Another example of such a mass customized product is Dell. A user can go to dell.co.in site and build a computer by themselves that has only what the user want, nothing more nothing less. Want more RAM? No problem, add more RAM. Need a DVD instead of a CD-ROM? Not a worry. Got to have that extra disk space for all those MP3s? Not a concern, just choose it. With only a few clicks of the mouse, the user gets the exact computer he/she desired for and not the one that used to be in stock. Thus, an entirely new shopping experience is provided where all the needs of customers are taken care of.

Market Turbulence

The primary indicator of the paradigm shift from mass production to mass customisation is the amount of market turbulence within an industry and firm. The greater the market turbulence, the more likely that the industry is moving to mass customisation and that the firm has to move in order to remain competitive. Market turbulence is an imprecise term but connotes the amount of instability, uncertainty and lack of control within a firm's market place. The prime reasons for market turbulence are as follows:

- The predictability or stability of demand levels did not exist. Demand became highly fragmented.
- Easily defined versus uncertain customer needs and wants. When the needs and wants of customers became uncertain, it became impossible to satisfy the entire market with a single product.
- Rate of change in customer needs and wants. If customer

needs and wants evolved very slowly, it may be possible for mass producers to continue with their system of production. But customer needs and wants changed rapidly and constantly, leaving no choice to mass producers.

- Customers started being more conscious on price, quality, and fashion/style. Thus, the firms were forced to move to non-standardized products and services. Total quality management was introduced and firms had to be flexible enough to change designs and production quickly.
- The intensity of competition was at its peak and in their battle for market share, customers had greater buying power.
- Price competition versus product differentiation. Consumers would literally pay not a penny more on differentiation, buying only from lowest priced producer.
- Vulnerability to substitute products accelerated the need for mass customisation. The logic here is that more vulnerable a firm's products are to substitutes, the more the firm is going to spend on meeting the needs of customer and it will ensure more variety and customisation.

In order to determine whether a shift was vital or not, a market turbulence map was introduced which would determine the turbulence was high or low on the basis of the above said factors. The following guidelines were used to determine the appropriate action:

- If current market turbulence in an industry is more than 60 points or if the change in turbulence has increased by 10 or more points in the past decade, then the industry is undergoing a paradigm shift right now.
- If current turbulence is between 40-60 points, or if the level has begun increasing and is expected to continue to do so, then the industry is on the threshold of the paradigm shift.
- If current turbulence is below 40 and has not been increasing, mass production remains a viable approach.

Approaches to Mass Customisation

Joseph Pine, II identifies four approaches to apply mass customisation (Gilmore and Pine, Four Faces of Mass Customisation, 1997, p. 92).

Collaborative Customisers: The organizations adopting this approach establish a dialogue to help customers specify their needs and identify offerings that suit their needs and then develop customized output. Dell is an example of this approach. It uses a collaborative approach to mass customize and assembles computers to customer's exact specifications. With only a few clicks of the mouse, the user gets the exact computer desired for. Nike and Levis are two other examples of this approach.

Adaptive Customisers: In this approach, customers buy a standard product and make modifications to it by themselves based on their needs. The adaptive approach is appropriate for businesses whose customers want the product to perform in different ways on different occasions, and available technology makes it possible for them to customize the product easily on their own. For example, Microsoft offers a package of software designed to run all activities of small businesses. But if a buyer (a small business) wants, for instance, to add more accounting functions into the package, it allows doing that because it uses a popular programming language that can be used by other programmers.

Cosmetic Customisers: Companies adopting this approach produce a standard product but present it differently to different customers. It is very close to customized standardization. For instance, a cell phone company might market their phone to teenagers claiming it perfect for instant messaging with their friends and on the same time market it to professionals by saying that it is great for downloading business files quickly. Although the company is manufacturing only one type of phone, they are presenting it to different customers in different way.

Transparent Customisers: It occurs when manufacturers

provide consumers with a unique product without the collaboration of the customer. These companies provide custom products without the customers' knowing that a product has been customized for them. For example, an online computer might track how each customer uses its service and then suggest additional features that the customer may find useful. In a similar fashion, Amazon.com provides book recommendations based on information about past purchase.

Potential Benefits of Mass Customisation

Manufacturers must adopt mass customisation as an enterprise-wide business strategy to:

- Provide best protection against the commoditization of products.
- Reduce/eliminate inventory.
- Provide opportunities for better value-added services.
- Provide for the portion of the business that is manufactured for inventory, more accurate market information on changing customer tastes and the actual tradeoffs they make in choosing products. Also offers opportunities for more accurate forecasting.
- Help redesign the operations and logistics, leading to processes that result in better, cheaper, and faster products and services.
- Help in developing and maintaining customer databases and allows better utilization of IT to implement "segments of one" strategies.
- Get the customer to spend more on the products and services.
- Build a relationship with customers, thus achieving higher customer satisfaction and loyalty.
- Offer opportunity for better channel management.
- Stimulate continuous innovation.
- Increase customer satisfaction and loyalty.
- Reduce time-to-market.
- Reduce internal costs to support evolving product

offerings.

- Eliminate artificial product constraints due to effort/complexity to modify or enhance a product line.
- Increase flexibility and responsiveness to "give customers what they want".
- Reduce overheads.
- Personalized and customized products and services will differentiate against commodity type products. With Lead customers will provide a rich source of new ideas that can also be exploited with other customers or with new prospects. As a result, NPD has lower risk of failure and a higher chance of beating the competition.
- On-going service can be adapted throughout the customer's life because it can be linked to the unique product.
- Companies will forge a close relationship with their suppliers, distributors and customers as they return time and time again for further unique products.

Mass Production versus Mass Customisation

One of the main debates within the literature on mass customisation regards the difference between mass customisation and mass production. This question is whether mass customisation and mass production are both parts of a continuum or do they have any operational and strategic differences.

Commodities from grain to gasoline are typically manufactured under mass-production systems. The great virtue of mass production is *economies of scale*. Production facilities are typically expensive and inflexible, but variable production costs are low. Also, after production, the finished product is stocked in inventory, which serves to meet customer demands. Mass production systems can be adapted to make several different varieties of a product. Items from automobiles to toothpaste are manufactured in that way. In addition to deciding what and when to buy, a customer selects one of the variants. The production facility must be somewhat flexible—

enough to switch between variants with few delays and at a low cost, thereby retaining economies of scale.

The basic structure of mass customisation is similar to that of mass production, but there are important differences. Instead of selecting one variety of a product, each customer provides unique information so that the product can be tailored to his or her requirements. The production process must be very flexible in order to meet those requirements. There is no finished-goods inventory if the product is really customized. The lack of inventory has advantages (low carrying costs) and disadvantages (customers have to wait). The technological differences between mass production and mass customisation, while considerable, are matters of degree: Mass customisation entails richer information flows and more-stringent requirements for process flexibility.

Pine, Victor and Boyton (1993) suggested that mass production and mass customisation are very different from each other and incompatible to be adopted within the same organization. They opined that there are great dissimilarities in fundamental aspects such as focus, goal, key features and structure of each approach.

Mass Customisation and Personalization

Personalization is the process in which the customer's names and other personal data are used in order to make a message or product more appealing. The purpose is to make the consumer feel that he or she is treated on one-to-one basis, increase the response rate and, henceforth improve the conversion rate. Mass customisation was alternatively used with personalization but there is a narrow line of difference between the two. Customisation appears when the standardized products are changed as per the customers request whereas personalization relates to active dialog with the customer.

Mass customisation occurs when the customer is in charge of making decisions, whereas personalization is more about gathering information, predicting and delivering customer needs. Customisation takes place only when customers are actively involved in providing information about their preferences and needs. They are influencing their profiles directly, for instance when filling a registration form with personal data (Huang and Lin, 2005). Another method of defining these two terms is that mass customisation requires active user involvement whereas personalization relates to passive user involvement. Analyzing the above mentioned concepts, it may seem that the same product is personalized and customized at the same time (Allain, 2006; Huang and Lin, 2005; Schilke, 2004). It depends which perspective—channel or end users—is considered.

My Yahoo is an example of customisation where the customer or browser specifies what they want. Amazon.com is an example of personalization where the latter learns your interests and proposes a new product on the basis of your preferences.

One-to-one Marketing

One-to-one marketing (also denoted as 1:1) is a type of relationship marketing. The basic idea behind this type of marketing is treat different customers differently. This approach concentrates on providing services to one customer at a time by identifying and catering to their individual needs. It is repeated many times with each customer, such that powerful customer relationships arc forged. As such it differentiates customers rather than just products. One reason so many firms are beginning to focus on one-to-one marketing is the fact that it creates high customer loyalty and enhances the profitability of the business. One of the successful implementers of 1:1 marketing is the Motorola Company.

The Motorola Company is using today's technology to customize its products quickly to serve the needs of individual consumers. Motorola co-designs pagers with customers and manufactures customized pagers to their specifications. To accomplish this, Motorola's pager sales force visits a potential customer and uses the customer's own specifications to design the pager system that will satisfy the individual customer's needs. Then the salesperson finalizes the specifications on a laptop computer and sends it via modem to the Motorola's factory. Incredibly, over 20 million types of pagers can be specified by a customer and manufactured by Motorola. More incredibly, it is possible for the factory to finish producing the first customized pager of any customer's order in two hours. That kind of customisation and speed create an amazingly strong relationship between the company and customers (Peppers and Rogers, The One to One Future 1993).

Niche Marketing

Niche marketing encompasses the rule of personalization. Niche marketing operates on the phrase—'you can't please all the people all the time'. Niche marketing is targeting a product or service to a small portion of a market that is not being readily served by the mainstream product or service marketers.

An Example: Toyota, a huge company with a global focus on the auto business, is an excellent niche marketer. They were one of the first companies to realize there was a group of car buyers who would be very interested in environmentally friendly cars. Toyota answered this need with development of the legendary Prius, the first mass customized hybrid car.

Where other car manufacturers saw Toyota taking a huge risk, Toyota saw it as an opportunity to identify a new niche and establish its brand in that niche. In marketing, it is often the first brand to market, if executed successfully, that can own the niche market with their brand. Once Toyota took the plunge, it pursued an effective niche marketing plan. It didn't promote the Prius in just any media. It focused on media outlets that were watched, read or listened to by people concerned about the environment. For example, it heavily promoted the car through environmental groups and their publications. As the only game in town at that time, Toyota not only dominated the niche——it was the niche.

Mass Customisation and Customerization

Customerization encompasses more activities and functions than mass customisation of products. It describes situations in which customers rather than the company take the lead in designing the product or offerings. Customerization process also includes redefining every employee of the firm as its internal customers and creating value chains of internal customers that would ultimately lead to the external customer. In fact it can be said that mass customisation is a step toward realizing customized marketing whereas customerization combines mass customisation with customized marketing. Now, the question is what is the difference between mass customisation and customized marketing?

There is a hairline difference between them. Customized marketing takes place when the manufacturer prepares an entirely new product from scratch for the buyer in a similar way done by a custom tailor. Mass customisation takes place when the company has established the basic modules in the product which can be combined or altered in different ways for the customer. Customerization suggests the convergence of customer needs with customisation of marketing message and medium. It is the most important means for micromarketing and reaching those companies that are still working under the old paradigm of mass marketing. It is very vivid that those companies will be grounded by those firms that have recognized the creative power of linking marketing efforts to individualized needs of the customers.

By adopting customerization, a firm can yield greater profits as it results in customer-led product design, value proposition and positioning. It is highly advisable for every company to offer its customers a customerization platform to minimize customer defection and maximize customer satisfaction.

To conclude, mass customisation is increasingly gaining momentum as a strategy in management. Today, several major firms like Dell, Motorola, General Motors, Toyota, and

Hewlett Packard are actively using mass customisation in their production. Even after much success stories, mass customisation is still not very popular. Nevertheless, the discussion about this subject is strongly increasing. It is to be remembered that this is happening against the background that mass customisation is globally considered as one of the best strategies to maintain and consolidate market position of enterprises in the future.

Mass customisation is undoubtedly the right approach for those companies who crave for a greater market share and higher competitive advantage. In this era of seamless product differentiation, customers are not willing to settle for the second best choice. The companies that will provide them with the personalized product exclusively designed for them will succeed and mass customisation is the only way to achieve this in a cost-effective way. This new approach will not only change the production process, but also the entire way products are marketed. Correctly applied, marketing the right way becomes the key enabler for mass customisation in an enterprise and the most important factor for sustainable market growth.

References

Boer, C.R. and Sergio Dulio (2007), Mass Customization and Footwear: Myth, Salvation or Reality? Springer Verlag London Limited, London, p. 115.

Claus, Rautenstrauch, Ralph Seelmann-Eggebert and Klaus Turowsk (2002), Moving into Mass Customization: Information Systems and Management Principles, Springer Publishing House, New York, p. 63.

Joseph, Pine and Stan Davis (1993), Mass Customization-The New Frontier in Business Competition, Harvard Business School Press, USA, p. 65.

Kelly, Rainer, Casey G. Cegielski, Introduction to Information Systems: Enabling and Transforming Business, Harvard Publishing House, USA, p. 96.

Klaus, Moser, Mass Customization Strategies: Development of a Competence-based Framework for Identifying Different Mass Customization Strategies, Klaus Moser Publishers, USA.

Sameer Kumar and Promma Phrommathed (2005), New Product Development: An Empirical Approach to Study the Effects of Innovation Strategy, Springer Publishing House, USA, p. 57.

Tage Skjott and Larsen (2007), Managing the Global Supply Chain, Copenhagen Business School Press, UK, p. 218.

10

Changing Face of Indian Retail Market

Ambilikumar V.

India has emerged as the fifth most favourable destination for international retailers according to A.T. Kearney's Global Retail Development Index (GRDI) (June) 2012. The report reads, *While the world's largest developing markets—particularly the BRIC nations of Brazil, Russia, India, and China—still tempt the largest global retailers and show no signs of slowing down, many smaller, untapped markets are providing new profit frontiers, particularly for regional and speciality players.* With consumer confidence improving and spending increasing, global retailers continued their expansion into these markets. In the past five years, US-based Wal-Mart, France-based Carrefour, UK-based Tesco, and Germany-based Metro Group saw their revenues in developing countries growing 2.5 times faster than revenues in their home markets." India remains a high potential market with accelerated retail growth of 15-20 percent expected over the next five years, highlighted the report by A T Kearney.

Ernst & Young's India Attractiveness Survey, 2012 states that the fundamentals that make India attractive to investors remain intact. The high potential of the domestic market driven by an emerging middle class, cost competitiveness and a mammoth pool of talent continue to make India one of the most preferred destinations. The country's domestic demand-driven growth model is playing a catalyst role in attracting foreign investments in the country. Although the ongoing global uncertainty stemming from recessionary concerns and sovereign debt crisis has prompted some discomfort among global investors to make long-term commitments, India's inherent advantages and its proven resilience to counter macroeconomic challenges far outweigh these concerns.

India remained very attractive for FDI in 2011. FDI projects increased by 20 percent in India during 2011, attracting 932 projects, which created approximately 2,55,416 jobs. This is despite a global economic growth that had not fully recovered from the financial crisis of 2008-09 and has begun to slow again, from over 5 percent in 2010 down to a projected 3.3 percent through 2012. The recent furore against allowing Wal-Mart and other western multinational companies into India's lucrative retail sector is based upon fears that it will bankrupt the small retailers who have been at the hub of this country's consumer sector. There are fears that these small family run businesses will be unable to cope against the titanic behemoths which will use their financial muscle, supply chain and political influence to destroy all competition.

Definition of Retailing

In 2004, The High Court of Delhi defined the term *retail* as a sale for final consumption in contrast to a sale for further sale or processing (i.e. wholesale). In other words, it is a sale to the ultimate consumer. Thus, retailing can be said to be the interface between the producer and the individual consumer buying for personal consumption. This excludes direct interface between the manufacturer and institutional buyers such as the government and other bulk customers. Retailing is the last link that connects the individual consumer with the manufacturing and distribution chain. A retailer is involved in the act of selling goods to the individual consumer at a margin of profit.

Division of Retail Industry

The retail industry is mainly divided into:

1. Organized; and
2. Unorganized retailing.

Organized retailing refers to trading activities undertaken by licensed retailers. These include the corporate-backed hyper markets and retail chains, and also the privately owned large retail businesses.

Unorganized retailing, on the other hand, refers to the traditional formats of low-cost retailing, for example, the local *kirana* shops, owner manned general stores, *paan/beedi* shops, convenience stores, hand cart and pavement vendors, etc.

The Indian retail market comprises of the following:

- Barter system.
- Street hawkers.
- Mom and pop stores (e.g. kirana stores).
- Departmental stores (Shopper's Stop).
- Discount stores.
- Speciality stores (Pizza Hut).
- Supermarkets.
- Hyper markets (Wal-Mart, Big Bazaar etc.).
- Convenience stores (in petrol pumps etc.).
- E-tailors (e-Bay, amazon.com).

The Indian retail sector is highly fragmented with 97 percent of its business being run by the unorganized retailers. The organized retail, however, is at a very nascent stage. The sector is the largest source of employment after agriculture, and has deep penetration into rural India generating more than 10 percent of India's GDP.

Pre-liberalisation Period

Historically, India had followed an extremely cautious and selective approach while formulating FDI policy in view of the dominance of 'import-substitution strategy' of industrialization. With the objective of becoming 'self reliant', there was a dual nature of policy intention—FDI through foreign collaboration was welcomed in the areas of high technology and high priorities to build national capability and discouraged low technology areas to protect and nurture domestic industries. The regulatory framework was consolidated through the enactment of Foreign Exchange Regulation Act (FERA), 1973 wherein foreign equity holding in a joint venture was allowed only up to 40 percent.

Subsequently, various exemptions were extended to foreign companies engaged in export-oriented businesses and high technology and high priority areas including allowing equity holdings of over 40 percent.

Moreover, drawing from successes of other country experiences in Asia, the government of India not only established special economic zones (SEZs) but also designed liberal policy and provided incentives for promoting FDI in these zones with a view to promote exports. As India continued to be highly protective, these measures did not add substantially to export competitiveness. Recognizing these limitations, partial liberalisation in the trade and investment policy was introduced in the 1980s with the objective of enhancing export competitiveness, modernisation and marketing of exports through transnational corporations (TNCs). The announcements of Industrial Policy (1980 and 1982) and Technology Policy (1983) put forward a liberal attitude towards foreign investments in terms of changes in policy directions.

The policy was characterised by de-licensing of some of the industrial rules and promotion of Indian manufacturing exports as well as emphasising on modernisation of industries through liberalised imports of capital goods and technology. This was supported by trade liberalisation measures in the form of tariff reduction and shifting of large number of items from import licensing to open general licensing (OGL).

Post-liberalisation Period

A major shift occurred when India embarked upon economic liberalisation and reforms program in 1991 aiming to raise its growth potential and integrating with the world economy. Industrial policy reforms gradually removed restrictions on investment projects and business expansion on the one hand and allowed increased access to foreign technology and funding on the other. A series of measures that were directed towards liberalizing foreign investment included the introduction of dual route of approval of FDI-RBI's automatic route and Government's approval (SIA/FIPB) route, permission for technology agreements in high priority industries and removal of restriction of FDI in low technology areas as well as liberalisation of technology imports, permission to non-resident Indians (NRIs) and overseas corporate bodies (OCBs) to invest up to 100 percent in high priorities sectors, Hike in the foreign equity participation limits to 51 percent for existing companies and liberalisation of the use of foreign 'brands name' and signing of the Convention of Multilateral Investment Guarantee Agency (MIGA) for protection of foreign investments.

These efforts were boosted by the enactment of Foreign Exchange Management Act (FEMA), 1999 [that replaced the Foreign Exchange Regulation Act (FERA), 1973] which was less stringent. This along with the sequential financial sector reforms paved way for greater capital account liberalisation in India. Investment proposals falling under the automatic route and matters related to FEMA were dealt with by RBI, while the Government handles investment through approval route and issues that relate to FDI policy *per se* through its three institutions, *viz.*, the Foreign Investment Promotion Board (FIPB), the Secretariat for Industrial Assistance (SIA) and the Foreign Investment Implementation Authority (FIIA).

Foreign investment in India is governed by the FDI policy announced by the Government of India and the provision of the Foreign Exchange Management Act (FEMA) 1999. The Reserve Bank of India (RBI) in this regard had issued a notification, which contains the Foreign Exchange Management (Transfer or issue of security by a person resident outside India) Regulations, 2000. This notification has been amended from time to time.

The foreign investors are free to invest in India, except few sectors/activities, where prior approval from the RBI or Foreign Investment Promotion Board (FIPB) would be required. FDI under the automatic route does not require any prior approval either by the Government or the Reserve Bank. The investors are only required to notify the concerned regional office of the RBI within 30 days of receipt of inward remittances and file the required documents with that office within 30 days of issuance of shares to foreign investors. Under the approval route, the proposals are considered in a time-bound and transparent manner by the FIPB. Approvals of composite proposals involving foreign investment/foreign technical collaboration are also granted on the recommendations of the FIPB.

A perusal of India's FDI policy vis-à-vis other major emerging market economies (EMEs) reveals that though India's approach towards foreign investment has been relatively conservative to begin with, it progressively started catching up with the more liberalised policy stance of other EMEs from the early 1990s onwards, *inter alia* in terms of wider access to different sectors of the economy, ease of starting business, repatriation of dividend and profits and relaxations regarding norms for owning equity. This progressive liberalisation, coupled with considerable improvement in terms of macroeconomic fundamentals, reflected in growing size of FDI flows to the country that increased nearly 5 fold during first decade of the present millennium.

New retail stores have traditionally started operations in cities like Mumbai and Delhi where there has been an existing base of metropolitan consumers with ready cash and global tastes. Cities in south India have taken to the supermarket style of shopping very positively and so far the maximum number of organized grocery and department stores are in Chennai, Bangalore and Hyderabad. The north has a long way to go to come up to par. International stores now prefer to gauge the reaction of the public in these cities before investing heavily in a nation-wide expansion. Milou, the Swiss children's wear retailer, recently opened up its first store in Chennai, bypassing Delhi and Mumbai.

Besides the urban market, India's rural market has just started to be seen as a viable option and companies who understand what the rural consumer wants will grow to incredible heights. The bulk of India's population still live in rural areas and to be able to cater specifically to them will mean generating tremendous amounts of business. Business, specifically retail business must focus on the most important factor in the Indian mind set—*value for money.*

Present Scenario

Retailing in India is one of the pillars of its economy and accounts for 14 to 15 percent of its GDP. The Indian retail market is estimated to be US$ 450 billion and one of the top five retail markets in the world by economic value. India is one of the fastest growing retail markets in the world, with 1.2 billion people. India's retailing industry is essentially owner manned small shops. In 2010, larger format convenience stores and supermarkets accounted for about 4 percent of the industry, and these were present only in large urban centres. India's retail and logistics industry employs about 40 million Indians (3.3 percent of Indian population). Until 2011, the Government of India denied foreign direct investment (FDI) in multi brand retail, forbidding foreign groups from any ownership in supermarkets, convenience stores or any retail outlets. Even single-brand retail was limited to 51 percent ownership and that too through a bureaucratic process.

In November 2011, the Government of India announced retail reforms for both multi-brand stores and single-brand stores. These market reforms paved the way for retail innovation and competition with multi-brand retailers such as Walmart, Carrefour and Tesco, as well as single brand majors such as IKEA, Nike, Starbucks, Adidas, Apple, Armani and Gucci. The announcement sparked intense activism, both in opposition and in support of the reforms. In December 2011, under pressure from the opposition, the government placed the retail reforms on hold till it reaches a consensus. In January 2012, the Government of India approved reforms for single-brand stores welcoming anyone in the world to innovate in

Indian retail market with 100 percent ownership, but imposed the requirement that the single brand retailer source 30 percent of its goods from India. But, due to objections from different parts, the government of India continued to hold on retail reforms for multi-brand stores. IKEA announced in January that it is putting on hold its plan to open stores in India because of the 30 percent requirement.

On September 14, 2012, the Government of India has cleared the most awaited reform allowing up to 51 percent in foreign direct investment (FDI) in multi-brand retail, paving way for the international multi-brand retailers interested to set up shop in India. However, the government has not defined the term multi-brand. FDI in multi-brand retail implies that a retail store with a foreign investment can sell multiple brands under one roof. The Cabinet meet on September 14, 2012 has approved the proposal of the Department of Industrial Policy and Promotion for permitting FDI in multi-brand retail trading, subject to specified conditions. The proposal had earlier been approved by the Cabinet in its meeting on November 24, 2011. However, implementation of the proposal had been deferred, for evolving a broader consensus on the subject.

The Minister for Commerce, Industry and Textiles, Government of India has announced 100 percent foreign direct investment (FDI) in single-brand retail. The policy prominently mentions that the FDI proposals beyond 51 percent investment in single-brand retail will have to procure at least 30 percent of their requirements from domestic companies. The Cabinet Committee on Economic Affairs (CCEA) also said that any company who is looking for a waiver to this condition will have to establish their manufacturing facilities in the country.

The Cabinet has approved the proposal of the Department of Industrial Policy and Promotion (DIPP) for amendment of the existing policy on FDI in single-brand product retail trading. Vide Press Note 1 (2012 Series) dated January 10, 2012, Government had permitted FDI, up to 100 percent, in single brand product retail trading, subject to specified conditions. The policy details of the government's amendments in the FDI in the single-brand retail trading are as follows:

- The foreign investor should be the owner of the brand.
- In respect of proposals involving FDI beyond 51 percent, 30 percent sourcing would mandatorily have to be done from SMEs/village and cottage industries artisans and craftsmen. 'Small industries' would be defined as industries which have a total investment in plant and machinery not exceeding US$ 1 million. This valuation refers to the value at the time of installation, without providing for depreciation. Further, if at any point in time, this valuation is exceeded, the industry shall not qualify as a 'small industry' for this purpose. The compliance of this condition will be ensured through self-certification by the company, which could be subsequently checked, by statutory auditors, from the duly certified accounts, which the investors will be required to maintain.

The CCEA has approved modification of the above mentioned conditions, for the activity of single brand product retail trading, as under:

Only one non-resident entity, whether owner of the brand or otherwise, shall be permitted to undertake single brand product retail trading in the country, for the specific brand, through a legally tenable agreement, with the brand owner for undertaking single brand product retail trading in respect of the specific brand for which approval is being sought. The onus for ensuring compliance with this condition shall rest with the Indian entity carrying out single-brand product retail trading in India. The investing entity shall provide evidence to this effect at the time of seeking approval, including a copy of the licensing, franchise and sub-licence agreement, specifically indicating compliance with the above condition.

In respect of proposals involving FDI beyond 51 percent, sourcing of 30 percent, of the value of goods purchased, will be done from India, preferably from MSMEs, village and cottage industries, artisans and craftsmen, in all sectors, where it is feasible. The quantum of domestic sourcing will be self-certified by the company, to be subsequently checked, by statutory auditors, from the duly certified accounts which the company will be required to maintain. For the purpose of ascertaining the sourcing requirement, the relevant entity would be the company, incorporated in India, which is the recipient of FDI for the purpose of carrying out single-brand product retail trading.

Amendment in the condition relating to brand-ownership has been felt necessary, in view of the fact that, globally, single brand retailers often adopt a variety of business models, wherein the brand owning entity and investor entities are kept separate, even though in some cases, they may be having the same parent. Some single brand retailers adopt models where there is no link between the investing arm and the brand owning arm. In such cases, the brand owner entity could issue an exclusive license/franchise to the investor entity, to use the brand for the purpose of retail trading, either globally or for a specific region, through appropriate agreement/(s). Such business models were not found to be in consonance with the condition that the foreign investor should be the brand owner.

In view of the fact that the global business models do not strictly conform to this condition, a number of investors, who would otherwise have looked at investments in India, may not be able to do so. Therefore, keeping in view the constraints being faced by genuine foreign investors with different business models, as mentioned above, it would facilitate investment if this condition is liberalised.

However, in order to address the concern that more than one franchisee/licensee may apply for undertaking SBRT for the same brand, which could lead to difficulties in monitoring compliance and fixing responsibility for non-compliance of the specified conditions, it has been mandated that, only one non-resident entity, whether owner of the brand or otherwise, shall be permitted to undertake single brand product retail trading in the country, for the specific brand, through a legally tenable agreement, with the brand owner in respect of the specific brand for which approval is being sought. The onus for ensuring compliance with this condition shall rest with the Indian entity carrying out single-brand retail trading in India. The investing entity shall provide evidence to this effect at the time of seeking approval from government, including a copy of the licensing/franchise/sub-license agreement, specifically indicating compliance with the above condition.

Regarding the condition that 30 percent sourcing be mandatorily done from Indian small industry, investors have pointed out that it would be difficult to comply with this condition in the case of very specialized/high technology items. Global single brand retailers are often engaged in the business of retailing specialty/high-tech products. Such products are niche products, wherein it may not be viable for the foreign investors to build capacities wherever they engage in retailing, owing to the specialized requirements of quality and precision which the local small industry may not be able to provide. Investors are, therefore, of the view that the condition of 30 percent mandatory sourcing from Indian small, village and cottage industries, artisans and craftsmen, is acting as a deterrent to the desired foreign investment in this activity.

The other category of products relate to the range from household appliances, utensils, furniture, crockery and furnishings. These products are far more amenable to sourcing from MSMEs, village and cottage industries, artisans and craftsmen. Therefore, the proposed modification of the condition is envisaged to take into account the circumstances of both the specialized/high technology niche products, as well as the general category, covering a wide range of items.

The fact that 30 percent domestic sourcing is being mandated would imply that the single brand retailers would have to build production capacities in the country, either in existing units, or set up new ones, catering specifically to their sourcing requirements. Hence, even the 30 percent domestic sourcing is expected to develop production capacities in the country, with the attendant global best practices, relating to design, production and quality. Since single brand retailers are global players, Indian suppliers and vendors to these retailers would have an opportunity of becoming a part of their global supply chains. Thus, Indian products could find their way in the stores of these single brand retailers located in other countries, thereby augmenting exports from India as well.

Thus, the amended condition relating to sourcing of 30 percent, of the value of goods purchased, being done from India, preferably from MSMEs, village and cottage industries, artisans and craftsmen, in all sectors is expected to benefit Indian producers, including the Indian handicrafts sector, which provides livelihood to millions and is important from the point of low capital investment, high value-addition and high potential for export, as also to meet the critical need to integrate Indian producers with the domestic and global markets.

Skill integration with craftsmen abroad is likely to help develop synergies with international brands and generate more employment. The consequential benefits, arising from the integration of global best practices in management, along with global standards in quality, design, packaging and production, would help build capacities of local producers, by making it worthwhile for them to scale-up their production, thereby creating a multiplier effect on employment and income generation. This would also lead to up-gradation of technology, which, in turn, would have a further multiplier effect on the economy.

The government notification that allowed 51 percent FDI in multi-brand retail is as stated below:

In pursuance of the afore stated decision of the Cabinet on December 7, 2011, discussions have been held with State Governments, representatives of consumer associations/ organizations, micro and small industry associations, farmers' associations and representatives of food processing industry and industry associations. The Chief Ministers of Delhi,

Assam, Maharashtra, Andhra Pradesh, Rajasthan, Uttarakhand, Haryana and Governments of the State of Manipur and the Union Territory of Daman and Diu and Dadra and Nagar Haveli, have expressed support for the policy in writing.

The Chief Minister of Jammu and Kashmir, through his press statements, has publicly endorsed the policy and asked for its implementation. The State Governments of Bihar, Karnataka, Kerala, Madhya Pradesh, Tripura and Odisha have expressed reservations. During the consultations with the stakeholders, views for and against FDI in multi-brand retail trading were expressed. On balance, however, the discussions generally indicated support for the policy, subject to the introduction of adequate safeguards.

Accordingly, the following proposals have been approved:

- Retail sales outlets may be set up in those States which have agreed or agree in future to allow FDI in MBRT under this policy. The establishment of the retail sales outlets will be in compliance of applicable State laws/ regulations, such as the Shops and Establishments Act etc.
- Retail sales outlets may be set up only in cities with a population of more than 10 lakh as per 2011 Census and may also cover an area of 10 kms. around the municipal/urban agglomeration limits of such cities; retail locations will be restricted to conforming areas as per the master/zonal plans of the concerned cities and provision will be made for requisite facilities such as transport connectivity and parking; In States/Union Territories not having cities with population of more than 10 lakh as per 2011 Census, retail sales outlets may be set up in the cities of their choice, preferably the largest city and may also cover an area of 10 kms. around the municipal/urban agglomeration limits of such cities. The locations of such outlets will be restricted to conforming areas, as per the master/zonal plans of the concerned cities and provision will be made for requisite facilities such as transport connectivity and parking.

- At least 50 percent of total FDI brought in, shall be invested in 'back-end infrastructure' within three years of the induction of FDI, where 'back-end infrastructure' will include capital expenditure on all activities, excluding that on front-end units; for instance, back-end infrastructure will include investment made towards processing, manufacturing, distribution, design improvement, quality control, packaging, logistics, storage, warehouse, agriculture market produce infrastructure etc. Expenditure on land cost and rentals, if any, will not be counted for purposes of back-end infrastructure.
- A high-level group under the Minister of Consumer Affairs may be constituted to examine various issues concerning internal trade and make recommendations for internal trade reforms.
- Other conditions/safeguards, approved by the Cabinet on November 24, 2011, would remain unchanged. The suspension of Government's decision taken in the Cabinet meeting on November 24, 2011 to permit FDI up to 51 percent in MBRT, therefore, stands removed.

The respective State Governments administer the Shops and Establishment Act within their territorial jurisdiction. "Trade and Commerce within the State" is a subject allocated to the State Governments, under the Constitution of India. State Governments are also responsible for aspects ancillary to MBRT, such as zoning regulations, warehousing requirements, access, traffic, parking and other logistics. As such, the policy provides that it would be the prerogative of the State Governments to decide whether and where a multi-brand retailer, with FDI, is permitted to establish its sales outlets within the State. Therefore, implementation of the policy is not a mandatory requirement for all States.

Retail sales outlets may be set up only in cities with a population of more than 10 lakh as per 2011 Census (including an area of 10 kms. around the municipal/urban agglomeration limits of such cities). On the other hand, States/Union

Terrritories, which do not have any city with a population exceeding 10 lakh, but are desirous of implementing the policy, would have the flexibility to do so. Thus, the revised condition gives primacy to the decision of the States in this regard, recognizing that the FDI policy constitutes, at best, an enabling framework for the purpose.

According to the government, adequate safeguards have been built into the policy, some of which have been further strengthened. A three year timeframe has been fixed for setting up the back-end infrastructure, which includes capital expenditure on all activities, excluding that on front-end units; for instance, back-end infrastructure will include investment made towards processing, manufacturing, distribution, design improvement, quality control, packaging, logistics, storage, ware-house, agriculture market produce infrastructure etc. Expenditure on land cost and rentals, if any, will not be counted for purposes of backend infrastructure.

This condition will bind the foreign investors to invest in critical back-end infrastructure, which is a felt need across the country. It would also make the foreign investors accountable for proper implementation of the condition. The government claims that, implementation of the policy will facilitate greater FDI inflows, additional and quality employment, global best practices and benefit consumers and farmers in the long run, in terms of quality, price, greater supply chain efficiencies in the agricultural sector and development of critical back-end infrastructure.

However, Indians are very curious by nature and will try everything at least once before rejecting it. The initial success of KFC in India proved that, the Indians could make a success of most new ventures entering India but reject a concept once they have tried and tested the offering and found nothing worth going back for. The menu at KFC was rather boring and insipid to the Indian consumer who is used to the innumerable combinations and permutations of street food. For their second run in India, KFC re-thought its menu and has been very successful marketing at specific groups within India, like the Punjabis who have quite a history of loving the chicken leg and have made the Chandigarh outlet a huge success.

A company entering India cannot have just one game plan to apply to the entire country as the people, their tastes, the lifestyle, the budgets etc. are all too divergent. International entrants must enter each market specifically focusing only on that area to be successful. The food and beverage segment is seeing increased activity from foreign players. Starbucks partnered with Tata Group to own and operate cafes, and Dunkin Donuts recently opened its first store in Delhi, in partnership with local franchisee Jubilant Food Works.

Grocery remains India's largest source of retail sales. Hypermarkets and supermarkets continue to dominate, but cash-and-carry is growing fast, with significant expansion planned from Bharti Wal-Mart, Metro Group, and Carrefour. Apparel is expected to grow 9 to 10 percent year-over-year for the next five years. Players such as Zara, Marks & Spencer, and Mango are actively scouting locations to open more stores across the country. The luxury retail sector saw 20 percent growth during 2011, with luxury malls becoming entrenched in Delhi, Mumbai, and Bengaluru.

Why FDI is Attracted to India?

India is becoming an exciting and dynamic retail destination due to the following:

- A large market size and low organised retail penetration.
- Strong GDP growth.
- Increasing personal incomes.
- Large number of aspirational consumers (middle-class, young Indians, rural population, etc.).
- Cost competitiveness remains another key characteristic of India. 45 percent of investors cite the availability of low cost labour and inexpensive manufacturing capabilities as a key attraction for their business. Although India has witnessed some increases in its labour cost, it remains a

highly attractive destination for investors who struggle to find the same mixture of low cost and high quality.

Foreign Investor's Concern Regarding FDI Policy in India

For those brands which adopt the franchising route as a matter of policy, the current FDI Policy will not make any difference. They would have preferred that the Government liberalize rules for maximizing their royalty and franchise fees. They must still rely on innovative structuring of franchise arrangements to maximize their returns. Consumer durable majors such as LG and Samsung, which have exclusive franchisee owned stores, are unlikely to shift from the preferred route right away. The companies which would adopt the route of 51 percent partnership must tie up with a local partner. The key is finding a partner which is reliable and who can also teach a trick or two about the domestic market and the Indian consumer.

Currently, the organized retail sector is dominated by the likes of large business groups which decided to diversify into retail to cash in on the boom in the sector—corporates such as Tata through its brand Westside, RPG Group through Food World, Pantaloon of the Raheja Group and Shopper's Stop. An arrangement in the short to medium term may work wonders but what happens if the Government decides to further liberalize the regulations as it is currently contemplating? Will the foreign investor terminate the agreement with Indian partner and trade in market without him?

Either way, the foreign investor must negotiate its joint venture agreements carefully, with an option for a buy-out of the Indian partner's share if and when regulations so permit. They must also be aware of the regulation which states that once a foreign company enters into a technical or financial collaboration with an Indian partner, it cannot enter into another joint venture with another Indian company or set up its own subsidiary in the 'same' field' without the first partner's consent if the joint venture agreement does not provide for a 'conflict of interest' clause. In effect, it means that foreign brand owners must be extremely careful whom they choose as partners and the brand they introduce in India. The first brand could also be their last if they do not negotiate the strategic arrangement diligently.

Impact on Real Estate

As India's retail industry is aggressively expanding itself, great demand for real estate is being created. The cumulative retail demand for real estate across India is expected to reach 43 million square feet by 2013. Around 46 percent of the total estimated demand between 2009 and 2013 is expected to come from tier-1 cities. For instance, Pantaloon Retail added 2.26 million sq. ft. of retail space during the fiscal 2011 and booked over 9 million sq. ft of retail space to fructify its expansion plans in the future.

Some of the key players in the Indian retail market, with a dominant share are:

- Pantaloon Retail Ltd., a Future Group venture: Over 12 mn. sq. ft. of retail space spread over 1,000 stores, across 71 cities in India.
- Shoppers Stop Ltd.: Over 1.82 mn. sq. ft. of retail space spread over 35 stores, in 15 cities.
- Spencer's Retail, RPG Enterprises: Retail footage of over 1.1 mn. sq. ft. with approx 250 stores, across 66 cities.
- Lifestyle Retail, Landmark Group venture: Has approximately 15 Lifestyle stores and 8 Home centres.

Other major domestic players in India are Bharti Retail, Tata Trent, Globus, Aditya Birla 'More', and Reliance Retail. Some of the major foreign players who have entered the segment in India are as follows:

- Carrefour which opened its first cash-and-carry store in India in New Delhi.
- Germany-based Metro Cash and Carry which opened six wholesale centres in the country.
- Walmart in a JV with Bharti Retail, owner of Easy Day

store—plans to invest about US$ 2.5 billion over the next five years to add about 10 million sq. ft. of retail space in the country.

Issues and the Facts

The Government of India gave green nod for the single brand FDI in the second week of January 2012, and the government held long meetings with consumer groups and tried to convince them that FDI will give them opportunity to buy discounted items, they will have lot of choices and they will find all items at one place. Consumer organizations (who are represented by upper middle and high income class, who largely live a luxurious life and never bothers what is happening with small vendors, farmers and other producers) are now in the government's court. As the next step, the government has finally decided to permit FDI in multi-brand retail up to 51 percent ignoring the interest of 60 million farmers and 93 million people (around 77 percent of the total population) who survive by spending less than US$ 0.40 per day.

Most of us are, by now, familiar with the basic modus operandi of these transnational corporate interests. They first make an entry into the manufacturing sector and once they have established their control over industrial production they take the next logical step, which is to capture the natural resources required to produce goods, such as minerals, water, land and forests. The way they achieve their objective is by exerting pressure on national governments to dilute or weaken laws and regulations that stand in their path of consolidation. In the Indian context, we have seen such dilution specifically in the case of the Special Industrial Areas (Development) Act as well as the Land Ceiling Act and the Land Acquisition (Industrial Areas) Act.

Once the multinationals have more or less established their supremacy over resources and manufacturing, their next step is to capture the space between the producer and consumer of goods. That's why they so eagerly eye India's retail sector. This space is presently occupied by hundreds of thousands of merchants, commission agents and retail traders. Their game-plan is to eliminate these intermediaries, forge direct links with consumers and gain control over the complete trade cycle from production to consumption.

The consequences of multinational corporations capturing the retail space in the country are fourfold. First, the profits that small retailers and commission agents presently earn will now flow into the hands of foreign entities. Second, once these giant companies establish their monopoly in the market, they will begin selling goods that fetch them the highest profits. Third, the push for higher profits will encourage them to produce only those goods that meet their economic objectives. And fourth, given their monopolistic position in the market, they can exert pressure on the government to demand land, water and energy at concessional rates to expand their trade base. This has been the worldwide experience wherever policies to corporatize retail have been implemented, as seen in the following examples:

- In Thailand, supermarkets run by multinationals charge 10 percent more for fruits and vegetables.
- In Russia, costs of goods available in supermarkets are 20 percent higher than in traditional outlets.
- In the US, supermarkets progressively raised the price of tomatoes by 46 percent between 1994 and 2004 even as tomato prices fell 25 percent in traditional retail outlets during the same period. The justification that small retailers would remain unaffected by the introduction of such a policy also appears to be false.
- In Argentina, there was a sharp fall in the number of small retailers over a 10-year period, from 64,198 to around 44,000.
- In Brazil, the share of small retailers in fruit and vegetable trade fell 27.8 percent between 1987 and 1996.

There is also a question mark about whether the farmers who collaborate with them actually benefit in the long-run. According to a study conducted by Oxfam, the prices of apples exported from South Africa fell 33 percent while tomato growers in Florida got 25 percent less for their produce even as consumers paid 46 percent higher prices for the vegetable in supermarkets.

The global retailer, Wal-Mart has a trading empire encompassing 85 crore sq. ft. of retail space around the world. Retailers in India use an average of 150 sq. ft. of retail space. If this is taken as a standard retail unit, we see that Walmart controls retail space equal to 56 lakh average retailers. It accounts for 40 percent of the retail trade in 20 countries yet gives employment to a mere 8,00,000 people. It buys its products direct from large manufacturers, bypassing the chain of wholesale and retail traders. Hence, small local traders are completely wiped out wherever it establishes its presence. And once its monopoly is established, it encourages only its preferred brands.

Typical family run stores, have been ravaged out of existence by the aggressive tactics and predatory pricing of Wal-Mart. A similar story is found in Britain where farmers have had their profit margins squeezed to the absolute minimum. Local shops have gone under, unable to compete against the superstores who have now opened their own metro stores in the very same areas where the small village style shop was once trading. All over Britain and in many small American towns, the once vibrant retail sector has all but been diminished by the activities of the faceless corporate leviathans. Urban centres lie decaying except for fast food eateries, pubs, nightclubs, pawn brokers, and establishments specialising in catering to those addicted to gambling and sex. These are the only places, along with the supermarkets, actually making a very nice profit in the midst of a global economic recession. Hence, one can understand the opposition to Wal-Mart and other such companies setting up shop in India.

Customer service is available only to the wealthy as opposed to brusque and often dismissive manner in which the much vaunted street traders deal with India's mass consumer base. A protected economy breeds apathy, lack of innovation and above all an incredible level of arrogance. In a country like India, where the social and political system favours the small ruling elite over the masses, the kleptocratic neo-colonialism saturates all thinking so that those with even the smallest amount of power leverage ensure that it is used. So it is not surprising that lack of customer service abounds along with bad quality goods, inflated prices and where the word 'refund' is not even in the traders' vocabulary.

In such an environment, it is simply impossible to enforce any semblance of trading standards where customers are at the mercy of merchants who feel that they are actually doing them a favour by even letting them buy their substandard produce and consumer goods. At the polar end of the social scale those with power and status, especially if they are part of the ruling kleptocracy, benefit from slavish sycophantism where all their petty needs are catered for. Yet this is also not customer service but a hangover from a feudal pre-modern past where servants put shoes on for their masters, made the tea, or chased away the peacocks. The multinational supermarket knows that the customer will return if treated in a respectful manner as well as finding all their consumer goods at an affordable price, of good quality and all under one roof without being constantly pestered by the merchant for simply trying to browse.

Arguments for FDI in Retail Sector

The government offers several justifications for permitting FDI in the retail sector. It is important to analyze these arguments if we are to get at the underlying truth. For example, the government claims prices of goods will fall once FDI flows into retail because there will no longer be any middlemen or commission agents. The truth is slightly different. Once large malls and centralized sales distribution centres are established, expenditures on cold chains, storage, warehousing, electricity, and so on will shoot up. This, in turn, will raise the prices of goods reaching the consumer. Like their foreign counterparts, Indian customers are entitled to receive quality products, produced, processed and handled under a hygienic environment through professionally-managed outlets. Speculative apprehensions that small retailers will be adversely affected are not reason enough to deny millions of consumers access to products that meet global standards.

Furthermore, today's intermediaries amid producers and customers add no value to the products, adding hugely to final costs instead. By the time products filter through various intermediaries and into the marketplace, they lose freshness and quality, and often go to waste. However, intermediaries garner huge profits by distributing these losses between producers and customers by buying products at low prices from producers, but selling at extremely marked-up prices to consumers. In an unbalanced system that incorporates multiple intermediaries simply for logistics, only intermediaries benefit. With organized retail, every intermediate step—procurement, processing, transport and delivery—adds value to the product. This happens because it uses international best practices and modern technology, ensuring maximum efficiency and minimum waste.

Organized retail enables on-site processing, scientific handling and quick transport through cold storage chains to the final consumer. Once modern retailers introduce an organized model, other vendors, including small retailers, would mechanically copy this model to improve efficiencies, boost margins and stay in business. Organized retail would thereby bring more stability to prices, unlike the present system where hoarding and artificial shortages by profiteering intermediaries push up product prices.

Safety Valves on FDI

There is concern about the competition presented to domestic competitors and the monopolization of the domestic market by large international retail giants. The Indian government feels that FDI in multi-brand retailing must be dealt with cautiously, given the large potential scale and social impact. As such, the government is considering safety valves for calibrating FDI in the sector. For example:

- A stipulated percentage of FDI in the sector could be required to be spent on building back-end infrastructure, logistics or agro-processing units in order to ensure that the foreign investors make a genuine contribution to the development of infrastructure and logistics.
- At least 50 percent of the jobs in the retail outlet could be reserved for rural youth and a certain amount of farm produce could be required to be procured from poor farmers.
- A minimum percentage of manufactured products could be required to be sourced from the SME sector in India.
- To ensure that the public distribution system and the Indian food security system, is not weakened, the government may reserve the right to procure a certain amount of food grains.
- To protect the interest of small retailers, an exclusive regulatory framework to ensure that the retailing giants do not resort to predatory pricing or acquire monopolistic tendencies.

To conclude, the retail market of India is the sector that provides employment to a large number of people, next to the agriculture sector. By opening this sector for the multinational giants, the source of revenue of 4 crore of people who are directly engaged in this sector and their dependants are going to be challenged. Besides this, a large number of farmers and other middlemen will also be affected adversely. It is possible that the increasing level of competition between the multi- nationals may lead to a totally ethics free marketing in the country. At the same time, as pointed out above, threat, exploitation and control of resources and decisions may be the ultimate result of permitting 100 percent FDI in the country.

References

Anand Dikshit (2011), The Uneasy Compromise-Indian Retail, *The Wall Street Journal*, August 12, p. 12.

Bannock, Graham et al. (2003), The Dictionary of Economics, Penguin Books, London, p. 15.

Majumder, Sanjoy (2011), Changing the Way Indians Shop, BBC News, 25th November.

McKinsey Global Institute (2007), The Bird of Gold-The Rise of India's Consumer Market, The McKinsey Quarterly: The Online Journal of McKinsey & Co.

RBI, Foreign Direct Investment Flows to India, a research Study prepared in the Division of International Trade and Finance, Department of Economic and Policy Research, Reserve Bank of India.

The Economic Times, FDI in Retail: Riders in FDI Policy to Delay Investment from Single-brand Retail Chains, January 14, 2012.

11

Data Mining for Talent Management in Business Enterprises

Usha P.M.

The role of human resources management (HRM) in an organization has been experiencing a cosmic change. Human resources are the prime assets for any organization. Managing human resources in an effective and efficient manner is essential for competitive advantage of any organization. In the previous decades, personnel management's role was clerical in nature. The thrust was on record keeping and maintenance providing administrative support to management. HR staff members were the custodians of the data. With the introduction of human resource information system (HRIS) in organizations, the reach became widened. In the current digitized scenario, there are employee self-service (ESS) portals through which an employee can access and maintain their personal data and manager self-service (MSS) portals allowing the manager to receive reports and perform operations like performance appraisal online. Digitization reduces time, effort and cost of operations.

Accessibility of right information at right time eased the process of decision-making in human resource management. This resulted in a major transformation of human resource management as a strategic partner in moulding the business. Aligning the workforce and their performance indices to match the mission and goal of organization is achieved through strategic human resource management. Organizations are heavily dependent on the knowledge, skills and abilities of the employees. Hiring and developing a talented workforce is the major challenge for any organization to acquire a competitive edge over other organizations.

It is undeniably evident that the transformation took place with the support of information technology. Information technology is an imperative resource for any organization. Information technology's role was limited as a support for data storage and reporting. The scenario changed drastically with the advent of Business Intelligence system. Human resource information systems store enormous data for handling various functions of HR department like recruitment, training, performance appraisal and the like. This explosive growth of data resources have paved the way for providing necessary support for intelligent decision making.

A centralized repository of selected HR data is stored in a data warehouse. Data warehouse is built from the operational HR data. Data mining tools are employed to discover hidden patterns of relationships among the policies, practices and the end result. Business intelligence systems facilitates in finding the links between talent management and productivity. Data mining is evolving as a promising technology for prediction and forecasting used in business intelligence systems. Organizations should be aware of the support of information technology in enhancing the effectiveness of human resource management.

Data Mining Processes

Business intelligence systems adopt analytical technology for decision making. Application domains utilize data mining techniques which are emerging as a tool for data analysis, extraction of hidden knowledge which facilitates qualitative decision making.

Data mining can be defined as, "*A process that uses statistical, mathematical, artificial intelligence and machine learning techniques to extract and identify useful information and subsequent knowledge from large databases*". Using data mining data can be analyzed with different dimensions and categorized to identify the existing relationships.

Problem Definition: Data mining is suggested to unearth solutions for any unstructured problem prevailing in the business. For exploration and clear definition of the problem, participation of experts from all dimensions is essential. Data mining experts, business experts and the domain experts discuss and formulate an appropriate problem definition.

Data Exploration: Data from various sources pertaining to the business problems defined, are collected, described and explored.

Data Preparation: Data mining is performed by software incorporating statistical tools. Data need to be presented in a prescribed format to be fed as input to the model. Attributes which are not going to make any significant impact in the decision making process are to be avoided. Data from different sources should be converted to a uniform format and similar representations should be adopted. For example, the gender of an employee might be represented as "M/F" in one data source and as 1 or 2 in another data source. Either one should be replaced with the other format to maintain uniformity.

Modelling: Models are developed to represent business situations using the data mining software selected. Various alternatives are tried and tested in the model to arrive at optimum solution. Various mining functions like clustering, classification, association are available in the software. Appropriate algorithm for the business problem is to be identified and implemented.

Evaluation: The developed model should be evaluated in the context of business objectives. Every aspect of the business problem should be incorporated in the model. In the pretext of more parameters to be included or change in existing parameters required, appropriate amendments are done and evaluated again.

Deployment: Model developed is implemented and the results thus obtained used for further operations. Knowledge inferred from the implementation should be presented in the format required by the end user.

Data Mining Techniques

Classification: Historical data available from various sources is analyzed to form classes. Behaviour of these classes helps in predicting future behaviour. Instances are assigned to predefined classes. Hence, it is considered as a supervised learning.

Supervised learning involves external source for performing supervision. It is based on some training data. This method is useful when there is limited number of classes. Model developed using the available training data promotes predicting the class to which the new observation belongs. It is a directed data mining approach. The target variable is well defined and the relationship between the dependent and explanatory variables is analyzed. For example, training data set about patients with cardiac problems can be selected. They can be classified according to age, blood pressure, heart rate and the like. After classification, prediction rules can be formed as IF (age=65 and heart rate>70) or (age>60 and blood pressure>140/70) then heart problem=yes. This will help in predicting the chances of heart problem for a new patient by checking the condition mentioned.

Clustering: A data base is divided into different segments based on the qualities shared by the data. Clustering is an unsupervised learning.

Unsupervised learning is not based on training data. The target is not well defined. Here, the clusters are not defined when the process starts. Once the clusters are formed, it helps in predicting future behaviour.

For example, by analyzing the attributes of customers like their age, income level, location, preferences etc. different clusters of customers with similar buying patterns can be formed.

Association: Databases are analysed to explore frequent if-then patterns occurring in the database through which most prominent relationships are identified. Association rules can be used for prediction.

One common application of association algorithm is "market basket analysis" to find the asso.'ation between the items purchased by a customer. Understanding the association between the items purchased by a customer will help in store layout of retailers. Same can be applied in book stores also by understanding the books purchased together often.

Sequence Pattern: Patterns are discovered by analyzing associations over time. Sequential pattern mining finds frequently occurring sequences to describe the data. Identified sequences facilitate in prediction of future data.

Customers follow a sequence in shopping at times. A person who purchased a TV might go for a purchase of DVD player next and then a memory card. A sequence of time gap might be prevalent between these purchases. Identifying the above pattern helps in prediction of the behaviour of next customer.

Data Mining Algorithms

Various algorithms are used to perform data mining techniques like clustering, classification and association like decision tree, neural network and k-means algorithm.

Decision Tree: *Decision trees are simple, but powerful form of multiple variable analyses.* The attributes used in decision-making are listed. Select an attribute to place at the root of the decision tree and make one branch for every possible value. Repeat the process recursively for each branch. A branch node denotes a choice between the alternatives and the leaf node represents the decision.

K-means Algorithm: K-means is a clustering algorithm used in data mining. In this method the observations are divided into k clusters of related observations. K is mentioned as an input parameter. Each new observation is added to the cluster which has the nearest mean. New mean value is calculated with the added observation. The step by step process can be explained as given below:

- The algorithm arbitrarily selects k points as the initial cluster centres ("means").

- Each point in the dataset is assigned to the closed cluster, based upon the Euclidean distance [1] between each point and each cluster centre.
- Each cluster centre is recomputed as the average of the points in that cluster.
- Steps 2 and 3 repeat until the clusters converge. Convergence may be defined differently depending upon the implementation, but it normally means that either no observations change clusters when steps 2 and 3 are repeated or that the changes do not make a material difference in the definition of the clusters.

Neural Network: Neural networks are analytical techniques used for representing the functioning of brain in information processing. In artificial neural network, a mathematical model is developed which is based on the principles of the original biological neural networks. The technique is based on the process of learning in the cognitive system where we are able to predict the outcome based on the learning developed from the existing data and the capability to generalize the learning. Sequential patterns are identified for future predictions from the experience learned from the historical data.

Applications of Data Mining in Industry

Data mining technology has been adopted by all functional areas of an organization in varied industrial sectors. The technique can be used to take unstructured decisions that require some intelligent analysis. Decision-making turns out to be a proactive and knowledge driven process.

Effective data mining gives a competitive edge to organizations. Data mining applications find its relevance in all functional areas of business. This includes applications in marketing management, human resource management, financial management, operations management and the like.

Data Mining in Human Resource Management

Human resources are imperative for any organization. The

earlier scenario witnessed human resource department in a supporting role only providing supporting functions for management of the firm. The situation has changed dramatically and currently HR professionals show their presence in strategic decision-making of the organization. Development of technology and techniques like data mining facilitate data analysis and qualitative decision-making. Automation of HR processes from recruitment to retirement in an organization provides ample source of data for analysis which can form input for data mining.

Data mining techniques can be widely implemented for talent management. Talent management is challenged to ensure right person at the right job at the right time. Data mining techniques like clustering, association, classification and prediction can be used for the management of the workforce in an organization. Data mining finds its application in all levels of HR activities which ranges from selection of employee, proper placement of employee through matching their skill sets with the requirement of job, preparing a well planned career path for the employee, training need analysis, correlation of training to retention rates, prediction of the performance of employees, attrition rate of employees and the like.

Data Mining for HR Planning

Strategic human resource planning is indispensable for any organization. Organization's strategic plan and human resource plan should go hand in hand. Whenever new strategies are developed by organization, the potential of the human resources available to accomplish the goal has to be identified. The association of the key talents available in the organization and their relationship to the proposed goal can be generated and analysed using association rule in data mining for a more focused planning. Association rules contain if-then-else rules which uncover relationships from the data in a data warehouse.

Data from transactional data bases can be used to create

data ware houses with hidden patterns. Hotel chains and restaurants keep track of the inflow of customers in a day, hour etc. from the billing system. This information is linked with the shift pattern of employees to verify the availability of right number of staff members at the right time to serve the customers.

Human resource planning depends very heavily on the available data store. Airlines and Railways stores details of booking in their database. This can be correlated with the staff details to fine tune the requirements, availability and prepare a well structured human resource plan. Workforce scheduling is essential for effective utilization of man hours and machine hours in an organization. The operating conditions in a production environment may not be always uniform to form a regular scheduling pattern. Situations change and the man power requirement also changes accordingly. Considering all the possible situations that would arise and developing different schedules befitting the situation is an impractical assignment to be completed manually.

Using sequential pattern mining, appropriate scheduling of human resources and machine time can be formed. Sequential pattern mining tries to find relationships between occurrences of sequential events and identifies whether any specific orders of the occurrences exist.

Data Mining for Recruitment

Finding the right person for right job is extremely important for any organization. Analysis of the profile of prospective candidates produces fruitful results which would be beneficial in the long run. Traits of successful employees as well as the background information like the educational background and expertise of top performing candidates can be mined to form clusters with similar traits and thus a hiring profile can be generated. Information generated would help to focus the recruiting efforts of the HR department. With the profile of successful employees a career path can be set for new recruits with proper information support obtained through data mining.

Employee turnover is very crucial for any organization. If the recruitment efforts can predict the chances of an employee continuing in the organization for a longer period, turnover can be reduced. Predictions can be realistic rather than guesses with the support of data mining. Again, traits of successful employees staying back in the organization are mined to predict the chances of new hire.

Various sources of recruitment are espoused by organizations. Organizations can search for patterns in the relation between recruitment source and the successful performance of employees. Decision trees could be put into operation for this type of classification and prediction. C4.5 is a classification algorithm is employed in the construction of decision tree. All the attributes to be measured are listed. According to values of the attributes the trees are drawn. Classifications in HR according to age, experience and other features help in arriving at the decision of hiring or not hiring. These decision trees are developed by data mining software.

Data Mining for Focused Training

To enhance the competitive advantage of the organization, the knowledge of the available human resources within the organization should be well utilized and opportunities should also bc made available for augmenting the knowledgebase for self and organization's advantage. Knowledge management is crucial for any organization. Data mining techniques provide the platform for a focused training for knowledge enhancement based on the requirements aligned with the goal of the organization. Web-based training systems like employee training expert system (ETES) is available for training existing talents. ETES uses mining technologies like association mining for understanding the association between the learning map of employees and the training strategies to be used. Materials are provided according to the learning aptitude of employees. Employees can be clustered to form groups for a targeted approach for nominating employees for various training programs.

Human resource information systems store details about the training programs conducted in the organization and also the employees who participated in each program. The effectiveness of training can be studied using data mining techniques by understanding the relationship between the training attended and post training performance of employees. Investment decisions for subsequent training programs can be formulated on the basis of information generated.

Data Mining for Performance Evaluation

For performance evaluation the parameters can be identified and data mining can be used to form clusters of employees with similar performance level. For example the parameters of faculty performance in an educational institute can be identified by performing data mining on the data which contains parameters like educational qualification, industry experience, subject knowledge, years of teaching, professional development etc. The association between the attitude of employee and the performance of employee can be critically analyzed with the association algorithm provided by the data mining packages.

Raymond S. Bermudez et al., in their research paper, employed regression model in data mining for predicting the faculty performance. Six attributes were used by the researchers to measure the performance of a faculty. The list is mentioned as given below:

- Faculty peer observation result.
- Faculty self evaluation result.
- Faculty student evaluation result.
- Faculty competency assessment.
- Student grade.
- Class pass rate.

Uniform scaling techniques were used to represent the

above mentioned parameters. Well prepared input file carrying the above mentioned parameters of the faculties are provided as input to the data mining software called as Weka 3.6. Clustering algorithm was used to form clusters of employees. The data mining technique, k-means clustering is employed for performing this clustering [Raymond S. Bermudez et al., 2011].

Data collected about each faculty in the above mentioned six parameters were summarized as a table. This is converted to the format compatible with the software for clustering process. After clustering the attributes of a training set of values, three clusters were formed indicating clusters of employees with high performance, medium performance and low performance. The average score value of these indicators could be used as performance predictor indicator. The output generated by Weka could be used to predict the performance of a new faculty by calculating the average score and comparing with the performance predictor indicator of the three clusters to identify whether the new employee belongs to high, medium or low performance category. The same clustering can be utilized for developing training programs based on the level of performance of the faculty members.

Data Mining for Retention

Retention of performing employees in the organization is as important as the recruitment of an ideal employee for the vacant position. The data mining software, SAS is used to develop an employee retention software program. Using this software the organization can identify the employees who are most likely to depart from the organization. The analysis explores the profiles of employees who have left the organization in the past five years. The profiles are generated through data mining. Profiles thus generated can be compared with the profile of current employees to identify the risk factor. Factors leading to attrition are identified from these profiles. Retention strategies are developed based on the finding of this analysis.

Prediction techniques are used to make unstructured decisions in talent management. Employee behaviour and attitude and its effect on performance are predicted with lesser errors using these techniques. Predictions are derived from the past experience or knowledge. Employees can be clustered into groups with similar characteristics using the clustering algorithm in data mining packages. These segments can be analyzed to understand the drivers of engagement which helps in talent retention. Facts embedded in the database are analyzed thoroughly to extract hidden patterns which generate new knowledge. The satisfaction level and performance of employees for an organization can also be predicted using data mining software algorithms.

Data Mining for Placement in Right Job

Knowledge about the association between the employee profile and the nature of the job with which they can be associated helps the HR manager to allot the right person to the right job. Existing employees should be scanned to identify the people possessing those key talents. Development activities can be concentrated on them to make them fit for accepting pivotal positions in the organization. Human resource management process should give sufficient importance to the task of recognizing the key performance areas in the organizations and the talents required to carry out those assignments. Identification of the right person with right skills for future roles will be a tedious process to be handled manually. Records of the performance details of the employees can be a valuable source of data for doing the above mentioned analysis and prediction.

Employee Segmentation

Majority of the techniques used above employs clustering algorithm for segmenting the employees which has given rise to a new concept, "employee segmentation".

Employees are the most coveted assets for any organization. Business benefits from a productive employee and productive behaviour is enhanced with employee satisfaction. Organization's survival and growth is highly dependent on the pool of talent force available. Identifying the right talents and retaining them in the organization is the greatest challenge for employers. Understanding the requirements of the workforce and developing strategies based on that is of prime importance for the organization.

Organizations are highly meticulous about sustaining customer satisfaction. Customer's requirements are catered to by the employees of the organization. Only committed employees will be successful in providing satisfiable service to a customer. Commitment is a by-product of employee satisfaction.

Majority of the employers consider employees as a homogeneous group. Organizations introduce monetary and non monetary benefits to the employees uniformly being unaware of the individual preferences. Employees form a heterogeneous group. Catering to the requirements of individual employees is practically unfeasible for any organization. Employee segmentation provides an amicable solution to this problem. The process of defining and sub-dividing a large group of employees into clearly identifiable segments having similar needs, wants, or demand characteristics is called as employee segmentation. The motivational factors catering to each segment is diversified.

Drivers of engagement will be different for each group. The parameters measuring the satisfaction of an employee will be diversified. Once segmentation is done, analysis is carried out to understand the factors of importance to each segment like work life balance, career development, monetary benefits etc. Motivational factors of one segment will not be encouraging the next segment.

Through employee segmentation organizations can improve the engagement level of employee at all functional areas, increase flexibility and welcome change, increase the efficiency of communication between management and employee and vice versa, reduce absenteeism and turnover and improve employee satisfaction and there by customer satisfaction. The segmentation process is done using clustering algorithms like k-means clustering in data mining.

Web Mining in HRM

Organizations are scrupulous about ensuring their presence in web to become noticeable by the customers and there by hastening their success in business. The mass storage of data in the websites has given rise to the web version of data mining called as web mining.

Web mining is the application of data mining techniques to extract knowledge from web data, including web documents, hyperlinks between documents, usage logs of websites, etc.

Web mining technologies can be categorized as:

- Web content mining.
- Web structure mining.
- Web usage mining.

Recruitment efforts of organization are made online. There are job sites which register candidates and inform them about the available vacancies. Numerous resumes get posted in these websites. The career opportunities available in a firm are also advertised in the company website. Scanning the resumes posted to decide on the most appropriate resume manually is impossible. Resume mining with web mining software does the task for the organization by filtering the list to find quality resume matching the requirements of the recruiter.

On the other hand, job seekers search for appropriate jobs matching their skills in the websites. Web usage mining analyses candidate's requirements to form personalized recommendation framework. Job seeker's searching pattern is studied by usage mining software to provide quality service to them.

Answering employee queries promptly is one among the responsibilities of human resource management. In the globalized world, employees of an organization are located at various geographical locations. To keep the employees well informed about the policies of the organization, particulars are included in the web site of the organization. If the website is not well designed, employees still seek the help of HR officers to clear queries. When there is abundant information stored in websites, it turns out to be a Herculean task to extract information aligning to the requirements of the user.

Web mining technology can reduce this bottleneck. Web mining techniques along with sequence similarity approaches used in bioinformatics are employed to develop a recommendation system. An employee will be prompted with a link to associated pages which can reduce the number of clicks to reach the desired content. Usage mining technology helps in unveiling a navigational path starting from a particular page. This improves the predictive power.

Weka: A Tool for Data Mining

In the current competitive scenario, Business intelligence tools have become inevitable in carrying out the business operations effectively and efficiently. Different kinds of data mining software are available for use by organizations like SAS, Rapid miner and Weka. Some features of Weka, the data mining software are explored here.

Almost all of the above algorithms discussed can be implemented using Weka—a popular machine language written in Java. Weka was developed at University of Waikato, New Zealand. It is available free under GNU General Public License.

Weka contains tools for pre processing data, clustering, classification, regression, association and visualization which are essential for business intelligence systems. The data is provided in the form of ARFF [2] files which contains header and data section.

Users interact with Weka using an interface called as Explorer. The explorer interface has many panels for functions like pre processing, classifying, associating, clustering and visualizing. The functions are carried out by selecting the appropriate panel.

- Pre-process panel performs the first step of loading the data from other sources. Data is usually stored as arff files described earlier. The file is selected and loaded to Weka. According to the application for which data mining is applied, the appropriate algorithm is chosen.
- Classify panel enables in applying classification and regression techniques which classifies the data according to the parameters specified.
- Associate panel extracts the interrelationships between the attributes in the input file specified.
- Cluster panel uses clustering algorithms like x-means, simple k-means to cluster the data.
- Select attributes panel selects the most pertinent attributes in the given data set.
- Visualize panel displays a scatter plot matrix of the current data set.

The employee data can be entered in 'arff' format to do clustering/association/classification on the data set to predict the future behaviour. The software is very user friendly to be understood by a non-programmer also because it is a readymade package.

In conclusion, it may be seen that human resource management elevated from the supporting role to participation in strategic management. Undoubtedly, this transformation occurred with the introduction of automated tools available in the human resource information system installed in the organization. Apart from the operational systems, analytical software also helps in the decision-making process of the top level management.

Data mining applications are widely used by marketing professionals for operations like customer segmentation, market segmentation, market basket analysis and the like. But now, this technology has extended its application to human resource management functions of the organization also. Recruiting, developing and retaining good talents in the organization are essential for the competitive advantage of the organization. Use of decision-making tools ensures the effectiveness of these functions. Implementation of data mining technology has contributed in achieving this mission. With the advent of cloud computing, a new approach of data mining called as 'cloud mining' has been introduced. In future, cloud mining will still enhance the business applications of data mining.

End Notes

1. The Euclidean distance between points p and q is the length of the line segment connecting them ($\overline{pq}$).
2. An ARFF (Attribute-Relation File Format) file is an ASCII text file that describes a list of instances sharing a set of attributes.

References

Chandrani Singh and Arpita Gopal (2010), Performance Analysis of Faculty Using Data Mining Techniques, *International Journal of Computer Science and Application.*

Efraim, Turban, Jay E. Aronson, Ting-Peng Liang and Ramesh Sharda (2007), Decision Support and Business Intelligence Systems, Pearson Education.

Hamidah, Jantan and Abdul Razak Hamdan (2010), Knowledge Discovery Techniques for Talent Forecasting in Human Resource Application, *International Journal of Human and Social Sciences,* 5:11.

Jihong, Yan and David Nembhard, *Discovering Assignment Rules in Workforce Schedules Using Data Mining,* Conference on Data Mining, DMIN'06.

Qasem, A. Al-Radaideh and Eman Al Nagi (2012), Using Data Mining Techniques to Build a Classification Model for Predicting Employees Performance, *International Journal of Advanced Computer Science and Applications*, Vol. 3, No. 2.

Rao, V.S.P. (2005), Human Resource Management: Text and Cases, Excel Books.

Roxanne, A. Ancheta et al. (2011), Predicting Faculty Development Trainings and Performance Using Rule-based Classification Algorithm, *Asian Journal of Computer Science and Information*

Technology.

Raymond, S. Bermudez et al. (2011), Predicting Faculty Performance Using Regression Model in Data Mining, Ninth International Conference on Software Engineering Research, Management and Applications.

12

Management Practices and Challenges of Healthcare Industry

Shamla N.K.

The healthcare industry has transformed dramatically over the last decade. It is noted that a number of key market drivers will continue to shape the future of healthcare for the prime reason of rising need for healthcare services—an aging population brings with it the challenge of maintaining quality of life against an increasing prevalence of conditions such as diabetes, cancer and obesity. There are also issues such as escalating cost pressures—the need for global cost containment is forcing pharmaceutical and medical technology firms to demonstrate value, creating demand for financial controls and operational efficiencies; and increasing technical advances—advances in molecular biology offer not only the potential of new therapies, possibly tailored to the individual, but also offer the potential for the rejuvenation of the healthcare industry through the development of new business models and strategies.

Despite enormous strides that have been made in informing the knowledge, diagnosis, and treatment of disease, the healthcare industry is yet to balance the need for new and effective therapies while addressing ever regulatory pressures on costs. It is high time the gap between strategy, management, and technology innovation is identified and measures taken to properly bridge the gap.

Indian Scenario

Healthcare industry in India is one of the largest in terms of revenue as well as employment, and the industry is expanding at a very rapid pace. India faces enormous challenges and opportunities as it builds its healthcare system to meet the rapidly growing needs and desires of a burgeoning middle-class that will increasingly want, expect, and ultimately demand world-class healthcare. An analysis of the current healthcare profile of India indicates the gaps and deficiencies in terms of service outreach, available resources, infrastructure and affordability as well as government expenditure, when compared to other developing nations. The healthcare expenditure in many of the global, developed and other similar emerging economies also represents a greater challenge absorbing a major share of their national income.

In comparison to the above, India's spend is significantly low (KPMG Analysis, 2011). During 2010, the value of the Indian healthcare industry was estimated at US$ 40 billion, which was US$ 34 billion in 2007 and by 2020; it is expected to reach at a level not less than US$ 280 billion. Private sector participation which account for more than 73 percent of the total market contribute significantly to the development of Indian hospital industry whereas the public funding remains a meagre 26 percent (KPMG Analysis, 2011).

The former percentage is amongst the highest in the world in percentage terms and the latter, the lowest. Life in India, with a population of 1.21 billion, out of which 26.1 percent is below the poverty line, is rife with many challenges like high income disparity, lack of basic infrastructure and the incidence of diseases. Despite this, the public sector provides only about 20 percent of actual care services. As a result, delivery of quality affordable healthcare is an enormous challenge as well as a whopping opportunity.

Opportunities

India now has abundant opportunities in the healthcare industry. These opportunities are driven by the results of growing population, changing demographics, rising disposable income, cheaper treatment costs as opposed to the western countries, increased personal awareness, increasing health insurance penetration, thrust in medical tourism, growth in telemedicine, unconventional thinking of healthcare providers for enhanced operation, government decision to implement public private partnership and provision of tax holidays. The following section details the implication of the above-mentioned factors.

Population and Density

India's population according to census, as on 1 March 2011 stood at 12109 lakh—increased by more than 181 million during the 2001-2011 decade. India accounts for a meagre 2.4 percent of the total world surface area of 1357.9 lakh sq. km. yet it occupies the position of the second largest populated country in the world with around 17.5 percent of the world's population. The United States Central Intelligence Agency (CIA) estimates the rate of population growth to be approximately 1.376 percent as of 2010 compared to only 0.49 percent annual population growth in China (CIA, 2010). By 2030, India is expected to surpass China as the world's most populous nation.

The density of population of India is 325 persons per square kilometre as per 2001 census and 384 according to 2011 census data. This shows an increase of 17.5 percent (Census, 2011). Even though the percentage increase shows a declining trend while examining the density figures over several decades, the absolute increase is still there. The increase in the density of population poses threats to the country in terms of both natural and man-made resources and will ultimately bring down the quality of life. This evil effect, on the other hand, opens up massive opportunities in the Indian healthcare industry.

Shift in Demographics

The age of population is one of the challenges India is going to face in the future. 60 percent of the Indian population in the year 2011 falls in the younger age bracket and an increase of geriatric population from current 96 million to around 168 million (0.75 percent increase) is expected by 2026. This represents a huge patient base and creates a market for preventive, curative and geriatric care opportunities (KPMG Analysis, 2011).

The shift of demographics may have an effect on the healthcare needs and services of this particular segment. The market for healthcare services will increase with the ageing of societies. Major proportion of the geriatric population will be suffering from chronic illnesses which require longer recovery time. This opens up great opportunities for long-term care services such as nursing homes, home health, and personal care and so on (Wiener and Tilly, 2002). Because, the ageing process will not end abruptly, the healthcare market and hospitals if adapt to the needs of this particular segment can sustain in the long-run too.

Changing Economy and Rise in Disposable Income

India traditionally has been a rural, agrarian economy, which has been transformed to a service-driven economy since the beginning of economic reforms in 1991. These reforms brought enormous growth potential in the country. The entry of private sector and deregulation paved way to the formulation of liberalized foreign direct investment and trade policy (Ernst & Young, 2011). These factors together with increased urbanization and modern technology have brought remarkable change in the lifestyle of the Indian population. This increase in the rate of disposable income and affordable pricing has led to the emergence of a highly aware and demanding customer base (Ernst &Young, 2009).

More women are entering the workforce as well, further boosting the purchasing power of Indian households. If the economy continues to grow at such a faster rate, a reasonable proportion of the population will be middle class by 2020 (ibid). These changing situations probably bring opportunities in the healthcare industry in general and private healthcare sector in particular.

Cost of Treatment

In comparison with other countries, India has no parallels in healthcare when it comes to cost effective medical treatments. There exist significant cost differences among US, UK and South Asian countries. Moreover, the waiting time is almost nil in case of India. In a cost comparison study conducted by American Medical Association, it is found that a heart bypass surgery would cost US$ 1,30,000 in US, US$ 18,500 in Singapore and US$ 11,000 in Thailand, while the same surgery would cost the person US$ 10,000 in India. Similarly, when the heart valve replacement surgery would cost US$ 1,60,000 in US and US$ 12,500 in Singapore, it would cost only US$ 9,000 per person in India. That gives India a cost-effective edge when it comes to medical treatments. In addition, Indian doctors are renowned all over the world for their expertise and skills (AMA, 2007). Thus, India is now considered as the low cost medical destination by the US, UK and many South Asian countries.

In the recent years, due to the increase in the literacy rate and the widespread health awareness campaigns to address health issues all over the country, people are becoming more aware of their healthcare needs. With this rising awareness levels both in the urban and rural areas and increasing disposable incomes, it is expected that the coming decade will witness increased demand for preventive healthcare.

Health Insurance Penetration

Healthcare insurance is slowly picking up pace in India. According to the 2010 statistics released by the Insurance Regulatory Development Authority (IRDA), the total health insurance premiums written by non-life companies and standalone health insurance companies grew by 25.2 percent in thc 2010 financial year over 2009 financial year. With the growing penetration of health insurance, healthcare is likely to become affordable to a larger proportion of the country's population. Many private and international insurance companies had entered in the scene as a result of the liberalization of insurance industry in 2000.

Despite having many insurance schemes including Central Government Health Scheme (CGHS), the Employees' State Insurance Scheme (ESIS), social and community health insurance schemes, other Government sponsored schemes and private health insurance, the country was able to cover only 25 percent of the population in 2010. Out of the total health insurance coverage, 75 percent is through Rashtriya Swasthiya Bhima Yojana and other state government sponsored schemes. Increasing penetration of health insurance is expected to increase healthcare demand in India in the forthcoming years.

Medical Tourism

Medical tourism, otherwise called *health tourism* or *wellness tourism* is a concept where people from all around the world travels to other countries for obtaining medical, dental, and surgical care and at the same time, experience the attractions of the countries they are visiting (George, 2012). Medical tourism is one of the major external drivers of growth of the Indian healthcare sector. The emergence of India as a destination for medical tourism leverages the country's well educated, English-speaking medical staff, state-of-the art private hospitals and diagnostic facilities, and relatively low cost to address the spiraling healthcare costs of the western world.

India offers a unique basket of services to an individual such as Yoga, Meditation, Ayurveda, Allopathy, and other systems of medicines that are difficult to match by other countries (CII, 2005). It is estimated that 1,80,000 medical tourists were treated at Indian healthcare facilities in the year 2004. This number is growing at a rate of 25 to 30 percent annually. On the promotion side, e-marketing of medical tourism services will help the medical tourism firm to reach the customer directly, bypassing the middlemen. This will help the firm to provide services at a lower price, on time, and in a highly customized manner. The government is also promoting the growth of medical tourism by providing various incentives, reducing the import duties, as well as expedited visas for overseas patients seeking medical care in India.

Medical tourism provides vast opportunities for growth in the healthcare industry through tapping the potential of the international patient market. To utilize these opportunities, healthcare providers should leverage on both business and clinical considerations. A sincere commitment and co-ordination of travel, hospitality, and healthcare allows each stakeholder to focus on self-competencies and may even ease the level of competition which ultimately bring better long run revenues throughout the entire sector (George, 2012).

Telemedicine

Telemedicine is the use of electronic information to communicate technologies to provide and support healthcare when distance separates the participants. The term 'telemedicine' came from the words *tele* meaning 'distance' and *mederi* meaning 'to heal'. The World Health Organization (WHO) defines telemedicine as:

The delivery of healthcare services, where distance is a critical factor, by all healthcare professionals using information and communication technologies for the exchange of valid information for diagnosis, treatment and prevention of disease and injuries, research and evaluation and for the continuing education of healthcare providers, all in the interests of advancing the health of individuals and their communities.

Telemedicine activities started in India in the year 1999. The concept has wide application in patient care, education, research, administration and public health. The Apollo group of hospitals was a pioneer in starting this concept in India. The implementation was done in a secondary level hospital in a village in Andhra Pradesh. They started off with simple web cameras and ISDN telephone lines. Afterwards, the village hospital has constituted a state-of-the-art videoconferencing system and a VSAT (very small aperture terminal) satellite installed by ISRO (Indian Space Research Organization).

Coupled with this, was the Sriharikota Space Centre project which formed an important launch pad of the Indian Space Research Organization in this field (Ganapathy, 2001). To further support telemedicine activities within the country, the Department of Information Technology has defined the Standards for Telemedicine Systems and the Ministry of Health and Family Welfare has constituted the National Telemedicine Task Force.

PPP (Public Private Partnership) Model

In the healthcare sector, public private partnership (PPP) is an instrument for improving the health of the population. In this model, the whole medical sector is viewed as a national asset with health promotion as the goal of all health providers, private or public. Public private partnership has now emerged as one of the options to influence the growth of private sector with public goals in mind. The most common PPP models are contracting ('in' and 'out'), build/rehabilitate, operate, transfer, demand/ supply side financing, joint ventures, mobile health units, telemedicine, franchising, social marketing and public-private mix (Venkatraman, 2009).

Tax Holiday

As per the sub-section (11C) in Section 80-IB of the Finance Act, 2008, a five year tax holiday was granted by the Ministry of Finance, Government of India to encourage hospitals to be set up anywhere in India, except certain specified urban agglomerations, and tier-2 and tier-3 towns (Greater Mumbai, Delhi, Kolkata, Chennai, Hyderabad, Bangalore, and Ahmedabad urban agglomeration; and Districts of Faridabad, Gurgaon, Gautam Budh Nagar, Ghaziabad,

Gandhinagar, Secunderabad). According to the Act, the hospital should be started functioning at any time during the period beginning on the April 1, 2008 and ending on the day of March 31, 2013 (Finance Act, 2008). The objective of this is to establish a fully functional community owned, decentralized health delivery system.

Existing Management Practices and Challenges

All the above mentioned aspects provide huge opportunities to the healthcare industry in India. The healthcare industry as a whole is also very keen on devising strategies to utilize these opportunities to withstand competition and to enhance growth in the long run. But a recent study conducted by the World Health Statistics (2010) exposed the shocking reality of Indian healthcare Industry. This report pointed out that India has 6.13 lakh physicians, against a requirement for 13.3 lakh. When compared to China (1.4 doctors per 1,000), India has less than one doctor per thousand people (0.6).

The British Association of Physicians of Indian Origin (BAPIO) estimates that the United Kingdom has over 40,000 doctors from India, who are treating about nearly 50 percent of the British population. Similarly, the American Association of Physicians of Indian origin (AAPI) reports the number of doctors practicing in US as 50,000. Moreover 20 percent of the doctors practicing in Australia have received their basic medical training from India (Duttagupta, 2011). The figures mentioned above clearly portray the current Indian situation. The government spends enormous amount of money and time for medical training and once the training gets complete, they trade in places away from their mother land. This brain-drain leaves a huge gap between supply and demand of healthcare and creates significant challenges in the healthcare industry both in terms of accessibility of healthcare service and quality of patient care.

Operations Management

The healthcare industry today is very complex due to the involvement of different stakeholders such as patients, physicians, hospitals, insurers, employers, communities, and government with ever changing relationships. Moreover, the environment offers more challenges due to intense competition, increasing expectations of customers and, reduced funding and utilization. The healthcare costs are increasing on one hand and on the other hand, healthcare industry is striving hard to improve the quality of care it provides to its consumers (Gaucher and Coffey, 1993, p. 4). This session provides an overview of the operations management practices in the healthcare sector.

Capacity Planning/Capacity Management

In order to improve the access of Healthcare outcomes and to reduce the effect of competition in healthcare, the hospitals are struggling in to lower their cost of offering. The strategies adopted by many includes downsizing of beds, cutting of staff and merging with other hospitals. These critical decisions are generally taken by the hospitals without the help of any scientific analysis and many of these decisions have found to be resulted in diminished patient access without any significant decrease in costs.

On the other side, patients are highly demanding improved clinical and service outcomes. All these factors together demands an organization to think of a more scientific and analytical approach that will help to identify capacity needs and ways to use the existing capacity more efficiently and effectively (Brandeau, Margaret L. et al., 2004).

The issues related to capacity are found in areas such as number of inpatient beds, quantity of manpower required, operating rooms and other major diagnostic equipments. In earlier days and even now in many places, hospital bed capacity decisions are made based on the average percentage of occupied beds which was not an accurate determinant of bed capacity. To overcome the manpower requirement problem, many healthcare organizations adopt the strategy of adjusting the available manpower in accordance with the patient arrival volumes. This strategy will reduce the quality of services. Hence, a match between the above two elements is substantial or even critical for providing timely care to the severely critical and injured patients. Lack of scientific analysis based on the criticality of operations is the reason for the bottlenecks in operating room scheduling and many a times, it is noticed that very expensive diagnostic equipments such as MRI (magnetic resonance imaging devices) remain unutilized or underutilized. All these are capacity related issues prevalent in healthcare organizations.

Process Design/Process Re-engineering

Even though the concept of BPR (business process re-engineering) is widely applied in the manufacturing sector, the application in the healthcare is still at its infancy. Since, BPR mainly performs radical redesigning or radical restructuring; it has limited scope in healthcare organizations. However, process improvement which emphasizes small and measurable refinements to an organization's process has been widely adopted by the whole of the healthcare industry (Walley, 2003). Mintzberg (1997) also given a similar statement that hospitals could better learn how to solve general problems systematically and this will require tangible changes in their collective behaviour rather than strategic planning and structural reorganizing.

Total Quality Management (TQM) and Six Sigma

Hospitals are by nature complex organizations and the complexity is compounded in service hospitals with perceived notion of service deficiencies. Quality has emerged as a major issue in healthcare sector and TQM has been accepted as a major long-term strategic initiative towards continuously improving quality of healthcare. Key concepts of TQM start with top management leadership with emphasis on process and customer focus. Implementation of TQM in service hospitals will require quality management awareness, training and framework development as well as development of customer awareness. TQM has been widely applied in clinical field with successful outcome. TQM is not a short-term solution, it has to be understood and practiced as a long-term strategic commitment.

Six Sigma is "a rigorous set of processes and techniques to measure, improve, and control the quality of care and service based on what is important to the customer" (Woodard, 2005, p. 229). The objective of Six Sigma approach is to bring procedures to defect-free levels by trying to eliminate variation in processes. This approach is quite successful in healthcare in areas such as medication error, lab turnaround time, supply chain management for supplies, claims reimbursement, nursing retention, patient condition outcomes, and others (Revere and Black, 2003). Six Sigma is directed by the DMAIC approach: define measure, analyze, improve, and control (Riebling and Tria, 2005).

Lean Thinking

Even though the application of lean principles in hospitals is not very common, it is gaining greater acceptance due to the reason that it will increase efficiency (Wysocki, 2004). In hospitals, wastages can arise in the form of medication errors, wrong patient ID and wrong procedures, incomplete admission information, poor clinical outcomes and retesting, misfiled reports/records; overproduction in the form of duplication of records; confusion in the form of unclear role expectations and wrong billing procedures; excessive waiting to get things done, excessive inventory piling up and so on.

In India, Aravind Eye Care System (AECS) has applied the principle of lean thinking successfully. The operational processes at AECS have been classified with planned precision and all the processes have been standardized. This ensures the same quality of care to all. Moreover, a *checklist* system has been put in place to monitor the different parts of processes and a flow chart explains the time for each process. This serves an impetus to the doctors and staff to monitor their performance and even informs the patients about the processes involved in the provision of care that they will receive.

Supply Chain Management (SCM) in Healthcare

SCM is the process of planning, implementing and controlling the operations of the supply chain for analyzing the customer requirements as efficiently as possible. It involves the planning and management of all activities involved in sourcing and procurement, conversion and all logistics management activities.

An integrated SCM for healthcare will enable lower fulfilment costs, shorter delivery lead times and improved ability to focus on service delivery rather than administrative processes. Healthcare organizations today are looking for opportunities to improve operational efficiencies and reduce costs without negatively impacting patient care. Creating a supply chain that connects employees in the medical facility, fosters collaboration and offers supplier's visibility into demand-and-supply is essential to reducing overall supply chain costs (Hanna and Sethuraman, 2005).

Quality of healthcare service in any hospital or clinic is considered to have far reaching implication in respect of growth and reputation of business. Undoubtedly, these aspects of quality control and maintenance play a pivotal role in the gross business perspectives of market expansion, brand image of healthcare facility and service standards. Over and above these reasons, quality is considered as the very heart and soul behind the excellence of any healthcare facility's reputation.

Challenges of Healthcare Industry

Human Resource Management: Human resource development and management is a vast domain. Today, due to the emergence of multi-speciality hospitals with enormous facilities, India is being viewed as an upcoming destination for medical tourism. Amidst this, human resource departments in various healthcare organizations face the challenging job of attracting, recruiting, training and retaining healthcare professionals. Moreover, human resource departments play a vital role in helping the organization meet its strategic goals by managing the workforce effectively and efficiently. Below mentioned are some of the human resources management practices followed by healthcare organizations in India.

Talent Hiring and Selection: If the healthcare facility is focusing on rendering best healthcare to the population, it cannot afford a shortage of qualified healthcare professionals. Hence, this is considered to be one of the most crucial and best HR practices for healthcare management. In the public sector, recruitment is done on the basis of various examinations conducted by the Central and State Governments. Placement consultants, walk-in interviews, references, internal circulars for vacancies via intranet, campus recruitment, advertisements in newspapers, job portal, data bank, referrals etc. are the major sources of recruitment in private healthcare organizations in India. The selection process includes screening of applications, written test and different rounds of interviews followed by medical test. The job offer letter is issued to the candidates after selection.

Induction: A very few healthcare organizations carry out induction programmes. Various induction programmes include issue of induction manual, briefing of HR issues by the head of the organization/superior, presentations by departmental heads, general tour of the hospital, and induction speech usually by vice-chairman/superiors. In addition to the above, certain organizations put their new employees through lecture sessions with the help of power point presentations covering aspects like, background of the hospital, customer following, services provided, general expectations from hospital staff, disciplinary matters, and personal benefits.

Compensation: A basic salary is provided with other

allowances. This base salary usually accounts for 40 to 50 percent of an employee's salary. The remaining salary is comprised of several allowances such as dearness allowance (DA), house rent allowance (HRA), and medical allowances. Certain organizations also provide leave travel allowance (LTA) which permits two tax-free travel opportunities in India within a four-year period. LTA is provided based on an employee's salary and level in the organization. This includes employees and their family members.

Training and Development: Many of the healthcare organizations in India identify the components of training after a thorough need assessment. However, in some organizations the Head of the department recommends as to who are the employees who need training. The HR manager or the training manager then prepares the training calendar which includes both in-house and external training. The in-house training generally comprise of behavioural etiquettes, soft skills, communication skills, hygiene aspects, personality development, team building and leadership. Certain organizations follow the policy of CME (continuous medical education). For administration and management, in-house training is adopted. In the external training, the employees are sent to outside agencies for training in professional areas. Only a very few healthcare organizations in India are conducting employee development programmes.

Performance Appraisal: Performance appraisal is carried out in organizations for different cadres during different time spans. The duration is normally quarterly, half-yearly, and yearly basis. The method employed by the majority is rating scales, both graphical and itemized. Certain organizations fix their performance through the management by objectives (MBO) system. These involve setting of goals through mutual consent which bring out various *key results areas* (KRAs) with time frames. Every employee is required to state his performance levels in a FORM on the basis of weightages depicted for the level of achievement in each KRAs. After each appraisal, scores are assigned to the employees and discussion is carried out with the concerned employee to ascertain the stated level of performance. In many organizations, performance appraisal forms the basis of rewards, performance and promotion.

Promotion and Reward: Employees are looking forward to compensation at par with industry standards, good work life balance, a sense of equity and justice and a robust performance management system linked to a well-balanced reward system. In India, the promotion and reward system is different in public and private sectors. In the public sector, the promotion is based on seniority levels whereas in the globally oriented private sectors, merit and performance linked promotion and reward system exists.

Career Planning: Organizations are facing shortages in their workforces due to retirement and exits for search of better prospects. Moreover, the tremendous growth in the healthcare industry adds to the workforce shortage to create vacancies that threaten survival of many hospitals. To prepare for this uncertainty, organizations are conducting career development programs to retain key employees, build their existing workforce to meet future needs, and remain competitive. In India, such development programmes seems to be very rare even in big organizations. Based on a systems perspective, issues in human resource management can be broadly classified under macro and micro environment.

From a macro perspective, the size and composition of the work force, its distribution among service levels and across the country; regulation of education and professional practice; and general parameters of working conditions, incentive systems, payment mechanisms, and labour relations are major concerns in the Indian healthcare industry. At the micro level, human resource management is more concerned with individuals than groups. Performance management, supervision, evaluation and conflict resolution are some of the micro level issues of HRM in India (WHO, 2007).

Information Technology in Healthcare

The Internet and web-based technologies have a significant impact on the healthcare industry. Many of the organizations are now adopting e-healthcare tools to provide better patient care.

Major improvements have been witnessed in key healthcare metrics due to information technology such as reduction of medical error rates, lowering of laboratory costs, administrative expenses and so on. A few popular IT application tools in the healthcare industry include the following.

Electronic Medical Record (Computer-based Patient Record): Healthcare is an industry which is heavily dependent on maintenance of data. For maintaining steady and smooth access to the information regarding the patient's treatment and medication, the electronic medical record or EMR plays a very important role. Thus, EMR is globally considered to be one of the best practices of healthcare management.

Web-based Order Entry Tools: Computerized provider order entry (CPOE) in its basic form is typically a medication ordering and fulfilment system. More advanced CPOE will also include lab orders, radiology studies, procedures, discharges, transfers, and referrals.

E-medicine: E-medicine is defined as the *use of telecommunication* to provide medical information and services. It may be as simple as two health professionals discussing a case over the telephone, or as sophisticated as using satellite technology to broadcast a consultation between providers at two distant locations, using videoconferencing equipment.

E-medicine uses multimedia technology incorporating elements of television, telecommunication, computers, engineering and medicine. The application of e-medicine is expanding at a faster pace in India. This is evident if considered the case of Kolkata. The people with heart conditions are now recording their own electro cardiograms on a machine installed at home and transmit the information over the phone to a specialist

(Dinesh and Reddy, 2012).

There are many activities that are going to contribute to the spread of e-medicine in India, of which, Apollo in Hyderabad and Asia Heart Foundation in Bangalore are emerging as key players. Madras Medical College is the first government medical college to have e-medicine installed in India. Organizations such as Indian Space Research Organization (ISRO), have taken innovative approach to facilitate healthcare delivery by launching an exclusive health satellite. It provides almost hundred percentage uptime, making it the best medium for a country such as India with diversity in terrain. General Electric and Wipro are also undertaking e-medicine stations in Chennai and Hyderabad (Saxena and Singh, 2010).

Telemedicine: Telemedicine is an upcoming field in health science arising out of the effective fusion of information and communication technology (ICT) with medical science having enormous potential in meeting the challenges of healthcare delivery to rural and remote areas besides several other applications in education, training and management in health sector. There are many independent organizations and government departments in India carrying out telemedicine activities. Some of them are Department of Information Technology (DIT), Indian Space Research Organization (ISRO), Ministry of health and family welfare (MOH&FW), All India Institute of Medical Sciences (AIIMS, Delhi), Apollo Telemedicine Networking Foundation (ATNF), Narayana Hrudayalaya (NH, Bangalore) and Centre for development of Advanced Computing (C-DAC).

Picture Archiving and Communications System (PACS): This technology captures and integrates diagnostic and radiological images from various devices (e.g., x-ray, MRI, computed tomography scan), stores them, and disseminates them to a medical record, a clinical data repository, or other points of care.

Cyber Knife Surgery: 'Cyber Knife' which was

developed by John Adler uses a mesh mask to stabilize the head. It represents an entirely new approach to radio surgery. It is the only system that combines robotics, and advanced image guidance to deliver frameless radio surgery. The technology tracks any unintentional movement on the part of the patient and adjusts the radiation path as necessary. The Apollo speciality hospital in India is using this technology for the past few years.

Micro Surgery: Micro surgery is a sub-speciality performed with the aid of a microscope on structures that are hardly visible to the naked eye. This sub-speciality mainly deals with 'replantations' (reattaching severed parts of the limb). In India, the micro surgery is performed at Apollo Hospitals for problems such as congenital abnormalities, carpal tunnel syndrome, arthritis, tumours and other finger related deformities.

Radio Frequency Identification Device (RFID): The use of RFID technology which was popular in the manufacturing industry is now increasing in the healthcare industry too. It is useful in tracking physical assets and the flow of patients. In patient management, identifying and tracking patients is much easier using RFID tags than any other technologies. The combination of RFID and sensor technologies is helpful in monitoring different biometrics and implanted devices. In the near future, patients could be discharged immediately after treatment because physicians can monitor their condition in real time from remote places. The major constraint associated with e-healthcare initiatives is financial viability. Moreover, patients also need to check and ensure legal, quality and safety implications of relying on the internet to meet their healthcare related informational needs.

Research and Development in Healthcare

The amazing advancements in the realm of medical science and technology over the globe have been largely possible due to the integration of medicine and technology. Millions of people across the globe have been able to enhance their quality of life through this and yet another billion are still waiting to enjoy the fruits of this revolution. Innovations in technology have led to spectacular advancements in medicine. The following are some of the research and development areas in healthcare.

Medical Imaging and Image Analysis: Medical imaging is the technique and process used to create images of the human body (or parts and function thereof) for clinical purposes (medical procedures seeking to reveal, diagnose, or examine disease) or medical science (including the study of normal anatomy and physiology). Extensive researches are being carried out in this area. The existing imaging technologies include radiography, magnetic resonance imaging (MRI), fiduciary markers, nuclear medicine, photoacoustic imaging, breast thermography, tomography, ultrasound, echocardiography and so on. The proposed or developed techniques under this area include diffuse optical tomography, elastography, electrical impedance tomography, optoacoustic imaging, ophthalmology techniques such as A-scan, B-scan, corneal topography, optical coherence tomography, scanning laser ophthalmoscopy and so on.

Medical Instrumentation: Medical instrumentation is the function and use of a device in the diagnosis, treatment and management of illness or in the assessment and preservation of health (Winters and Story, 2007). Many researches are being carried out in India on this topic.

Tissue Engineering: Tissue engineering is a discipline that aims at repair, replacement and regeneration of specific tissues. Recent advances of tissue engineering could develop several tissues in laboratory, but regenerating tissue-to-tissue interface is still a challenging proposition. Researches are going on in this area in IIT, New Delhi to investigate at the interface between fundamental and applied research, by combining the principles of textile technology and tissue engineering.

Biomaterials: A biomaterial is any matter, surface, or construct that interacts with biological systems. This concept is about 50 years old. Biomaterials are used in joint replacements, dental implants for tooth fixation, heart valves, and contact lenses. Researches pertaining to this area are expanding across the globe. In India also, extensive researches are carried out in organizations such as IITs, Society for Biomaterials and Artificial Organs under Sree Chitra Tirunal Institute of Medical Sciences and Technology, Trivandrum and many other healthcare institutions.

Bio-MEMS: Bio-MEMS, or biomedical micro electro mechanical systems, has emerged as a subset of MEMS devices for applications in biomedical research and medical micro devices. This is a multi-disciplinary approach wherein it draws concepts from electrical, mechanical, optical, chemical and biomedical engineering. The science of biomedical micro electro mechanical systems (Bio-MEMS) promises to deliver sensitive, selective, fast, low cost, less invasive, and more robust methods for diagnostics, individualized treatment, and novel drug delivery. The Bio-MEMS industry is increasing rapidly with a growth rate of 11.4 percent, with projected revenues of US$ 850 million in 2003 to over US$ 1 billion in 2006 [Rebello, 2004]. Centre for Nano Science and Engineering at Indian Institute of Science (IISc), Bangalore and IITs carry out research programmes in this area.

Reproductive Biology: Various researches are being conducted in India in the area of reproductive biology in institutions such as National Institute for Research in Reproductive Health, Mumbai and Department of Molecular Reproduction, Indian Institute of Science.

Drug Design: Design of a novel drug is one of the biggest challenges faced by the pharmaceutical industry. The use of computers accelerates the process of drug designing which is a time intensive process that reduces the cost of designing process. There are different forms of drug discovery such as QSAP, virtual screening and, structure-based drug designing methods, of which the Structure based method is gaining more importance. The Indian Institute of Technology, Delhi and

Bioinformatics Institute of India (BII) are the organizations in India conducting research in this field.

Medical Statistics and Informatics: Medical statistics deals with applications of statistics to medicine and the health sciences, including epidemiology, public health, forensic medicine, and clinical research. It develops statistical ratios for measuring the patterns of various disease and health conditions. HIV health indicators, counting radiation doses and forensic criminal investigation ratios are some of the newly developed ratios (Altman, 1991 and Armitage, 2002). Medical informatics is a combination of information science, computer science, and healthcare. It deals with the resources, methods, and techniques required for optimizing the acquisition, storage, retrieval, and use of information in health and biomedicine. In India, medical informatics is still in its infancy.

Nuclear Medicine: Nuclear medicine is a branch of medical science where radio-nuclides are used for diagnosis and treatment of human diseases. Various Indian Research organizations are involved in this field of research such as Advanced Nuclear Medicine Research Institute, Chennai, Society of Nuclear Medicine and Punjab University.

Healthcare Management: With the healthcare industry witnessing remarkable growth in the last few years, the concept of healthcare has gone beyond hospitals. Instead, it is now related to a gamut of quality services linked to hospitals. This in turn has increased the demand for quality healthcare professionals in India. A major challenge for the Indian healthcare industry would be not only to retain the healthcare workforce, but also to develop an environment that would encourage the NRIs to come back. The area of research under healthcare management includes the application of management principles and best practices to healthcare delivery, improving the process of innovation, employment of principles of strategy and consumer choice in healthcare, identification of regulatory mechanisms for emerging healthcare fields, development of approaches for delivering high-impact healthcare in developing nations.

Marketing Management

The concept of marketing is same in product and service industry, the only difference that exists is that a product is tangible which can be seen, felt, and touched whereas services are perishable and intangible. Consumers can come up with desirable parameters for rating a tangible product whereas it is very difficult to rate an intangible product.

In the healthcare industry, marketing today has become a vital component owing to the rise in the number of hospitals and immense competition. Marketing of healthcare services includes the analysis and management of four factors essential to the delivery of healthcare product, place, price and, promotion.

In other words, it is important to understand the type of healthcare service to be offered, location and mode of access, how the service will be delivered to the patient, what is the worth of the service delivered, how and what the prospective patient learns about the organization and the services it offers. The healthcare being a service industry with a noble cause cannot utilize advertising techniques in the way other industries do. Marketing strategies in the hospital industry would include the various aspects of retaining and growing profitable external direct customers.

In the public sector, *healthcare promotion* is the term best suited for healthcare marketing. Development of community-wide education programmes and other health promotion activities are undertaken by the government in different areas to promote healthcare. Various health related programmes are organized on days like Diabetes day and Heart day in different places including villages to help create awareness at the grass root level. The private sector players adopt different marketing strategies to attract their customers of which, pharmaceutical and big insurance companies use mass advertising as primary marketing channel.

Local physicians and hospitals give newspaper advertisements to make consumers aware of their health specialty and location. Many hospitals also have online presences in websites that act as digital brochures. Drug companies and insurance companies have also established websites for physicians and patients to visit. The major objectives of healthcare marketing are: (a) to generate preferences among public regarding the brand and services offered by the healthcare provider, (b) to retain customers, (c) to educate consumers about medications, including how to take them and what to avoid when using them, and (d) Government compliance. There are different types of marketing approaches followed by healthcare organizations.

Referral Marketing: Healthcare is a personal service that inherently relies on trust, bonds and personal recommendations. Perhaps more than any other industries, consumers rely on word-of-mouth marketing and referrals to find quality doctors and healthcare specialists. Healthcare business-to-business sales also rely on positive referrals and word-of-mouth.

Social Marketing: Social marketing is widely used to influence health behaviour. Social marketers use a wide range of health communication strategies based on mass media; they also use mediated (for example, through a healthcare provider), interpersonal, and other modes of communication; and marketing methods such as message placement (for example, in clinics), promotion, dissemination, and community level outreach. Social marketing encompasses all of these strategies.

Relationship Marketing: Building relationships with patients is critical to the success of every healthcare organization. Healthcare relationship marketing techniques focus on the customer. As consumers have become more educated about their options, relationship marketing (RM) techniques are geared toward encouraging increased communication in order to foster brand loyalty, retain trust and provide better healthcare. This approach emphasizes getting to know the customer on a personal level and creating channels of communication that the customer feels comfortable enough to use.

Data-driven Marketing: This approach incorporates available evidence-based information regarding the provider's services into the marketing message, according to the entrepreneur business resource site. A data-based marketing message also enables consumers to compare a particular provider's success and outcome rates with other competing service providers. In effect, data-driven marketing helps healthcare organizations communicate useful information to the consumer within their marketing message.

Technology-driven Marketing: This approach incorporates the communication networks through the internet. This approach enables healthcare organizations and providers to work around uncomfortable marketing messages by making themselves directly accessible to the consumer.

Healthcare marketing ethics state that medical professionals should not recommend or prescribe treatment that is not essential for the patient's health, just to increase profits. Marketers should provide complete transparency in their marketing techniques so that the public may see the fairness and honesty in the marketing policies. Their advices should be in the best interest of the individual patient welfare.

Financial Management

The health sector reforms in India are taking place under the broad umbrella of Structural Adjustment Programs (SAP) or the New Economic Policy (NEP). The two major aspects of the SAP are 'privatization' and 'liberalization'. The major impediment under Structural Adjustment Programmes at present is the issue of under-funding of health services. The investment by the Government of India in healthcare has always been insufficient to meet the demands of the people. The government has over the years committed not more than 3.5 percent of its resources to the health sector.

That is only one percentage to gross domestic product (GDP)

against the World Health Organization's recommendation of 5 percent. The grants from Central Government to the State Governments went down drastically from 19.9 percent in 1974-82 to 3.3 percent in 1992-93 which affected the central and centrally sponsored programs adversely. Following are some of the financial management practices in Indian healthcare industry.

Allocation of Health Expenditure: Investment on Health and Family Welfare, AYUSH and Health Research for Eleventh Plan (2007-12) stood at ₹ 1,31,650.92 crore, ₹ 3,988.00 crore and ₹ 4,496.08 crore respectively. Total budgetary allocations under health sector was ₹ 1,40,135.00 crore. This shows an increase of 6.49 percent from 3.97 percent of total plan investment. The fund flow is high from private funds (76.74 percent) as opposed to public funds (20.97 percent). In 2009, private expenditure in India accounted for 67 percent of the total expenditure on health. With this very little available amount, the government's prioritization and allocation of health expenditures are misplaced. The foremost priority of the government lies in the population control program followed by family planning and welfare activities. On the one side, this prioritization has led to the neglect of many critical areas and on the other side; this has not reduced the population growth rate and total fertility rate (TFR) to a greater extent. The severe consequence happens to be a loss of faith in the public sector particularly for curative care and it led to the expansion of private sector to a very large extent.

Health Financing Alternatives: The mobilization of funds for healthcare has gained prominent attention around the world. Billions of dollars in new funds are flowing into healthcare in low- and middle-income countries. India relies mostly on individual out-of-pocket payments. The government increases the outlay of health sector through several methods under structured adjustment programs. These include aid from bilateral and multilateral sources, loans from World Bank and other international agencies, and taxes imposed through user charges.

Government Support for Private Sector: The National Health Policy encourages the private participation in healthcare to establish an integrated network of evenly spread specialty and super-specialty services (MoHFW, 2002). The indirect support include financial concessions in the form of subsidized sale of land, reduced import duties, tax concessions for medical research (Baru, 2000), reduced utility charges, discounted or free land, and low-interest loans (Chakraborty, 2003). Moreover, the corporate hospitals in the private sector receive huge amounts of public funds in the form of reimbursements from public sector undertakings and the State and Central governments [e.g., the Central Government Health Scheme CGHS] (Rao, 2012).

Sources of Financing: The private sources for healthcare financing in India encompasses debt financing from banks and financial institutions, foreign direct investment, external commercial borrowings, individual investors, foreign institutional investors, and venture capital. The public sources include Annual Government budget for rural and urban health sectors, government funding for community programmes, incentives and subsidies, approval for large special economic zones in some areas, government facilitations and removal of red tape and other community-based schemes.

Financial Regulation: The private health sector in India works practically unregulated and unaccountable to the people or any authority. There are no standards of medical practice prescribed for private hospitals in terms of qualification of staff employed, equipment needed, administration and treatment offered. Only recently, the private practitioners and hospitals were brought under the purview of the Consumer Protection Act, a policy which was met with great resistance from the medical fraternity. The existing regulations which are too few are obsolete, insufficient and not being carried out.

Household Expenditure on Health: Households contribute 71.13 percent of total health expenditure with social insurance funds at 1.13 percent and firms at 5.73 percent. A significant portion of their income and consumption expenditure is spent on health. It is estimated that the house hold expenditure had shown a rate of increase of 13.9 percent in the year 2004 (Cbhidghs, 2005).

Conclusion

The proven management tools, techniques, and methodologies combined with industry expertise uniquely position the industry to help medical technology, biopharmaceutical, and associate businesses around the world. The qualified team members having significant capabilities and experience in working must be able to shape the direction and future of R&D, marketing, and strategy for pharmaceuticals, biotechnology, drug delivery, and fine chemicals. In order to realize the potential and improve performance, each unit should identify and diagnose the source of weakness.

Once the weakness has been mitigated, the unit must align its operations with its strategies, optimize its processes and manage required changes. Improving performance and realizing potential requires corporate commitment as well as an innovative approach to the process. For the transformation of units from within, they must integrate the components such as business process optimization, organizational and resource planning and design, supply chain optimization, complexity and change management, knowledge management, benchmarking and execution in a fruitful manner.

References

Altman, D.G. (1991), Practical Statistics for Medical Research, CRC Press.

Andreasen A. (1995), Marketing Social Change, San Francisco, CA: Jossey-Bass.

Armitage, P., Berry, G. and Mathews, J.N.S. (2002), Statistical Methods in Medical Research, Blackwell.

Bhat, Ramesh (1999), Characteristics of Private Medical Practices in India: A Provider Perspective, *Health Policy and Planning*, 14(1), pp. 26-37.

Brandeau, Margaret L., et al. (2004), Operations Research and

Healthcare- A Handbook of Methods and Application, Kluwer Academic Publishers, London, pp. 15-42.

CBHI, DGHS, MoH&FW (2007), Managing Human Resources for Health in India, WHO, New Delhi.

Central Bureau of Health Intelligence (CBHI) (2010), Health Finance Indicators, National Health Profile.

Central Intelligence Agency (2010), *The World Factbook*, CIA.

Chakraborty, S. (2003), Private Health Provision in Uttar Pradesh, India, in A.S. Yazbeck and D.H. Peters (eds.), Health Policy Research in South Asia: Building Capacity for Reform, World Bank, Washington, DC, pp. 257-277.

Dasgupta, A. and Deb, S. (2008), Telemedicine: A New Horizon in Public Health in India, *Indian Journal of Community Medicine*, January; 33 (1): 3-8.

Duttagupta, I. (2011), Indian Healthcare: Stop the Brain Drain of Doctors, *ET Bureau*.

Karnik, Gaurav (2011) (ed.), Doing Business in India, Ernst and Young.

Ganapathy K. (2001), Telemedicine in India: The Apollo Experience, Neurosurgery on the Web.

Gaucher, J.G., and Coffey, J.C. (1993), Total Quality in Healthcare, *Jossey Bass*, San Francisco.

George, Babu P. (2006), Medical Tourism: An Analysis with Special Reference to India, *Journal of Hospitality Application and Research* (JOHAR).

George, J. (2012), Challenges of Medical Tourism in "Vulnerable" India, *International Journal of Business and General Management* (IJBGM) Vol. 1, Issue 1, August, pp. 1-10.

Gopalakrishnan, S. (2007), India's Healthcare Hurdles, *ISB Insight*, Vol. 9, Issue 2, Indian School of Business (ISB).

Hanna, V. and Sethuraman, V. (2005), The Diffusion of Operations Management Concepts into the Healthcare Sector, ANZAM Conference proceedings, Australia.

India Brand Equity Foundation (2007), *Healthcare*, Ernst and Young, October.

Jack M. Winters and Molly Follette Story (2007), Medical Instrumentation: Accessibility and Usability Considerations, CRC Press.

KPMG, *A Journey from Bench to Bedside, Report of the summit on Emerging Trends in Healthcare*, ASSOCHAM, 2011.

Kumar, Dinesh, N. and Reddy, V.S.K. (2012), E-Medicine: Best Solution for Healthcare of Remote and Rural Reach, *Global Journal of Advanced Engineering Technologies,* Vol. 1, Issue1, p. 18.

Mazumder, B. et al. (2011), Total Quality Management in Pharmaceuticals: A Review, *International Journal of Pharm-Tech Research,* Vol. 3, No. 1, pp. 365-375, January-March.

Ministry of Health and Family Welfare (MoHFW) (2002), *National Health Policy 2002,* New Delhi, Government of India.

Ministry of Law and Justice (2008), The Finance Act, 2008, Government of India, New Delhi.

Mintzberg, H. (1997), Toward Healthier Hospitals, *Healthcare Management Review*, 22(4), 9-18.

Pricewaterhouse Coopers (2012), Healthcare Infrastructure and Services Financing in India: Operation and Challenges, *Healthcare Financing Report MS 384*, Indian Chamber of Commerce, September.

Pricewaterhouse Coopers LLP (2007), Emerging Market Report: Health in India 2007, pp. 1-22.

Raman, Venkat, A. and Bjorkman, J. W. (2009), Public Private Partnership in Healthcare in India: Lessons for Developing Countries, Routledge, London, 2009.

Riebling, N. and Tria, L. (2005), *Six Sigma Project Reduces Analytical Errors in an Automated Lab, Medical Laboratory Observer.*

Rao, M.G. and M. Choudhury (2012), Healthcare Financing Reforms in India, Working Paper No. 2012-100, National Institute Of Public Finance and Policy, March.

ASCI (Administrative Staff College of India) (2012), *Journal of Management,* 41(2), pp. 14-39.

Revere, L. and Black, K. (2003), Integrating Six Sigma with Total Quality Management: A Case Example for Measuring Medication Errors, *Journal of Healthcare Management,* 48:6.

Saliterman, Steven S. (2006), Fundamentals of Bio-MEMS and Medical Micro-devices, The International Society for Optical Engineering, Bellingham, Washington, USA.

Saxena, G. and Singh, J.P. (2010), E-medicine in India: Hurdles and Future Prospects, seminar paper, The International Institute of Professional Studies, Devi Ahilya University, India.

Shah, D. (2010), Learning from Arvind: How Improved Processes

Leads to Operational Efficiency, Access Health International, December.

Shah, U. and Mohanty, R. (2010), Private Sector in Indian Healthcare Delivery: Consumer Perspective and Government Policies to Promote Private Sector, *Information Management and Business Review*, Vol. 1, No. 2, pp. 79-87, Mumbai, December.

Walley, P. (2003), Designing the Accident and Emergency System: Lessons from Manufacturing, *Emergency Medicine Journal*, 20(2), 126-130.

Woodard, T.D. (2005), Addressing Variation in Hospital Quality: Is Six Sigma the Answer?, *Journal of Healthcare Management*, 50:4.

13

Management Practices of Co-operatives in the Globalized Era

M. Sarngadharan

An organization in the co-operative sector is globally viewed as an association of persons, who have voluntarily joined together to achieve a common end through the formation of a democratically-controlled organization, making equitable contributions to the capital required and accepting a fair share of the risks and benefits of the undertaking in which the members actively participate. While trying to narrate the general ideas behind the co-operative concept, it is imperative to look back to the earlier years with a view to developing a clear vision for the future.

India has been basically an agrarian economy with 70 percent of its total population residing in rural areas. The rural people need a lot of services in their daily life which are met by the village co-operative societies. The seeds of co-operation in India were sown in 1904 when the first Co-operative Societies Act was passed. Since then, the co-operative movement has made significant progress, that too in all the spheres in the economy. Co-operatives have extended across the entire country and there are currently an estimated 550 million members nationwide. The co-operative credit system of India has the largest network in the world and co-operatives have advanced more credit in the Indian agricultural sector than the commercial banks.

The village co-operative societies provide strategic inputs for the agricultural sector, consumer societies meet their consumption requirements at concessional rates; marketing societies support the farmer to secure remunerative prices and co-operative processing units help in value additions to the raw products. In addition, co-operative societies are helping in building up of warehouses including cold storages, rural roads and in providing facilities like irrigation, electricity, transport and health. Various development activities in agriculture, small industry marketing and processing, distribution and supplies are now carried on through co-operatives.

In fertilizer production and distribution the Indian Farmers Fertilizer Cooperative (IFFCO) commands over 35 percent of the market. In respect of the production of sugar, it can be noted that the co-operative share of the market is about 60 percent and in the marketing and distribution of cotton they have a share of around 65 percent.

The co-operative sector accounts for about 55 percent of the looms in the hand-weaving sector. Co-operatives process, market and distribute 50 percent of edible oils.

Dairy cooperatives operating under the leadership of the National Dairy Development Board and through state co-operative milk marketing federations has now become the largest producer of milk in the world.

The groundwork for this was laid in the early 1970s when the largest dairy development programme in the world—Operation Flood—was launched.

The co-operative societies in India, in fact, have been playing multi-functional roles both in rural and urban areas. An Expert Group constituted by the Government of India in 1990 recommended facilitating the integrated co-operative structure; to make the co-operative federation organizations responsive towards their members; to minimize Government interference and control in the functioning of co-operatives and to eliminate politicization from the co-operative sector.

Based on the recommendations, the central government enacted the Multi State Co-operative Societies Act, 2002 which provided for democratic and autonomous working of the co-operatives and this came into force with effect from August 2002. Various development activities in agriculture, small industry marketing and processing, distribution and supplies are now carried on through co-operatives. The co-operatives in India have made an all-round progress and their role in, and contribution to agricultural progress has particularly been remarkable.

The co-operative structure in India consists of different constituents. At the bottom of this structure are the primary societies which render varied services. Of this, about 80 percent is concerned with agriculture and most of these societies deal with credit only. Thus, a chunk of the primary societies are directly engaged in agriculture and credit. They perform various functions such as credit, irrigation, marketing and transports. These are generally divided into two groups—credit societies and non credit societies. Each of these two sub-groups can be further split up into two: agricultural societies and non-agricultural societies.

Agricultural societies—both credit and non-credit—are found in rural areas and non-agricultural societies—both credit and non-credit—are mostly located in urban areas. There are central banks and state co-operative banks to supervise and provide financial support to the cooperative credit societies. The central banks supervise the functioning of the primary societies of a district or part of a district and offer financial assistance to them. Their capital is drawn by way of public deposits, share capital and loans from other sources. Since there are varied sources for these banks to augment financial resources, they act as a link between co-operative societies and the financial market. They function as balancing centres by diverting funds of surplus societies to the needy societies. They also make available ordinary banking functions.

The agricultural co-operative credit structure is broadly divided into two sectors, one dealing with the short-term and medium-term finance and the other with the long-term credit. The short-term and medium-term credit structure is based on a three-tier system, i.e., the apex co-operative bank at the State level, the central co-operative bank at the district level and the primary agricultural credit societies at the village level. The major objectives of the primary agricultural credit service societies are to supply agricultural credit to meet the requirements of funds for agricultural production, distribution of essential consumer commodities, storage and marketing facilities and for light agricultural implements and machinery.

At the top of the co-operative credit is the state co-operative bank, at the state level, known as the apex bank. It controls the working of central banks and provides finance to them. It also acts as the link between NABARD (considered as the rural Reserve Bank of India) from which it borrows and the central banks and primary societies. It directs the co-operative movement in the state. Its capital comes from share capital, public deposits and loans and advances from the state and Reserve Bank of India.

The National Cooperative Union of India is the apex organisation promoting the co-operative movement in the country. All the above three types of institutions are concerned with short and medium term credit of people. Long-term loans are given by land development banks, which have a unitary structure having branches at different places. These banks obtain their funds from share capital, reserves, deposits, issue of bonds and debentures. However, the major part of their resources is drawn from the floating of ordinary debentures in the market.

Changes in the Globalized Era

It is now increasingly recognized that the co-operative system in India has the capacity and potentiality to neutralize the adverse effects emerging from the process of globalization among the lower income and middle income strata. Since the adoption of economic liberalization under the new economic environment, co-operatives at all levels have been taking efforts to reorient their functions in accordance with the market demands. The failure of the public sector in several cases has been creating problems in the economy in areas such as equitable distribution of essential commodities, price control mechanism, reinvestment of surplus for general welfare, reduction of regional imbalances and state assuming the role of an entrepreneur in enhancing the production and distribution of goods and services needed internally in the economy. Privatization has also failed to make an impact on the development of rural economy.

Therefore, there have been great expectations on the co-operative sector. The co-operatives are now considered an important plank of development and the government is committed to co-operative development. The co-operatives have inherent advantages in tackling the problems of poverty alleviation, food security and employment generation. Co-operatives are also considered to have immense potential to deliver goods and services in areas where both the state and the private sector have failed.

However, there arises urgent need for revamping the administrative mechanism of the co-operative sector in tackling the inherent problems such as over dependence on government, dormant membership, failure to conduct elections on time, lack of strong human resources policy and absence of professionalism. There should be strong communication and public relations strategies which can promote the concept of co-operation among the masses. It should also push forward by developing effective strategies to overcome existing weaknesses and for continuing growth of the sector.

Despite rapid growth the overall progress of co-operative movement during 109 years of its existence, it has not been very impressive. People are not well informed of the objectives of the movement, the contributions it can make in rebuilding the society and the rules and regulations of co-operative institutions.

Adding fuel to fire, factors such as unhealthy politics of the region and factional politics in it management, caste ridden elections to the office bearers of co-operative societies, bureaucratic attitudes of the government officials, mismanagement and manipulation of the board and the staff, functional weaknesses, restricted coverage of the operational area, inadequacy of trained human resources, size of the societies, and single or limited purpose of societies and lack of co-ordination among various divisions of the co-operative structure have contributed unfavourably to the performance of faster growth of co-operative movement in India.

However, a supportive climate has been created for the development of co-operatives as democratic and autonomous business houses providing them with the opportunities for diversification. The co-operatives have long been demanding that the Central Government introduce democratic reforms in their regulation, supervision and functioning. With the persistent efforts of the National Cooperative Union of India, the Central Government have passed the Multi-State Cooperatives Societies Act and also formulated a national co-operative policy that provides greater autonomy to co-operatives. As result, there has been more co-operation and co-ordination among different constituents of the co-operative structure.

- The scope of co-operatives have extended and diversified.
- Emphasis is given on multipurpose societies.
- Maximum number of societies is now run on the basis of limited liabilities.
- The size of the societies is extended on the basis of scientific principle.
- It is perceived as the powerful strategy of economic growth.

It is widely observed that the formulation of National Policy on Co-operatives is likely to uphold the values and principles of co-operation recognizing its autonomous characters and attaching priority to professionalism, human resource development and to act as preferred instrument for execution of public policy in rural areas and in the sectors engaged in effective delivery system. To strengthen their competitive edge in the market, total quality control initiatives, management initiatives and cost reduction initiatives will also be taken up.

New Management Practices

As stated earlier, co-operatives were invented as organizations having a high potential of innovation in times of rapid change, just like companies were invented for augmenting large sums of money for investment from varied sources. They were instrumental to gain access to new ideas, new technology, new opportunities and new institutions, which the individual acting alone would never have. Following the footsteps of company form of ventures, the co-operatives offer protection within a group of persons having common needs and aspirations, making it possible to try innovations even against the general trend. A co-operative is a tested model of organized collaboration, offering a set of rules which make it possible to reconcile conflicting elements in a well-balanced synthesis, that usually create conflicts in the society: freedom and dependence, tradition and progress, individual self-reliance and group solidarity and unity and social responsibility

In such a backdrop, it is highly imperative that new management practices are easily adaptable to the co-operative sector, particularly the co-operative law and to the needs of survival of co-operative enterprise in a highly competitive market evolved in Indian scenario. It is felt that these practices must be structured in such a way as to overcome the structural weaknesses of the co-operative organizations, by bringing them more close to the company model. This means:

- Providing managers professional competency and skill with more autonomy to manage the co-operative enterprises and minimizing the interference of members and the elected representatives on matters related to execution and routine administration.
- Nominating external professionals with expertise to serve on the board of directors to determine the overall policy of their co-operative and to instruct the professionals to execute this with a view to gaining maximum benefits to the organization and to the society.

- Facilitating merger by way of amalgamation and absorption of small co-operative entities into large societies rather than propagating functional integration or networking among smaller societies.
- Giving more emphasis of co-operatives concentrating on financial audit in the company style rather than concentrating on performance audit/management audit for achieving the aims and objective of the promotion of members and of the organization;
- Promoting and widening the scope for business with non-members as a key and indispensable part of co-operative business, leaving dividend on share capital as the main incentive for membership as has been practiced in companies.
- Minimizing the gravity of political intervention in setting the goals for joint action and determining the rules to be employed for controlling the elected leaders democratically.

Need for Functional Revamping

It is high time for the co-operatives in India to overcome their functional weaknesses in managing the areas such as operations, marketing, human resources, finance, research and development and information.

Operations Management: Operations management deals with the design and management of products, processes, services and supply chains. It considers thc acquisition, development, and utilization of resources that the organizations need to deliver the goods and services their clients demand. The purview of OM ranges from strategic to tactical and operational levels. Representative strategic issues include determining the size and location of manufacturing plants, deciding the structure of service or telecommunications networks, and designing technology supply chains.

Tactical issues include plant layout and structure, project management methods, and equipment selection and replacement. Operational issues include production scheduling and control, inventory management, quality control and inspection, traffic and materials handling, and equipment maintenance policies. Every cooperative organization, depending upon its size and nature of activities should evolve a scientific methodology for managing its operations irrespective of the fact whether it is engaged in industrial, agricultural or service activities.

Technological innovations have paved the way to use energy and raw materials more effectively or to substitute scarce raw materials by new artificial products. Transport and communication systems have made it possible to transfer jobs to places where labour is cheap, to separate production and assembly plants. Thanks to modern technology, fewer farmers can produce more food than ever before and are even paid by the State to reduce their production to avoid surpluses.

On the other hand this high productivity is brought about by heavy use of chemicals which in turn contribute to the pollution of water, soil and air. In the developing countries industrial development programmes are still favouring capital intensive, labour saving ("advance") technologies, although these countries are short of capital but rich in cheap labour. Appropriate technologies have been developed for use of solar energy e.g. to cook food without using firewood, to catch rainwater to be used during the droughts, to introduce sophisticated irrigation schemes, new high-yield varieties of plants; however, all this known technology is not reaching the masses.

Marketing Management: Marketing is observed to be a serious bane for the organizations in the co-operative sector in India, especially in the globalized era of stiff competition. For the co-operative ventures, there can be several organisational approaches to marketing. There arises the need for instilling a marketing led ethos throughout the business; researching and reporting on external opportunities; understanding current and potential customers; managing the customer journey (customer relationship management); developing the marketing strategy and plan; management of the marketing mix; managing agencies; measuring success; managing budgets; ensuring timely delivery; writing copy; approving images; developing guidelines; and making customer focused decisions. Marketing managers need to have a good knowledge of the customer. This means building up an accurate picture using the resources that are available. Information can be gathered from questionnaires, focus groups, the internet, interviews, buying habits and many more sources, but it's important that the information is examined in a scientific way using proper quantitative methods.

There is the need for preparing a detailed marketing plan containing: (i) Situation Analysis—where are we now?; (ii) Objectives—what do you want to achieve?; (iii) Strategy—how are you going to get there?; (iv) Tactics—what are the details of the strategy?; (v) Actions—who is going to do what, and by when?; and (vi) Controls—how are you going to measure success? The marketing plan should provide direction for all relevant members of the organization and should be updated throughout the year. The main reason for the marketing plan is that it provides a structured approach that forces the marketing manager to consider all the relevant elements of the planning process which might be missed if a more rushed approach is adopted.

Human Resource Management: Human resource management encompasses the management of people in organizations from a macro perspective i.e. managing people in the form of a collective relationship between management and employees. This approach focuses on the objectives and outcomes of the HRM function. What this means is that the HR function in contemporary organizations is concerned with the notions of people enabling, people development and a focus on making the employment relationship fulfilling for both the management and employees. The key difference is HRM in recent times is about fulfilling management objectives of providing and deploying people and a greater emphasis on planning, monitoring and control.

In the 21st century organizations, the HR manager or the people manager is no longer seen as someone who takes care of the activities described in the traditional way. In fact, most organizations have different departments dealing with staffing, payroll, and retention etc. Instead, the HR manager is responsible for managing employee expectations vis-à-vis the management objectives and reconciling both to ensure employee fulfilment and realization of management objectives.

Financial Management: Management of funds has assumed greater significance in the management world, irrespective of the fact whether the organization in question has profit motive or service motive. As far as co-operative ventures are concerned funds management, especially working capital management has become a crucial affair. Management of funds covers planning, organizing, directing and controlling the financial activities such as procurement and utilization of funds of the enterprise. It means applying general management principles to financial resources of the enterprise.

The financial management is generally concerned with procurement, allocation and control of financial resources of a concern with the main objectives such as ensuring regular and adequate supply of funds to the concern; ensuring adequate returns to the shareholders which will depend upon the earning capacity, market price of the share, expectations of the shareholders, ensuring optimum funds utilization. Once the funds are procured, they should be utilized in maximum possible way at least cost; ensuring safety on investment, i.e., funds should be invested in safe ventures so that adequate rate of return can be achieved; planning a sound capital structure. There should be sound and fair composition of capital so that a balance is maintained between debt and equity capital. In the day-to-day operations, cash management demands due attention keeping a trade-off between profitability and liquidity

Research and Development: Research and development is one of the means by which business can experience future growth by developing new products or processes to improve and expand their operations. While this is very important, the development of existing products is of equal significance because consumer preferences are continually changing. The task of product research and development is to come up with the goods and services that meet the needs of tomorrow's customers.

In any well-run organization, research and development have strictly commercial functions—to further the business objectives by creating better products, to improve operational processes and to provide expert advice to the rest of the organisation and to customers. Research and development is an investment for future benefits. Depending upon the size of the organization and the nature of activities carried out, a co-operative venture can either have its own research and development wing or rely on outside agencies through outsourcing the research work.

Management Information System: We are living in a time of great change and working in an information age. Managers in the co-operatives, together with their counterparts in other forms of organizations, have to assimilate masses of data, convert that data into information, form conclusions about that information and make decisions leading to the achievement of business objectives. For an organization, information is as important as other resources like money, materials, methods, machinery and manpower. This situation has tempted the creation of management information system as a separate functional area in all the organizations.

It provides several benefits to the business organization in terms of effective and efficient coordination between the functional areas; quick and reliable referencing; access to relevant data and documents; use of less labour; improvement in the organizational and departmental techniques; management of day-to-day activities (as accounts, stock control, payroll, etc.); day-to-day assistance in a department and closer contact with the rest of the world. MIS provides a valuable time-saving benefit to the workforce.

Employees do not have to collect data manually for filing and analysis. Instead, that information can be entered quickly and easily into a computer program. As the amount of raw data grows too large for employees to analyze, business analysts can build programs to access the data and information in response to queries by management. With faster access to needed information, managers can make better decisions about procedures, future directions, and developments by competitors, and make them more quickly.

In the developed countries well-established and highly developed system of co-operative societies are in existence with the support of liberal constitution guaranteeing human rights, social security networks and effective labour laws. They are fighting unemployment by forming self-managed enterprises for self-employment or developing innovative forms of job-sharing and part-time employment leading to a more equitable distribution of work and income; organizing community co-operatives, where public funds usually provided as unemployment benefits are pooled with the work force of unemployed persons to create hybrid forms of self-help organizations providing jobs with the help of public funds for carrying out work in the interest to the community and for the benefit of the public (e.g. the community co-operatives in the United Kingdom or co-operatives for social solidarity in Italy).

They are in a joint action against exploding cost of health insurance by organizing preventive health care on a co-operative basis, while the public and private health sector is firmly oriented towards high-tech and high cost curative Medicare. This could be done by forming medical co-operatives employing their own doctors or running their own hospitals as already practiced in countries like Japan, Spain and Singapore. They have succeeded in mobilizing citizens for joint action against further destruction of the environment by giving preference the ecologically safe products and technologies, by pooling consumer power through consumer co-operatives, shareholders' associations and pressure groups to force producers for consumer goods to adopt ecologically sound production methods.

In conclusion, it is pertinent to add that at present, the Government of India is in the process of formulation of National Policy on Co-operatives which is likely to uphold the values and principles of co-operation recognizing its autonomous characters and attaching priority to professionalism, human resource development and to act as preferred instrument for execution of public policy in rural areas and in sectors where they provide the most effective delivery system. With a view to strengthening their competitive edge in the market total quality control initiatives, management initiatives and cost reduction initiatives will also be taken up.

It is now increasingly recognized that the co-operative system in India has the capacity and potentiality to neutralize the adverse effects emerging from the process of globalization and liberalization, and continue to play an important role in employment promotion and poverty alleviation, both as production enterprises—mainly of the self-employed—and as providers of services to members. Co-operative organizations must have the best talented managers in order to succeed in the hypercompetitive and increasingly complex global economy. Along with the understanding of the need to hire, develop, and retain talented people, organizations are aware that they must manage talent as a critical resource to achieve the best possible results. Careful planning, culminating in a sound talent strategy that is tightly connected to the organization's overall business strategies and business needs, is required for talent management to become ingrained in an organization's culture and practices. Only when this happens, is it possible for co-operatives to be both effective and sustainable.

References

Gupta, S.P. (2006), Globalisation, Economic Reforms and Employment Strategy in India.

Hanumantha, Rao and Bhattacharya, Siddharthan (2005), Indian

Economy and Society in the Era of Globalisation and Liberalisation, Academic Foundation, Delhi.

Radhakrishna, Rao, S. Mahendra Dev and K. Subbarao (2006), India in a Globalising World Some Aspects of Macro Economy, Agriculture and Poverty, Academic Foundation, Delhi.

Samantaray, P.C. (2004), Hundred Years of Co-operative Movement: Emerging Issues and Challenges, *Orissa Review*.

Thorat, Y.S.P. (2005), Keynote address, Centenary of Indian Co-operative Movement, Round Table on Co-operative Banking, Pune.

14

Environmental Management for Sustainable Development

Anil Kumar K. and Ajesh S.R.

While focusing on economic development and growth factors, businesses are increasingly confronted by the effects of their business on the environment. Green is the colour of our modern age. Recent public awareness of resources and its competing and conflicting use has prompted the sustainable development as a desired goal in the decision making process. The need for new approaches to sustainable management such as adaptive environmental management arises from the relatively new demands posed by the concept of sustainable development.

Sustainable Development

Sustainability is defined as the ability to carry forward or support or maintain for a prolonged period approaching perpetuity. Sustainability means meeting the needs of today without compromising the ability of future generations to meet their needs (Brundtland report, 1987). In business terms, this is something that has traditionally been aspired to in terms of economic factors as businesses strive to balance inputs and outputs to maintain a profitable enterprise.

Sustainable development has become a widely used term that goes beyond economic security to include issues of environmental impact and sustainable use together with social effects. The triple bottom line created by this approach is what is now commonly meant when the term is used and this is the definition adopted. However, pressures are growing rapidly to adopt such an agenda and indeed to assess performance and report against such issues. Key business decisions are being increasingly taken with environmental and social concerns alongside economic ones as crucial parts of total value.

Sustainable Development stands for meeting the needs of present generations without jeopardizing the ability of futures generations to meet their own needs—in other words, a better quality of life for everyone, now and for generations to come. It offers a vision of progress that integrates immediate and long-term objectives, local and global action, and regards social, economic and environmental issues as inseparable and interdependent components of human progress.

Sustainable development will not be brought about by policies only: it must be taken up by society at large as a principle guiding the many choices each citizen makes every day, as well as the big political and economic decisions that have. This requires profound changes in thinking, in economic and social structures and in consumption and production patterns.

The concept of sustainable development began to emerge towards the end of the last century and its importance started to prick the social conscience, helped by publicity surrounding issues such as the thinning of the ozone layer, widespread destruction of rainforests, drought and famine, urban pollution and the threat of extinction to a number of the world's best loved and most recognizable species.

Sustainable development is about:

- Balanced and equitable economic development.
- High levels of employment, social cohesion and inclusiveness.
- A high level of environmental protection and responsible use of natural resources.
- Coherent policy making in an open, transparent and accountable political system.
- Effective international co-operation to promote sustainable development globally.

Figure 14.1: The Protection of Queensland's Environment Achieved by an Integrated Management Programme that is Consistent with Ecological Sustainable Development

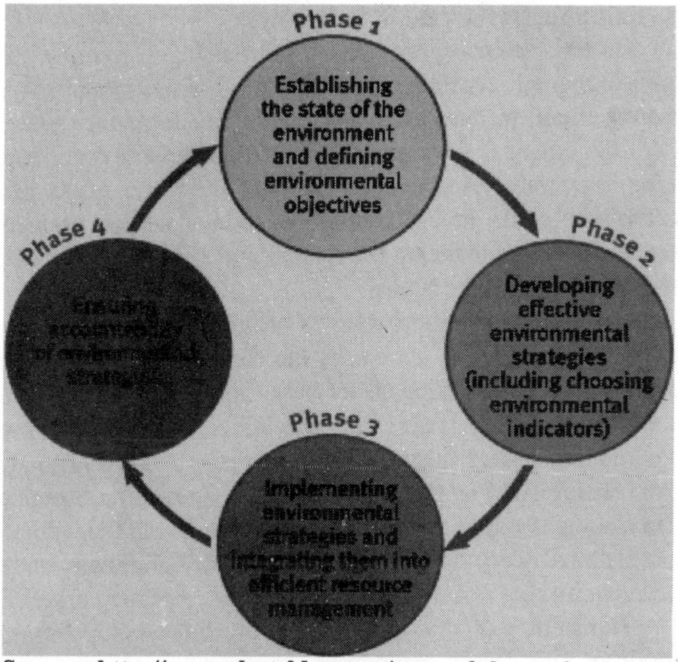

Source: http://www.ehp.qld.gov.au/state-of-the-environment/ report-2007

The above figure depicts the ecologically sustainable development (ESD) program of Queensland. ESD is defined in the EP Act as 'protecting the environment while allowing for development that improves the total quality of life, both now and in the future, in a way that maintains the ecological processes on which life depends'.

Under the EP Act, state of the environment reporting is an integral part of a four-phase planning and management cycle which includes establishing the state of environment and defining environmental objectives, developing effective environmental strategies, implementing environmental strategies and integrating them into efficient resource management and ensuring accountability of environmental strategies.

Sustainable Development in Business

Global Industry is on a three-stage journey from environmental compliance, through environmental risk management, to long-term sustainable development strategies. For the business enterprise, sustainable development means adopting strategies and activities that meet the needs of the enterprise and its stakeholders today while protecting, sustaining and enhancing the human and natural resources that will be needed in the future.

One Prominent Approaches to sustainable development used by global industry is known as the triple-bottom line—a term coined by John Elkington (1997), author and management consultant, which refers to the three prongs of social, environmental, and financial accountability. It is a term that has been championed by the World Business Council on Sustainable Development and is finding increasing and widespread international acceptance within the corporate community and one that is informing and transforming corporate reporting practices.

The notion of reporting against the three components (or 'bottom lines') of economic, environmental, and social performance is directly tied to the concept and goal of sustainable development. Triple bottom line reporting, if properly implemented, will provide information to enable others to assess how sustainable an organisation's or a community's operations are. The perspective taken is that for an organisation (or a community) to be sustainable (a long run perspective) it must be financially secure (as evidenced through such measures as profitability); it must minimize (or ideally eliminate) its negative environmental impacts; and, it must act in conformity with societal expectations. These three factors are obviously highly inter-related.

Conducive Environment for Sustainable Enterprises

An environment conducive to the creation and growth or transformation of enterprises on a sustainable basis combines the legitimate quest for profit—one of the key drivers of economic growth—with the need for development that respects human dignity, environmental sustainability and decent work.

The enabling environment for sustainable enterprise development comprises a large array of factors, the relative importance of which may vary at different stages of development and in different cultural and socio-economic contexts. However, there are some basic conditions that are generally considered to be essential. These inter-connected and mutually reinforcing conditions are the following:

- Peace and political stability.
- Good governance.
- Social dialogue.
- Respect for universal human rights and international labour standards.
- Entrepreneurial culture.
- Sound and stable macroeconomic policy and good management of the economy.
- Trade and sustainable economic integration.
- Enabling legal and regulatory environment.
- Rule of law and secure property rights.
- Fair competition.
- Access to financial services.
- Physical infrastructure.
- Information and communication technologies.
- Education, training and lifelong learning.
- Social justice and social inclusion.
- Adequate social protection.
- Responsible stewardship of the environment.

China has overtaken the US as the world's largest greenhouse gas emitter. Rapid industrial development has depended upon increasing inputs of energy, natural resources, and environmental services. As a result, resource depletion and environmental pollution have become serious problems that require the rethinking of governmental policies. Recognizing the unsustainability of its growth model, the Chinese government has called for a major policy shift to address the environmental impacts of economic growth. In fact, China claims it is one of the first developing countries to propose and implement sustainable development as a national strategy.

The government has achieved substantial advancements in sustainable development, including poverty reduction and population control. These efforts are not pure political slogans; they are important policy experiments in sustainable development. China still faces numerous challenges. Most of the country is in the early to middle stages of economic development and must deal with critical natural resource and environmental constraints. Significant economic and social structural problems also remain. The inadequacy of China's existing strategies can be explained in part through universal shortfalls of the concept of sustainable development, which is difficult to define and measure.

Suggestions

- Creating the requisite harmonized policy environment, as well as legal and regulatory frameworks to promote regional cooperation on all issues relating to environment and natural resources management including trans-boundary ecosystems.
- Promoting environmental mainstreaming in order to ensure the responsiveness of all policies, strategies and programmes for sustainable development.
- Regular assessment, monitoring and reporting on environmental conditions and trends.
- Capacity building, information sharing and awareness creation on problems and perspectives in environmental management.

- Ensuring coordinated positions in the negotiations and implementation environment management programmes.

To sum up, sustainable development can be defined simply as a better quality of life for everyone, now and for generations to come. The issues that would act as hurdles can be numerous and varied for attaining sustainable urban development and city form. But all of them should consider economic, social and environmental aspects of development. In the end it can be said that economic growth does not mean economic development. True economic development should contribute to increase in efficiency and quality of life of a community.

It is to be seen that positive externalities (such as more employment) of economic growth of a city does not give rise to negative externalities like air pollution, traffic congestion and so on. It is also to be remembered that such an effort should be made at local, regional and global level. Sustainable development is a vision of progress that links economic development, protection of the environment and social justice, and its values are recognized by democratic governments and political movements the world over.

References

Arvind Kumar (2009), Economics of Sustainable Development, *Southern Economist*, June, pp. 5-7.

Bhose, Joels, (2003), NGO's and Rural Development: Theory and Practice, Concept Publishing Company, New Delhi, p. 57.

Lisa, Segnestam (2002), Indicators of Environment and Sustainable Development Theories and Practical Experience, World Bank Environment Department-Environmental Economic Series, December.

Laxmi Kumar (2009), Economics of Sustainable Development, *Southern Economist*, June, pp. 5-7.

Murali, Vallabhan T.V. (2007), Protection of Environment and Promotion of Development, Environment Protection and Development: Emerging Issues, Reforms and Strategies, Deep and Deep Publications Pvt. Ltd, New Delhi, pp. 22-27.

Sankaran, S. (2007), Environmental Economics, Marcham Publication, Chennai, pp. 100-108 and pp. 404-408.

Suresh, S. (2009), Economics of Sustainable Development, *Southern Economist*, September, pp. 5-7.

Index

Index